中译翻译文库

中英同声传译

卢信朝 著

Chinese-English
Simultaneous
Interpreting

中国出版集团
中译出版社

图书在版编目(CIP)数据

中英同声传译 / 卢信朝著． -- 北京 ： 中译出版社，2024.6
ISBN 978-7-5001-7576-6

I. ①中… II. ①卢… III. ①英语－同声翻译－教材 IV. ① H315.9

中国国家版本馆 CIP 数据核字 (2024) 第 033361 号

中英同声传译
ZHONGYING TONGSHENG CHUANYI

出版发行 / 中译出版社
地　　址 / 北京市西城区新街口外大街28号普天德胜主楼4层
电　　话 / (010) 68359827，68359303（发行部）；68359725（编辑部）
邮　　编 / 100044
传　　真 / (010) 68357870
电子邮箱 / book@ctph.com.cn
网　　址 / http://www.ctph.com.cn

出 版 人 / 乔卫兵
总 策 划 / 刘永淳
出版统筹 / 杨光捷
策划编辑 / 刘瑞莲　钱屹芝
责任编辑 / 钱屹芝
营销编辑 / 董思嫄　吴雪峰

排　　版 / 冯　兴
封面设计 / 潘　峰
印　　刷 / 三河市国英印务有限公司
经　　销 / 新华书店

规　　格 / 710毫米×1000毫米　1/16
印　　张 / 18.25
字　　数 / 270千字
版　　次 / 2024年6月第1版
印　　次 / 2024年6月第1次

ISBN 978-7-5001-7576-6　定价：78.00元

版权所有　侵权必究
中 译 出 版 社

PREFACE 前言

　　同传是一种认知负荷极高的双语加工任务。同传能力是与生俱来，还是后天学得？主要靠遗传禀赋还是专业训练？这些有关同传学能与能力发展的问题尚待深入研究，但学界、业界的基本共识是：专业译员＝口译学能＋口译训练，即专业译员培养需要两个条件：具备口译学习能力（口译潜质），且经过专业训练。

　　同传学能包含数十种要素，但最为重要的是语言资源、话语信息加工能力与口齿伶俐性。在接受同传培训前，学员应具备丰富、可用、灵活的词句资源，高效理解、加工及双语转换话语信息的能力，与精准、流利表达话语的能力。这三者相互联系，共同影响同传学习的效率、效果，甚至决定着同传能力的上限。此外，与交传相比，同传是边听边译的工作模式，对反应速度与抗压能力要求较高。

　　同传训练包含两块：分项技能训练与整体能力训练。国际主流做法是：学员在具有丰富同传职业经验的教师指导下进行实景训练，教师对学员的口译表现进行评估、诊断、反馈，学员也要对自己的口译表现进行评估、反思。无论是分项技能还是整体能力训练，反思性刻意练习都是最主要的训练方式。反思性刻意练习是指学员聚焦具体阶段性训练目标，将源语与译语录音转写为文字并对齐，基于录音和文字，评估译语内容、语言、发布质量及整体可用性，发现问题与不足，再从同传学能、同传分项能力、同传认知过程等方面反思原因，制定针对性训练计划，持续精进。同传能力与乐器演奏技能、体育运动技能一样，数千甚至数万小时的刻意练习，是获得专家能力的必由之路。

《中英同声传译》正是基于上述理念与实践编写。全书包括同传简介、同传技能讲、练、评与同传实战三部分。书中所有会议素材均来自作者曾参与过的会议同传项目，学员训练录音、转写、反思及教师点评等来自中英同传课程（一年级下）的教学实践。训练部分的内容包括会议资料，源语与译语片段的转写、学员反思、教师点评，教师提供的参考译语，译语片段音频和源语完整音频。本书配套音频请通过扫描二维码使用。需要指出的是，同传边听边译，时间压力大，认知负荷高，且影响同传质量与过程的源语因素、场景因素与译员因素多种多样，同传译语质量常常存在多种问题，即便专业译员也在所难免，多维、深入、细致的译语转写与录音分析有利于全面、充分发现问题。

　　使用本书时，建议读者先学习同传的能力构成、中英同传重、难点等知识，再进行分项技能训练，最后进行实战训练。训练时，先根据所提供的会议资料，如会议议程、发言材料、嘉宾介绍、行业报告等，进行充分的译前准备；然后播放源语音频进行口译训练；之后听学员译语音频，看教师点评与学员反思，并转写自己口译的部分译语片段，发现问题与不足，反思原因，制定改善计划，坚持针对性训练。

　　同传能力，几分"天注定"，几分靠"打拼"？这一问题，有待各位读者探索、回答。

卢信朝
2024 年 4 月 1 日

CONTENTS 目 录

第一章 同声传译简介 … 1
- 一、同传起源与发展 … 1
- 二、同传工作方式特征 … 2
- 三、同传译员能力构成 … 3
- 四、中英同传学习重、难点 … 7
  1. 同传方向与中英不平衡性 … 7
  2. 中英语言结构差异 … 8
  3. 中国特色话语 … 9
  4. 中文发言特点 … 10

第二章 中英同声传译技能讲、练、评 … 11
- 一、听译同步 … 11
  1. 讲解 … 11
  2. 训练与点评 … 13
- 二、顺句驱动 … 17
  1. 讲解 … 17
  2. 训练与点评 … 18
- 三、断句顺接 … 26
  1. 讲解 … 26
  2. 训练与点评 … 29

I

四、信息听辨 34
  1. 讲解 34
  2. 训练与点评 37

五、信息加工 48
  1. 讲解 48
  2. 训练与点评 59

六、纵/横加工 86
  1. 讲解 86
  2. 训练与点评 88

七、译语发布 101
  1. 讲解 101
  2. 训练与点评 102

八、英语提升 104
  1. 讲解 104
  2. 训练与点评 106

九、质量监控 117
  1. 讲解 117
  2. 训练与点评 119

十、译员意识 131
  1. 讲解 131
  2. 训练与点评 132

第三章 中英同声传译实战 148

一、译前准备 148
  1. 了解口译项目 148
  2. 获取相关资料 148
  3. 熟悉发言材料 149
  4. 利用网络资源 149
  5. 现场译前准备 150

6. 资源整合加工　　151
二、会议类型与同传策略　　151
　　1. 政务会议、政务典礼仪式　　152
　　2. 商业典礼仪式　　152
　　3. 发布会、推介会、媒体招待会　　152
　　4. 行业会议　　154
　　5. 学术会议　　154
　　6. 企业会议（年会、客户会、销售会、采购会、环境健康安全会、培训会、董事会会议等）　　155
　　7. 咨询会　　156
三、商务话语同传　　158
四、学术、技术话语同传　　208
五、互动话语同传　　236
六、政务话语同传　　256

第一章 同声传译简介

一、同传起源与发展

  同声传译（下称"同传"）指的是译员边接收源语，边近乎同步发布译语的一种口译形式。20 世纪 20 年代初，美国波士顿商人 Edward Filene 在目睹国际会议中使用交替传译（下称"交传"）费时费钱后，给国际联盟秘书长写信，建议设计同传系统，以节省会议时间，避免发言被打断，确保听众同步理解发言，总体提升国际会议效率。1928 年的国际劳工组织会议全部使用同传系统，涉及 7 种语言。1945—1946 年的纽伦堡审判正式使用同传，效果良好。受这一使用经验启发，1946—1947 年联合国开始试用同传，发现同传效果优于交传，绝大多数交传译员开始接受同传工作模式。此后，同传使用逐渐普及，成为国际会议最常用的一种口译形式。

  同传在我国较早的一次大规模使用是 1995 年 9 月在北京召开的联合国第四次世界妇女大会，该会议的主会场设有中、英、法、西、阿、俄同传。普通民众对同传的较早认识源于 2003 年中央电视台对伊拉克战争直播报道，央视首次采用多语种同传，同步现场直播了美国总统布什电视讲话、白宫新闻发布会以及境外电视台新闻。随后的 2008 年北京奥运会、2010 年上海世博会以及中国主办的 APEC 峰会、G20 峰会等重要国际会议进一步推动了同传的使用。近年来，随着我国逐步走近世界舞台中央，发起或承办的各类国际交往活动日益增多，同传使用日益普及。

除了借助同传工作间（又称同传箱/厢）与专业设备所进行的一般意义的同传外，新的同传工作模式不断出现，如使用无线手持设备为游览、参观人员提供的无线导览同传，以及不借助设备，在听众耳边提供的耳语同传。得益于信息通信技术发展，除现场同传外，远程电话、视频会议同传应运而生，在全球新冠疫情流行期间发挥了重要角色。此外，计算机辅助同传、人工智能同传、人机协作同传等新模式也在快速发展中。

二、同传工作方式特征

同传时译员边听边译，听、译同步，是同传工作方式的最主要特征。这一特征又决定了其他三个特征：时间限制、渐进加工与节奏受控。由于译员需要边听源语边产出译语，其用于源语理解和译语表达的时间十分有限。听、译同步与时间限制又要求译员必须采用渐进性加工的工作方式——译员常常不是等到源语句子完整，而是在听到句子的一部分时便开始进行理解、转换及译语表达等加工，同时进一步对句子的后续部分进行理解等加工，以渐进方式推进源语理解和译语产出。听、译同步与渐进加工又使得译员的译语产出时间和节奏受控于发言。发言节奏变化时，译员需调整自己的产出节奏。

上述四点是同传与交传的区别性特征，使得同传工作颇具挑战，译员需通过相应策略加以应对。首先，边听边译时，听和译在语音、语义等层次上会相互干扰，因此学习同传的第一步便是要学会分配协调好听和译的精力，让耳朵、大脑和嘴巴能够协同工作，做到一边理解源语信息，一边进行译语表达。时间限制特征要求译员进行高效理解和表达，理解、转换和表达能够做到（半）自动化，双语转换与译语表达不能过分追求文采，而要注重效率与可听性，以简洁高效的语言表达源语信息。此外，渐进加工方式下，译员听辨理解的源语资源随着句子的推进呈累加式增长，译员要将逐步听到的源语的意义进行整合，以便获得更加准确、清晰、完整的理解，同时要基于部分源语资源进行译语产出。对译员来说，源语句子信息是逐步明晰的，译员最初的预测、理解、表达等可能会出现错误，译语表达中的句式结构或词汇搭配等也可能要随时调整，这就要求译员在遵循顺句驱动原则的基础上，合理断句，恰当调整，保持译语的衔接和连贯。再者，由于发言人常常会改变说话节奏，译员需要通过调整自己的 EVS（Ear-Voice Span，听－说时差，译员听某部分源语到译出该部分源语之间的时间差）及译语表达节奏等加以应对。

此外，同传（耳语同传等除外）中，译员在专用工作间中借助专业设备提供翻译，与发言人、听众一般没有互动，源语转瞬即逝，译员往往无法请发言人重复之前的话语，或者降低语速，也无法就理解、表达等环节的困难向发言人或听众求助。这对译员的语言能力、知识储备、口译技能与临场应变能力等提出了极高要求。

三、同传译员能力构成

同传译员能力指胜任同传工作所应具备的，由语言能力、职业素养、知识储备、口译技能、特质及元认知能力所构成的职业能力体系。5 个大类中，语言能力最为重要，其次是知识、技能和职业素养，特质及元认知位列最后。从具体能力要素看，外语听力等 13 项要素为"核心"要素，百科知识等 19 项要素为"重要"要素，公众演讲能力等 4 项要素为"一般"要素，具体见表 1。

表 1　同传译员能力要素层级

层次	级别	项数	要素大类	要素项
核心	1	1	语言	外语听力
	2	3	语言	外语表达、母语表达、外语阅读
	3	9	职业素养、技能、语言、特质及元认知	职业道德、多任务处理、脱离语言外壳、母语听力、有效传达信息、双语快速转换、知识和信息获取能力、自我学习提升能力、专注力

续表

层次	级别	项数	要素大类	要素项
重要	1	7	知识、职业素养、语言、技能、特质及元认知	百科知识、专业知识、临场应对策略、母语阅读、工作记忆、抗压能力、会议情境知识
	2	5	技能、特质及元认知	意群切分、反应敏捷、耐力、适应能力、自信心
	3	7	职业素养、技能、知识、特质及元认知	同传工作间工作能力、顺句驱动、文化知识、渐进式加工、语言转换策略、元认知能力、译语产出监控
一般	1	2	特质及元认知	公众演讲能力、好奇心
	2	1	特质及元认知	声音悦耳
	3	1	特质及元认知	喜欢挑战自我

同传译员能力是一种职业能力，有不同于其他职业能力的区别性特征和专属能力要素，如边听边译的多任务处理、顺句驱动、渐进式加工技能及同传工作间工作能力等。同传译员能力是由多项能力要素集成的能力体系，不是各项能力要素的简单相加，而是各要素相互协同形成的整体，其中某些关键能力的不足直接影响整体同传表现。同传译员能力不仅包括同传操作技能，还包括保障和促进技能有效运用的语言能力、知识储备、生理与心理特质、职业素养，等等。

特别值得一提的是，同传教学不可忽视语言能力（尤其是外语能力）的基础地位，在学员语言能力（尤其外语理解和表达能力）未达到较高水平时［根据国际会议口译员协会（AIIC），进行双向互译的语言应为 A 语言或 B 语言］，技能教学往往事倍功半，专业译员培养可能也无从谈起，这一问题在非双语或多语社会的我国尤其应得到重视。有些教师认为知识最为重要，但是没有良好的语言能力和口译操作技能，片面追求知识学习，可能会本末倒置。正如译员所服务的很多领域专家，相关领域知识远比译员丰富，却并不具备同传能力。此外，专注力、抗压能力、反应敏捷、耐力、适应能力、自信心等均处于比较重要的位置。

从技能角度看，同传中，译员听译同步，时间压力大，认知负荷高，其瞬间可用语言资源丰富性、双语转换迅捷度、信息理解和传递效率等须达到较高水准。多任务处理、脱离语言外壳、有效传达信息、双语快速转换，尤其是"边听边译多任务处理"技能是同传区别于交传的关键能力要素。这些技能在交传学习阶段均可得到有效训练。从时间压力稍小、先听再译的交传训练中先习得这些技能，为接受下一阶段高强度同传训练打下基础，无疑比直接学习同传更易操作。倘若不经过大量交传训练，如听辨理解源语时的脱离语言外壳训练、边听边记忆边记录的多任务训练、双语转换训练、高效传达信息而非寻求字面对译的训练等，学员往往一下子难以跟上同传教学节奏，无法有效学习同传，笔者在教学中曾经碰到过这一情况。此外，在交传学习阶段，学员的语言能力、专注力等也会得到提升。因此，建议先学好交传再进阶到同传学习。

从同传学习门槛角度看，有三点可供参考：口头表达伶俐性（verbal fluency），即认知与时间压力下精准、流利表达话语的能力；话语信息加工能力（control over message），即在认知与时间压力下高效理解、表达话语信息的能力；语言资源丰富性（linguistic resourcefulness），即在认知与时间压力下双语词汇、句式资源的丰富性、可用性、灵活性。其中，前两点可能与遗传因素较为相关。

从学员成为译员的过程，就是构成同传能力的各个子能力逐渐发展、最终全面运用的过程。近年，笔者研究团队针对同传译员和学员的能力开展了一次问卷调查，请译员和学员对自己的 36 项子能力进行自评（1-5 分），共收到 49 名译员和 108 名学员（MTI 口译专业学生）的有效数据。结果见表 2。

表 2　译员与学员子能力自评

排序	译员（均值）	学员（均值）
1-5	职业道德 4.76，母语阅读 4.73，母语听力 4.67，同传工作间工作能力 4.65，会议情境知识 4.57	职业道德 4.25，母语阅读 3.77，母语听力 3.77，会议情境知识 3.64，好奇心 3.56

续表

排序	译员（均值）	学员（均值）
6–10	母语表达 4.49，知识和信息获取能力 4.41，适应能力 4.35，抗压能力 4.31，自我学习提升能力 4.29	知识和信息获取能力 3.56，适应能力 3.53，母语表达 3.48，自我学习提升能力 3.47，声音悦耳 3.44
11–15	双语快速转换 4.27，反应敏捷 4.24，脱离语言外壳 4.22，专注力 4.22，好奇心 4.22	抗压能力 3.43，元认知能力 3.40，专注力 3.37，耐力 3.34，喜欢挑战自我 3.28
16–20	元认知能力 4.20，顺句驱动 4.20，外语阅读 4.20，临场应对策略 4.20，多任务处理 4.16	外语阅读 3.26，公众演讲能力 3.23，同传工作间工作能力 3.23，反应敏捷 3.19，自信心 3.15
21–25	自信心 4.16，渐进式加工 4.14，外语听力 4.14，意群切分 4.14，声音悦耳 4.12	临场应对策略 3.11，外语表达 3.11，意群切分 3.07，外语听力 3.06，顺句驱动 3.06
26–30	有效传达信息 4.06，语言转换策略 4.04，耐力 4.04，工作记忆 3.98，外语表达 3.98	工作记忆 3.05，文化知识 3.04，脱离语言外壳 3.04，语言转换策略 2.98，双语快速转换 2.94
31–36	译语产出监控 3.96，喜欢挑战自我 3.96，文化知识 3.94，公众演讲能力 3.90，百科知识 3.80，专业知识 3.69	百科知识 2.91，有效传达信息 2.86，译语产出监控 2.85，多任务处理 2.71，渐进式加工 2.66，专业知识 2.60

两组排序差异主要包括：译员技能子能力排序显著高于学员，而学员特质及元认知子能力排序较为靠前，前 20 项中此类过半。译员排序最高的技能子能力分别为"双语快速转换"（11）、"脱离语言外壳"（13）、"顺句驱动"（17）、"多任务处理"（20），学员排序最高的为"意群切分"（23）、"顺句驱动"（25）；"有效传达信息""多任务处理""渐进式加工"均列最后 5 位。特质及元认知子能力中，译员的"反应敏捷"（12）明显高于学员（19），学员的"好奇心"（5）、"声音悦耳"（10）、"耐力"（14）明显高于译员（15、25、28）。译员职业素养子能力中"同传工作间工作能力"显著高于学员，"临场应对策略"略高。学员的"外语表达"（22）、"文化知识"（27）排序明显高于译员（30、33）。

学员与译员评分差异最大的 10 项子能力分别为：渐进式加工、多任务处理、同传工作间工作能力、双语快速转换、有效传达信息、脱离语言外壳、顺句驱动、译语产出监控、临场应对策略、专业知识。这些子能力也许应该成为学员同传学习和训练的重点。

四、中英同传学习重、难点

1. 同传方向与中英不平衡性

国际会议口译员协会将译员的工作语言分为三种：A 语言、B 语言和 C 语言。A 语言指译员的母语或能如母语一样运用的语言；B 语言指译员接近母语运用水平，听、说自如的语言；C 语言指译员能如母语一样，可以完全听懂的语言。关于同传方向，东西方存在两种不同观点。会议口译传统比较悠久的欧洲社会一般认为：译员应该（甚至必须）从 B 语言或 C 语言译入 A 语言，译入 B 语言的质量要低于译入 A 语言，译语地道表达非常重要，译入 B 语言时需要投入额外精力在 B 语言中寻找对应表达，从而影响到翻译中的意义构建，译入 B 语言应该尽量避免，除非因为一些语言缺乏相应 B 语人才或使用不广，如汉语和阿拉伯语虽为联合国官方语言，必须先译入 B 语言，以供其他译员接力。东方社会一般支持译入 B 语言，认为理解 A 语言比理解 B 语言更为容易，译语内容上忠于源语比译语表达是否地道更为重要，B 语言理解困难或错误造成的问题更为严重。

现有同传方向性研究的一些发现也基本支持译入 A 语言比译入 B 语言更容易、质量更高：译入 A 语比译入 B 语语言质量高，反应时间短，更轻松灵活；译入 B 语言时，大脑激活区域更广，认知负荷更高；译入 B 语言时碰到如下问题：B 语言习惯性表达有限、更容易疲劳、听众对 B 语言口音不满；许多译员在译入 B 语言时目标有所降低，更加注重信息的传递而非表达风格；译员译入 B 语言时表现欠佳，使用的策略更多，而译入 A 语言时更自如，错误和困难更少；译入 A 语言时的意义类错误比译入 B 语言时多，而译入 B 语言时的语言和表达类错误比译入 A 语言时多。国际会议口译教学界也广泛认为译入 A 语比译入 B 语更容易，译入 A 语教学应先于译入 B 语教学。尽管如此，近年来译入 B 语言的需求在上升，客观需求使得译入 B 语言逐渐为更多人接受。在韩国、中国、日本等市场及其他一些市场，译入 A 语言与译入 B 语言几乎平分秋色，译入 B 语言已经广为接受，加上欧盟扩张也增加了译入 B 语言的需求，译入 B 语言已经日益成为满足实际需要的客观必然选择。

在当下我国社会语境中，绝大多数中英同传学习与实践者是不平衡双语者，中文是 A 语言，英文是 B 语言，中英语言能力不平衡，中译英是 A 语言译入 B 语言，英语词汇、句式资源的丰富性，高压力下的词句资源可用性及运用效率等是同传双语转换的关键。因此，中译英同传学习的重、难点之一就是要持续提升英语作为口译工作语言（而非一般日常交流英语，后面会详谈）的能力，提升英语语言资源的丰富性、可用性、表达的正确性、准确性、地道性和传递信息的效率。

2. 中英语言结构差异

同传一般以句子及句内更小结构为加工单位，顺句渐进加工，因此，两种语言间的句法、词汇在有限空间（往往不超过一个句子）与时间内高效转换显得格外重要。英语重形合，汉语重意合，相较英语来说，汉语句子结构一般比较松散，逻辑关系不依赖关系词进行表达，不如英语清晰凸显。因此，中英同传时，中文源语信息的听辨理解比较关键。此外，中英句法结构不对称，尤其是词序差异较大。在双语转换中有效应对语言结构性差异是中英同传的又一重、难点。例如，汉语句子往往是主题突出（topic-prominence），而英语句子是主语突出（subject-prominence），翻译时需将汉语的"主题 + 评论"（如：这一行业许多人都觉得很有发展前景）恰当转换为英语的"主语 + 谓语"（This sector, to many, is quite promising）。再如，汉语是"定语 + 中心语"顺序，而英语的定语既可前置也可后置，恰当处置定语非常关键。针对结构性差异带来的挑战，译员需通过预测、等待、断句、（非实质性）填充、压缩、句式重构、EVS 调整等策略来应对。一般来说，两种语言结构性差异越大，译员越倾向于基于意义和信息的翻译策略。此外，中英语言结构性差异还会影响数字和部分专有名词的翻译，译员需要采取具体策略加以应对。

3. 中国特色话语

中国特色话语包括中国特色当代政治话语和中国特色传统文化话语。中国特色当代政治话语指我国政府表达、阐释政治、经济、社会、环境等治理方针策略时所使用的权威、正式用语及相关专有名词，包括治理概念（名词词组）、治理举措（动词词组）、引语（句子）、职务、机构名、会议（报告）、规划、倡议名、政策、法律、法规名、区域名、项目、活动名等。政治话语主要见于党和国家领导人及其他政治参与者的著作、演讲、谈话、媒体发布，党章、政府工作报告、政策法规文件、白皮书等。中国特色传统文化话语指蕴涵中国传统文化信息的表达，如与文化人物、事件、现象、理念、实物、习俗等有关的文化负载词、习语、诗词、引语等，常出现在各类讲话中。由于中外语言与文化差异巨大，要让中国话语为国际社会听得见、听得懂、听得进，翻译尤为重要，其中，会议同传是一个重要渠道。中国特色话语高质量同传对讲好中国故事，传播好中国声音，构建融通中外的话语体系具有重要意义。

然而，中国特色话语言简意赅而意蕴丰富，且具有一定的领域专业性，使用时常常缺乏语境铺垫，且产出流利，语速、信息密度高，有些话语使用了修辞手法，这些特征不仅导致译员可用加工时间短，记忆负担重，导致认知精力不足，而且会增加译员理解、转换与表达难度，导致其认知能力不足，两者相互影响。这一挑战对于非政府机构译员尤其明显。由于政府机构译员往往接受过机构内部有关特色话语翻译的专业培训指导，长期从事此类话语翻译，此类话语及其译语的记忆储备多，译前译中资料充分，在同传中往往是通过将此类话语与其对应译语语块进行记忆配对，或者口头产出笔译译文的方式进行翻译，视译、视听译、视听读等方式更为常见。而非政府机构译员对政治话语及其译语的储备少，翻译的会议主题庞杂，发言风格与源语特征更不可控、更难预测，面对即兴发言或者读稿但自己未获稿件的情形多，完全依赖源语语音进行即兴听译的口译方式更多。

4. 中文发言特点

中文发言常常点多线少，曲线思维，迂回间接，语言形式多，信息少或不明晰。此外，据笔者多年会议口译观察发现，不少中文发言人不善演讲，缺乏听众意识和被翻译意识，过于关注演讲任务而非演讲效果，照着引经据典、结构复杂、辞藻华丽、数字和专有名词多的讲稿快速阅读，甚至直接阅读论文；有些发言人（主要是主持人）的讲话经过精心加工和准备，语速极快，极为流利；有些发言接近脱口秀，语言流利、幽默、活泼，主题跳转快，格言警句使用多，双关、比喻等修辞手法多；在互动性强的环节，有的发言缺乏逻辑性，主题跳转快，语言破碎凌乱，断句多，折返多，重复多，口头语多，语言形式多，思想和信息不够凸显，甚至吞吞吐吐，语无伦次等。上述发言特点给中英同传中的源语听辨理解、双语转换等增加了难度。

上述所谈的中英同传学习的重、难点归结起来主要包括以下三点：在边听边译模式下，在有限可用时间和有限可加工语言空间范围内，实现中文源语信息的准确听辨理解，中文结构向英文结构的高效正确转换，清晰简明高效的英语译语产出。

第二章　中英同声传译技能讲、练、评

一、听译同步

1. 讲解

分配协调听和译的精力（又称分心、注意力分配等），做到边听边译、听译同步，是同传学习的第一步。其中的关键是了解如何恰当使用耳朵，培养双耳分听的习惯。

双耳分听可通过两种模式实现：一种是让两只耳朵分别听源语和译语（如左耳听源语，右耳听译语，或反之）；另外一种是两只耳朵根据同传任务的具体情形随时调节听源语和听译语所用精力。第一种模式中，译员将两只耳机中的一只覆盖在一只耳朵上，以该只耳朵为听辨耳，另一只耳朵不戴耳机，作为监听耳，两只耳朵可轮换。

第二种模式中，译员两只耳机都戴上，其中一只主要进行听辨源语，另外一只的一部分精力用于听辨源语，其余部分用于监听译语。译员根据源语情况随时调节其中一只耳朵的覆盖程度。当源语听辨负荷极高时（如英译中且有口音时），译员可能完全用两只耳朵听源语，以提升源语听辨理解效率和效果，当源语听辨负荷较低时（如中译英时），译员可用一只耳朵听源语，另一只耳朵监听译语，以提升译语表达质量，但是大部分时候，应该总有一只耳朵同时听辨源语和监听译语，只是用于听源语和译语的精力会有所变化。如果用于听的总精力量化为两只耳朵，那么听源语的耳朵为1–2只，听译语的耳朵在0–1只。笔者在实践中发现，大多数译员采用这种模式。

除了这两种模式外，也有译员不使用覆盖耳朵的头戴式耳机，而选用小耳塞。此时，如果源语声音不太大，一般都可以听见自己的译语，听辨源语和监听译语的任务分配不再根据耳朵进行选择，而是将总精力的一部分用于监听。

在确定自己比较适应的用耳模式后，便可以进行分听训练。传统的同传培训一般将影子练习（即边听边跟读）作为分听的入门训练。有时还在此基础上增加任务来提升难度，如边听边跟读边在纸上写数字、画圈等。但由于影子练习是语音跟读，而非语义和信息层面的加工，与真实同传工作模式不同。因此，笔者在教学中并不推荐该练习，而是直接进行听意译意训练——边听源语意思，边翻译其主要意思，先不苛求非重点信息翻译的准确性和英语质量，将重点放在大意的同步理解和翻译上。通过训练，逐步减少听辨源语、产出译语和监听译语三者间的干扰。如果学员经过了专业交传训练，有过边听边记忆或记笔记的分心训练，一般很快（往往1个月左右）便能基本适应这种工作模式。

听译同步实际上并非完全同步，译语需要稍稍晚于源语，以便译员协调听辨理解、记忆、转换和发布。该晚多少，即EVS该多长，是动态可调节的。听译同步训练时，可以尝试不同EVS，体会其对理解、记忆、转换和发布精力和质量的影响。由于同传加工过程主要是以句子/命题为单位推进的（具体见"信息听辨"部分），EVS最常见的情形是包含1个命题，即译员晚于发言人1个命题（1个主谓结构或者1个句子）的时间，译员开始口译时，已经听到该部分完整命题，或者通过预测基本可以确定该命题信息内容（也包括可还原为命题的省略表达）。发言人通常是以命题为单位表达信息，而译员也是以命题为单位传递源语信息，只是译员比发言人晚1个命题，以便既能更好理解即将要译的命题信息，又能有精力妥善转换和产出上一命题信息。

但在实际工作中，源语特征丰富多样，译员认知状态不断变化，源语命题和译语命题并非一对一的映射关系，而是一对多或者多对一，译员需要根据源语特征、自身状态等，动态调节 EVS，以确保自己处于理解即将听到的发言内容与转换、发布刚刚听过的内容的状态。调节方式总体包括两大类：1）源语命题信息内容较少，表达松散，结构简单，源语多个命题可压缩为译语 1 个命题；2）源语命题信息内容较多，表达凝练，结构复杂，源语 1 个命题可拆分为译语多个命题或多个独立结构译出。因此，具体看，EVS 调节还常存在以下情形：1）源语口语化特征明显，语速较快，信息冗余性较高时，EVS 可包含 2–3 个简单、意思清晰且同属一个小意群的几个小命题，译员可以将几个命题压缩成一个命题译出；2）源语书面特征明显，读稿较慢，信息内容较多时，尤其是定语或状语较长时，EVS 可包含任何一个在源语中并不独立，但可处理为相对独立译语结构的源语成分；3）源语语速中等或较慢，源语中含有时间、地点、原因、目的、让步、程度、条件等可相对独立理解、表达的状语时，EVS 可仅包含该状语；4）源语出现数字、术语、专有名词、词组等罗列时，由于罗列成分冗余性低，记忆负担重，转瞬即逝，EVS 包含 2–3 个罗列成分，译员往往需要在预测到罗列成分或听到第一个罗列成分时，迅速缩短 EVS，紧跟发言快速译出。

刚开始同传训练时，需要警惕交传模式影响，尽量避免因担心自己不理解，而使 EVS 过长，即需要等超过 1–2 个句子，语境信息丰富明确时再开始翻译，将同传变成同传式交传，也需要警惕另一极端，即因担心自己来不及翻译，而使 EVS 过短，跟源语太紧，导致译语理解不正确，表达支离破碎。

2. 训练与点评

> 会议：第 16 届中国国际教育年会——国际化与学生流动论坛，主持词，主旨演讲：新时期来华留学的质量挑战，教育部国际合作与交流司领导

1A：EVS 过短

源语：大家都知道，来华留学经过了 60 多年的发展，我们取得了丰硕的成果，在 2010 年，中国发布了《留学中国计划》。我们的目标是要到 2020 年成为亚洲最大的留学目的国，当年我们的留学生规模要达到 50 万，当然这个数字我们已经非常熟悉了，但是我们的目标不仅仅是一个数字，在这个数字背后是来华留学质量的提高，是我们中国教育、高等教育的发展和我们整体的教育对外开放的程度的不断深入。

译语：We all know that the students who would like to come back to China to study has been developed for about six decades with fruitful results. In 2010, China issued the Study in China Program. Our destination is to by the end of 2020, become the largest destination country of study in Asia. Back then, our in that year, the foreign students in China will be like 500 thousand. It is a very familiar goal. But our goal is more than a figure. Behind the figure, it will be our quality of improvement of Study in China. It is the development of the high-end education in China and the opening up of China's education industry.

教师点评：该译语 EVS 过短，跟发言太紧，语速过快，语流不稳，音韵不佳，削弱了译语可听性。此外，因为急着追赶发言，译员只能紧贴原文字面翻译，缺乏足够的听辨分析和理解，不仅导致多处理解错误（尤其"在这个数字背后……"一句），还导致了句子切得太碎，啰唆，而且因为句子太长，短期记忆饱和，出现不少语法错误。

1B：EVS 较为合理，发布平稳

源语：那么我们要实现这个目标，要实现来华留学的一个健康可持续发展，我们要靠的不仅仅是我们综合国力的支撑，经济社会的发展，政策环境的不断优化，当然还有我们方方面面的各界同人的努力，最核心的我们是要提高我们来华留学的竞争力，也就是我们最核心的质量竞争力。那么在质量建设方面，我们这么多年有哪些宝贵的经验，在新形势下我们又面临着哪些挑战和困难？今天我们非常高兴地邀请到国内

的政府、学校还有学界几方面的专家来一起和我们大家共同探讨这个问题。

译语：To achieve this aim and the sustainable development of Study in China, we shall not only rely on the comprehensive national strength, but also the development of our economy, and the optimized policies, and the efforts from all quarters of this sector. And the most important thing is to boost our competency, and that is our quality. To develop our quality, our experiences over the decades...what are those? And what are the challenges we have faced? Today we are lucky to have the experts from the government and academia to discuss this question.

教师点评：该例中的 EVS 较为合理，译员发布的节奏较为平稳。"我们这么多年有哪些宝贵的经验"一句可以处理为 what are our best practices over the years。

1C：听与译协调不够，EVS 动态调节不足

源语：一些老牌的有着非常优秀的高等教育资源的发达国家，包括德国、法国这样的，他们都要政府拿很多的钱，你像德国、法国和意大利，国际学生基本不收学费或者收很少的学费来吸引国际学生，所以，对它们来讲，国际学生经济上它不是一个资源，而且要国家要投入很多的国力来往里投入，所以从这个角度来看，就是我们国家也不是英语国家，所以现在能做到我们的规模已经很不容易。但是其实要真正往里看……

译语：And those great countries with great education resources have attracted many overseas students because they are given many subsidies for overseas students. And for for them overseas students is not a resource. They are instead given much more resources to these students.

教师点评：和 1A 的情况相反。译员同传中存在明显的交传加工模式、特征，比如较长等待，翻译深层意思，颠倒语序（attracted...given many subsidies...they are instead given...）。这种追求源语理解深度和译语表达质量的深度加工模式易消耗译员精力，导致理解和记忆跟不上发言，尤其是发言语速较快时，可能引起大段信息丢失，甚至同传中断。此外，译员语速也应适当提高。刚学同传时，要深入理解同传与交传加工模式差异，确保听译同步。

1D：交传的纵向 / 深加工模式 / 特征明显

源语：英语本身是吸引留学生一个极大的不可比拟的一个优势和资源。你看所有的，就从经济角度来讲，能够从国际学生身上能够大量的有外汇收入的都是英语国家，美国、英国、澳大利亚、加拿大，（还有）新西兰这样的只有450万人的小国家，一些老牌的有着非常优秀的高等教育资源的发达国家，包括德国、法国这样的，他们都要政府拿很多的钱，你想德国、法国和意大利，国际学生基本不收学费或者收很少的学费来吸引国际学生。所以，对它们来讲，国际学生经济上它不是一个资源。

译语：English countries is a unique tool to attract these international students. Like America, US, America, New Zealand, UK and so on. Some traditional countries with uh higher education, premium higher education like Germany and France can, can, need, depend on government spending to attract international students.

教师点评：由于听与译的精力不够协调，加上部分地方的中英转换带来挑战，导致译员未能同步、流利表达，出现一些讹误。译语中的第一句，译员转换与表达出现困难，占用了一定精力，影响了第二句的理解，而且第二句的长定语结构给译员造成转换困难（可以脱离框架，提取信息，译为 international students bring/generate lots of revenue to/for...），导致漏译。而后一句，译员开口稍稍有些早，加上关键信息没有理解，误译为 traditional...（可译作 some leading countries with...）。译语最后一句可处理为 these governments spend a lot to.... 该例中可见，语言资源的丰富性、灵活性和可用性对于同传比较重要。

二、顺句驱动

1. 讲解

顺句驱动，又叫顺译，是为应对同传时间限制挑战，实现边听边译而被迫采用的一种策略，具体指同传时以句子及句内更小结构为加工单位，总体按照源语语序进行翻译，并且保证译语和源语信息一致。由于中英表达方式差异较大，克服中英结构性差异是关键。

总体上，英语重形合，汉语重意合，相较英语来说，汉语句子结构一般比较松散，逻辑关系不依赖关系词进行表达，不如英语清晰凸显。汉语句子多使用动词，动作感强，多用重复、排比等，常用流水句，节奏感强，话语组织得犹如竹节，英语则较依赖名词，表达偏静态，词汇表达注重多样性，在一个主谓结构上衍生出介词、名词等构成的短语，各种非限定分句及从句等，话语组织得像是枝繁叶茂、盘根错节的参天大树。中译英时，既要将中文源语信息总体按照其呈现的顺序译出，又要充分尊重英语表达习惯进行适当的词句调整。

如"我们的目标是要到 2020 年成为亚洲最大的留学目的国，当年我们的留学生规模要达到 50 万，当然这个数字我们已经非常熟悉了，但是我们的目标不仅仅是一个数字，在这个数字背后是我们来华留学质量的提高"可处理为：We aim at making China by 2020 Asian largest host country, with 500 thousand international students, a number quite familiar to you but we will aim beyond quantity for quality.

由于汉语句子往往是主题突出，而英语句子是主语突出，翻译时常常需要进行两种语言组织方式的调换，将汉语的"主题＋评论"转换为英语的"主语＋谓语"。如："这一领域，很多企业都在投资"可处理为 This area is one in which many enterprises are investing in/This area is attracting investment from many enterprises/This is an area that many enterprises are investing in。

此外，中英词序差异也带来挑战，如汉语是"定语＋中心语"顺序，而英语的定语既可前置也可后置，恰当处置定语非常关键，中译英时，长定语可用简洁英语＋中心词进行表达，如果无法完全表达修饰语的意思，也可在中心词后再追加修饰语。如："我们把这样的一个技术应用到我们的商业领域，甚至是跟金融本身已经没有太大关系的这样一个我们常规的企业业务里边"可译为 We apply the technology to our businesses, specifically in non-financial scenarios, the day-to-day operations of our ordinary businesses。

顺句驱动是同传基本的一种语言加工方式，学员要熟悉中英结构差异，再通过预测、等待、断句、（非实质性）填充、移位、压缩、句式重构、EVS 调整等相应策略加以应对（详见后文）。

值得注意的是：口译理解和表达过程往往比较强调摆脱源语语言形式束缚，表达和传递意义、信息。交传中，这一操作的空间往往更大。同传中，顺句驱动是基本原则，传递意义、信息常常要以顺句驱动为前提。当然，顺句驱动和传递意义、信息的具体运用常常受源语类型影响。源语语言结构较为书面，表达严谨，结构复杂时，往往更多采用顺句驱动，而当源语松散，结构简单，短句较多时，往往更多地进行意义、信息加工。专业译员能够根据不同源语类型灵活把握和调节。可参考后文"纵／横加工"部分。

2. 训练与点评

1E：

源语： 目前作为世界第二大经济体，我国的综合国力的提升和高等教育的发展使中国成为国际留学生的重要的留学目的国。从规模上看，英国媒体《金融时报》宣称中国已经成为美国和英国以后的第三大这个留学生这个 host 的这个国家。但是这个数字呢，坦率讲啊，我个人认为，如果再往下看，我们远远没有达到第三位，因为很多的因素，这个吸引留学生远远不能拿 GDP 来看，因为你从一个很简单的现象看啊，我个人的观察啊，英语本身是吸引留学生一个极大的不可比拟的一个优势和资源。

译语：As the second largest economy in the world, China has developed a lot in terms of education. We have been a very important host country for international students. *The Financial Times* from UK has said that China has become the 3rd largest host country in the world, just after UK and USA. I think we haven't been the 3rd yet, because of a lot of reasons. We can't use GDP as a criteria to see those things. Because I have discovered that English-speaking country is actually a huge attraction for those international students.

源语：你看所有的，就从经济角度来讲，能够从国际学生身上能够大量的有外汇收入的都是英语国家，美国、英国、澳大利亚、加拿大，（还有）新西兰这样的只有450万人的小国家。一些老牌的有着非常优秀的高等教育资源的一些老牌的发达国家，包括德国、法国这样的，它们都要政府拿很多的钱，你想德国、法国和意大利，国际学生基本不收学费或者收很少的学费来吸引国际学生，所以，对它们来讲，国际学生经济上它不是一个资源，而且要国家投入很多的国力来往里投入，所以从这个角度来看，就是我们国家也不是英语国家，所以现在能做到，一方面，我们的规模已经很不容易。

译语：We can see that countries earned a lot of foreign exchange from international students are all English-speaking countries. For example, UK, USA, Canada, and so on. Several countries, they have a lot of well-known resources, educational resources, such as Germany. But they have to spend a lot of money to attract more international students. For example, they may charge no tuition for international students. For those countries, international students are not a resources, but a spending for the government. So, on this point, China is also not an English-speaking country. It is very difficult for us to have the achievements we have got now.

教师点评：该译语总体能够保持顺句驱动，但是仍有一些可作调整：

（1）"世界第二大经济体"可处理为 world's second largest economy，"国际留学生的重要的留学目的国"可以省略语境冗余信息 for international students，或者前置为 international students' major (study abroad) destination；

（2）"英国媒体《金融时报》"可处理为 Britain's *Financial Times*；

（3）China has become the 3rd largest host country in the world, just after 可调整为 China has, following UK and USA, become the third largest host country；

（4）countries earned a lot of foreign exchange from international students are all English-speaking countries 可顺句调整为 international students are/bring/generate a major source of foreign exchange revenue to/for English-speaking countries；

（5）对于"美国、英国、澳大利亚、加拿大、新西兰"这样的罗列，建议缩短 EVS，结合笔记，按照原来语序快速译出；

（6）"能做到我们的规模已经很不容易"可顺句处理为 the current scale is/means a significant achievement。

顺句驱动可以有效降低译员记忆负担，使其能够腾出更多精力用于双语转换和译语发布。

1F：

源语：但是呢，同时呢，我们看到呢，来华留学生，刚才我说的质量和我们国家的世界的影响力和经济地位呢，还不相称。一方面呢，学历教育的竞争力有待于提高，从学生层次看，学历生总数占来华留学生比重较低，仅为43.6，研究生数量占12.7%，从学科分布来讲，文科比重较大，占61%，汉语比重尤其是大，约一半左右，理工农经占的比例仅为25%，分布不均匀。另一方面，学分生的多元化水平有待改善，来华留学生当中，学分学生人数比较少，就是到中国来短期学习然后拿着学分回国的学生比较少，来自周边国家和非洲国家的生源比重占到70%。来华留学目前主要还是依靠地缘、文化和性价比等优势来吸引国际学生。

译语：But, Meanwhile, we have seen that the quality of our international students have not matched with our national strength and image. We have a long way to go to improve our competitiveness and the scale of our international students, which is not very large in terms of our record students, which is 43.7%. We have a large proportion of students of liberal arts, especially the Chinese language major, much lower than that of mechanics, engineering and science. We have a lot of room for improvement in diversifying our demographics. We have less long-terms students. However, we have more students who have to return home after graduation. We have already 70% of international from Asia and Africa. We can only attract students for our geographical advantages.

教师点评：译语顺句驱动问题不少：有几处源语是无生命名词作主语，可以直接顺句译出，无须使用we句型颠倒语序，如"学历教育的竞争力有待于提高"可以顺句处理为 degree education needs to be more competitive，"学历生总数占来华留学生比重较低"可处理为 degree students take a small percentage/proportion，"文科比重较大，占61%"可处理为 liberal arts students account for 61%，文中漏译，"学分生的多元化水平有待改善"可处理为 non-degree students need to be further diversified，"来自周边国家和非洲国家的生源比重占到70%"可处理为 neighbouring Asian and African countries' students account for 70%，"来华留学目前主要还是依靠地缘、文化和性价比等优势来吸引国际学生"可处理为 geographic, cultural and cost efficiency advantages are major attractions for international students。

此外，译语有些啰唆，语言问题也不少，存在多处讹误。

> 会议：联合国教科文组织国际工程教育中心理事会暨顾问委员会2018年会议，互动环节发言，西安交通大学校长

> 2A：

源语：然后很高兴来自于西安交通大学，我像钱院士一样，还是用中文说，更清楚地表达我的意思。工程教育我提几个观点，第一个我作为大学校长感觉到特别地担忧，因为现在当今世界，科学技术发展之快远远超出我们的想象。很多企业的研究，甚至走到了大学的前面，很多颠覆性的技术来自于校园之外，而不是来自于大学之内。这让我们大学的教育面临着一个巨大的挑战。那么这个原因在什么地方？我觉着当今世界在第四次工业革命到来的这个浪潮中，社会对技术、对人才需求的研究，那种人力、物力资金的投入要远远大于大学，在这个方面，实际上在很多方面大学已经落后于社会的发展，那么大学的存在价值就受到了挑战！

译语：It's a pleasure to be here. I'm from Xi'an. I want to use Chinese to present this speech. First, as a university principal, I have my concern. Since now the world faces rapid technological advancement. And some researchers from enterprises outpace university researchers, and a lot of cutting-edge technologies come from outside of the universities. So this poses a serious challenge to us. What's the cause? I think because the world is now at the stage of the 4th industrial revolution and the society has an elevated need for research and talents, for the resources in every aspects. We need more investment like the universities that cannot fulfill alone. In this context, universities' values are challenged.

源语：大学本来是应该引领社会的发展，现在是社会走在了我们大学的前面，那我们大学的价值存在价值就值得社会的怀疑，所以这是我们一个非常非常大的挑战。那么基于这个情况，我想整个市场的变化是随着社会的需求来变化的，企业的追求是满足市场的需求，所以它不断

地有新技术的研发，那么大学需要做的是用什么样的知识来满足市场所需要的新的技术所需要的基础知识。但是往往在这个方面，我们没有及时地快速地响应社会的需求，为企业提供满足社会需求的基本知识，反倒是企业等不及，干脆你提供不了，那我们自己来研究就算了。所以你看现在很多高新技术企业类，就像IBM，像很多大的企业公司，他们所做的研究，无论从理念还是技术的实现程度都远远走在了大学的前面。

译语：Now the society outpaces universities in development. So people question the values of universities, higher level education. So from my perspective, I think we need to change with the times. The enterprises fulfill societies' needs timely. So we also need to consider how to fulfill these needs. However, we kind of lag behind this immediate response like the enterprises side in basic knowledge. So the enterprises do not wait for us and they engage in their own researches that like IBM and other like big tech companies. They have a high level of technology, research and development.

教师点评：（1）该译语有些地方能够顺着源语句子，但有不少地方存在听辨理解不足，随意增、删、改源语意思，这种尺度过松，不尊重源语内容的工作方式，初学同传时须避免。
（2）译语的语言问题较多，语音、语调、语气、节奏等方面有较大提升空间。
（3）部分句子的处理建议如下：
科学技术发展之快远远超出我们的想象。很多企业的研究，甚至走到了大学的前面。
Science and technology grow faster than expected/unexpectedly fast. Many businesses' research is leading/outpacing that of universities/Many businesses are doing better research than universities.
那种人力物力资金的投入要远远大于大学
Society invests more in research than universities do.

整个市场的变化是随着社会的需求来变化的，企业的追求是满足市场的需求，所以它不断地有新技术的研发，那么大学需要做的是用什么样的知识来满足市场所需要的新的技术所需要的基础知识。

Markets respond to societal demands. Businesses seek to meet market demands with new technologies. Universities meet market demands for technologies/enable that process with basic knowledge.

我们没有及时地快速地响应社会的需求，为企业提供满足社会需求的基本知识，反倒是企业等不及，干脆你提供不了，我们自己来研究就算了。

We failed to address pressing societal needs with basic knowledge, and businesses can't wait and do their own research.

2B：

源语：所以这也是我作为一个大学校长我非常非常担忧的地方。所以最近我在做了几件事，一件事就是在中国工程院的支持下，完全打破了现在的这种常规的传统的教学模式。所以我采取了短训的模式，当然更多的是奔着很多国家，所以现在我涵盖了150多个国家的学生，包括一些企业的人员，我一年办了40多期的短训班，把最新的知识和工程师结合起来，一起为这些渴望得到这些知识的年轻的孩子们和工程师来提供这种培训。我跟周院长报告现在我都有点担忧，因为每次报名都大大地超出了我的容纳程度，所以现在有很多很多的年轻人特别喜欢听到来自于社会现实和第一线的工程师所给予他们的知识的传授，尽管有很多并不成熟，但是他们特别渴望能够得到这种知识的更新。

译语：So this is what I'm most worried about. So, I've, we've done some things. First, we broke the limits of this current education scheme. And we have incorporated students from 150 countries, including some enterprise employees. We hosted over 40 workshops, incorporating latest development in this industry and some new theories and knowledge. And

I'm really worried about the fact that many more people have applied for this program and many young people like to hear from the people directly involved in this change. Some of the knowledge remain immature, but still they want to know more about this industry.

源语：另外，我们也是像清华一样做了一个慕课网，现在我们上线的远远超出我的想象，我请了很多世界上各行各业的包括工程师来给他们讲课，现在在线学习的都超过一千多万了，所以这个远远超出我的想象，有那么多的青年人希望能够得到最新的知识。所以我也希望通过这样一个教学模式反过来来促进大学自身教育模式的改革，因为现在我真的觉着我们的教育模式太过于落后了，落后于社会发展的需求，这是第一个观点。

译语：And we invited engineers from all around the world to give lectures and online learn learners, reached over 10 million people. It's beyond my imagination that so many young people want to learn more. And I think engineering education can help change the education in scheme currently adopted by many Chinese universities.

教师点评：（1）本例译员与前面 1D 译员的翻译风格有些类似，加工过程比较谨慎，注重发布质量，这是优点，但与 1D 拉长 EVS 进行较深加工导致信息丢失所不同的是，本例译员总体在语言层面寻求对应，因为同传中过于谨慎地尊重源语语言，导致出现贴字面翻译、中式或不当表达（比如 broke the limits, incorporated，remain immature, invite），且一些地方消耗精力过多，导致信息理解错误或丢失。

（2）"打破了现在的这种常规的传统的教学模式。所以我采取了短训的模式，当然更多的是奔着很多国家，所以现在我涵盖了 150 多个国家的学生"可以处理为 we replaced the conventional training approach with brief sessions that span across numerous countries, reaching students from over 150 countries.

（3）"很多很多的年轻人特别喜欢听到来自于社会现实和第一线的工

25

程师所给予他们的知识的传授，尽管有很多并不成熟，但是他们特别渴望能够得到这种知识的更新"可以处理为 many youngsters love to learn from seasoned front-line engineers the hands-on knowledge. Despite being young, they just love to remain/be up-to-date/informed.

（4）help change the education in scheme currently adopted by many Chinese universities 可调整为 help reshape current higher education model/drive...reform./be a driver for...reform?

三、断句顺接

1. 讲解

为了赢得时间，保持边听边译，同传时译员采取渐进加工方式，即听一点儿译一点儿，听辨理解的源语资源随着句子的推进呈累加式增长，译员要基于一部分源语资源进行译语产出。这种加工方式要求译员必须能做到断句顺接：确定开译点，即决定听到多少源语时将所听源语作为一个相对独立的可译单位进行翻译，并通过词句恰当调整，把断开的成分顺接起来，确保语言衔接，意思连贯。从克服中英结构差异角度来说，断句顺接也是必要的。

一般来说，常见可以开译或断句的情形包括：位于句首、形式稳定（不受随后结构影响）、意义确定的部分非独立主谓结构，如时间、地点状语，部分介宾结构，状语从句；宾语或补语虽未完整发布，但是意义基本确定的独立主谓结构；完整发布的独立主谓结构；嵌入复杂结构的非独立主谓结构；具有较多或重要信息、可译为独立句子的非独立主谓结构；当源语口语特征明显，不够规范、明晰，或者结构较为复杂时，译员要迅速搜觅、抽取类似于上述几种情形中的有关结构。确定开译点本质上就是确定 EVS，也就是确定加工单位。EVS/加工单位的确定和调节是同传的核心问题之一，也是同传能力的核心指标之一，对同传质量影响深刻，后面的信息听辨、信息加工及纵/横加工等部分还会再谈。

论坛为我们提供了一次回顾发展历程和关注未来挑战的机会。

开译点为"论坛为我们"时，可处理为：At the forum, we looked…

APEC是他们了解各经济体领导人对国际经济形势判断和发展战略的构想的窗口。

开译点为"APEC"时，可处理为：During APEC events, they hear member country leaders' insights/perspectives regarding…

刚学同传时，可尝试在不同位置断句。

参与APEC对于当时绝大部分的中国企业家来说，更多的只是一个聆听者。

若开译点是"参与APEC"，即保持较短EVS，那么译语可处理为：A role in/ Being part of/ Attending APEC events for most Chinese business leaders is/means (being) more often a listener/an observer.

若听到"中国企业家来说"时开始翻译，稍稍拉长EVS，那么译语可处理为：Most Chinese business leaders attended APEC events then more often as listeners/observers.

如果等到听完该句（听到"聆听者"）再译，EVS为一个句子。那么译语可处理为：Most Chinese business leaders were more often just listeners/observers at APEC events.

一般而言，断句稍晚，即EVS稍长的工作模式下，译员所听源语较多，意思相对明确、完整，译语产出会也相对较为衔接、连贯、流利且易理解，但短期记忆负荷较大；断句较早，即EVS较短的工作模式下，译员的短期记忆负荷较小，但因为所听源语较少，对源语的理解往往不如EVS较长时，翻译时往往止步于词语层面直接对应，译语的衔接、连贯、流利性、可理解性等，往往也不如EVS较长时。

影响断句/EVS的因素很多。首先是技能熟练度，新手因技能不熟练、协调能力弱、短期记忆容量小，往往EVS较短，随着训练增加，同传技能熟练度增加，EVS 会适当变长。由于语言水平、知识储备、认知特质等差异，译员会逐渐形成自己的断句/EVS 风格，个体差异较大。此外，源语发布方式和特征，如是读稿还是即兴发言，主旨发言还是互动讨论，语速快慢，是否有明显口音，句子结构是否复杂，专业性程度强弱等也影响断句/EVS。译员生理心理状态等也会产生影响。

一般而言，初学者要避免两种不当加工模式：一是译语跟源语过紧，即听即译，不断句，没有明显、稳定 EVS，译员对源语几乎没有加工，对译语缺乏监管，译语被源语带着，表达凌乱，音韵感差，不易理解，另一种是译语离源语过远，译员听一截译一段，先听再译，难以同步翻译，导致大量漏译。

要提升顺句驱动、断句顺接能力，可以进行词句灵活度训练。先进行句式灵活度/句式重构训练，尝试用丰富多样的主语、谓语表达源语信息。随着训练的推进，在句式变换基础上进行重要词汇的替换。需要注意，词句变换后要确保语法正确，语言地道，源语信息基本未变。下面以一个例子说明如何进行句式灵活度训练。

> 由于两国经济互补性强，今年，双方政府签署有关协定，以促进两国在全球经济低迷的大背景下实现共赢。

该例中，几乎每一个中文词汇都可作为主语，再搭配恰当谓语，将句子译出。

"由于": The fact that both economies are strongly complementary led this year to an agreement...

"两国": The two countries enjoy strong economic complementarity so that...

"两国经济": The two economies' strong economic complementarity led this year to...

"互补性": The strong complementarity between two economies...

"强": The strength of economic complementarity...

"今年": This year saw both governments sign an agreement...

"双方"/"双方政府": Both sides/governments signed...

"签署"：The signing of an agreement between two governments is to give full play to their economic complementarity...

"有关协定"：An agreement was signed...

"以"：The purpose of achieving a win-win pushed two countries to sign...

"促进"：Promoting a win-win is the goal of two countries...

"全球经济"：Global economic context pushed...

"低迷"：Recession of global economy...

"大背景"：The macro context of...

"实现共赢"：Achieving a win-win...

除了主语变换外，谓语及其他部分也可变换和组合，再加上关键词汇的变换，该例的英语译语可达数十种。当然，每种译语在传递信息的效果、效率方面可能存在细微差异，训练中可加以体会。长期坚持这一训练，有利于提升同传过程中的语言资源丰富性、灵活性，双语转换迅捷度、便捷度，提升译语质量。

2. 训练与点评

会议：第二届"一带一路"国际合作高峰论坛，数字丝绸之路分论坛，对话：数字经济助力包容性增长和可持续发展，阿里巴巴首席执行官

3A：

源语：非常荣幸来参加今天这个活动。听了前面这几位的分享，我是非常有共鸣。我觉得今天大家都有一个共识，我们已经在一个数字经济时代，可能5年以前我们讨论更多的是我们在走向一个数字经济，但今天其实我们已经在这个数字经济当中了。其实我们每个人都是已经被数字经济的运作方式所影响，所改变。那么今天的主题是数字经济和包容性和可持续发展，那么在对于整个的数字经济的发展，它带来的基础，其实有一个基础，在前面几位分享当中都讲到了，我想大家都

有这个高度的共识,就是整个经济行为的数字化是整个数字经济的基础和带来后面无穷变化的前提条件。今天我们所有的无论是过去20年在整个世界范围内发生的大量的数字,围绕数字技术的创新、数字商业的创新,无论是电商,无论是数字金融,无论是各种大数据的处理的能力的发展,其实都带来了整个的数字经济行为的数字化的这样的一种前提条件。而在这里我特别想讲一点,就是阿里巴巴20年的发展,我们最大的感受是这样的一个数字,这样的一个经济行为的数字化以后,给这个世界特别是中小企业和个人的创业者带来一种新的天地,就使得他们突破了原有经济秩序当中,原来我们一直把它称为一个树状的经济结构。

3A 译语:I am happy to be here at this conference. And I've listened to the sharing of some of analysis. I have some resonance. And we have reached a consensus that we already lived in the digital era. And five years ago, we talked more about moving towards the digital economy, but today we already live in digitalized era. Actually, we are part of the digital economy and affected by it, changed by it. Our topic today is the digitalized, the inclusive and the sustainable development and the development of the digital economy. The foundation of it has been shown by the previous speakers. We have reached high degree of consensus that the economy is the foundation of the digital economy and also the changes. Today or in the past 20 years, all of the digital economy innovations, whether the e-commerce, the digital finance, or the big data computing have been digitalized and been the premise of that. And I would like to stress that in the past 20 years, Ali group that digital in the digitalized era which make the world, especially SMEs and the personal entrepreneurs, a new area, make them break through uh the economic regulations.

教师点评:译员的操作方式基本类似于前面所说的不良模式:跟源语过紧,即听即译,主要进行语言对译,对源语的加工不足,对译语质量缺乏监管。这一操作模式的好处是短期记忆负担轻,在源语表达比较规范、明晰的时候，译语可以保持一定的准确度。然而，由于缺乏源语深加工，在源语表达不够明晰、流利，口语特征明显时（如该段后半部分），译语会受源语影响变得凌乱、碎片化，不能透过语言形式传达信息。此外，由于基本没有明确的断句操作，听众很难听出译语中短语和句子边界，难以理解源语意思，而且由于缺乏译语监管，语言错误较多，发布音韵不佳，加上译员需要快速跟着源语，部分单词发音不准确、不清晰、不完整。总体上，译语内容不够准确，语言错误与不规范表达较多，发布质量也一般，不易理解。

3B：

3B 译语：Today I am very honored to attend this today's event. I've listened to these the previous speakers. I resonate with them. I think we've reached a consensus that is we are living in a digital era. Five years ago, we talked about that we talked about the things that we are moving to a digital economy, and now we are living in the digital economy. And we are actually shaped by the digital economy. The topic is the digital economy, inclusiveness and sustainable development. It has laid a foundation for the digital economy, which has been addressed by the previous speakers. We have reached consensus that the digitalization has laid a foundation for our economic growth. In the past 20 years around the world, we have seen a lot of digital innovation and business innovation, including e-commerce, digital finance, and the improvement of digital capabilities. This has laid foundation for the digitalization of the economy. And I want to mention one point that is in the past 20 years, we have developed a lot at Alibaba. The digitalization has shaped the world, especially the SME and entrepreneurs. It brings them new opportunities and new breakthroughs. And in the past, we call this a tree-like structure.

教师点评：译员有明显的断句顺接操作意识、源语加工意识、译语监管意识。译员 EVS 基本为一个主谓结构（即命题）或一个确定的状语结构，能够及时将所听到的源语中的部分信息独立成句译出，以句子为单位推进。虽然个别地方处理过度，如 we have developed a lot at Alibaba，个别地方受源语影响，表达不清晰，如 it has laid a foundation。但与译员 A 相比，内容更准确，语言质量更高，流利性和音韵更佳，更易理解。初学同传时，要培养顺句、断句和顺接的意识和习惯。刚开始时，可能会出现断句过早，产出不了完整句子，为了译语完整而添加内容，或者断句太晚，造成译语凌乱、臃肿、意思不明确或者漏译。经过循序渐进训练，能够逐渐找到较为普适的断句顺接规律与适合自己的操作方式。

部分源语的处理建议如下：

听了前面这几位的分享，我是非常有共鸣。
The sharing of the previous speakers has resonated with me.

由于源语句子非常短，语速快，不建议处理为：I have listened to the previous speakers. I strongly resonate with their ideas. 或者 After listening to the sharing of the previous speakers, I strongly resonate with their ideas.

那么在对于整个的经数字经济的发展，它带来的基础，其实有一个基础，在前面几位分享当中都讲到了，我想大家都有这个高度的共识，就是整个经济行为的数字化是整个数字经济的基础，和带来后面无穷变化的前提条件。

"带来的基础"属不规范表达，不知道是否是"到来"的口误，但是根据会议主题和语境不难理解，指数字经济发展的基础。该句处理方式有多种：
1) As for the development of the digital economy, there is a foundation which previous speakers touched upon. They all agreed that the digitalization of economic behaviour is the foundation of digital economy and a prerequisite for the endless transformations that follow.

2) The development of the digital economy is based upon something previous speakers touched upon. They all agreed that the digitalization of economic behaviour is the cornerstone of the digital economy and a prerequisite for the endless transformations that follow.

3) The development of the digital economy is built upon a foundation that previous speakers have touched upon and agreed upon—the digitalization of economic behaviour. This is the cornerstone of the digital economy and a prerequisite for the endless transformations that follow.

今天我们所有的无论是过去 20 年在整个世界范围内发生的大量的数字，围绕数字技术的创新……

1) Today, we can see that over the past 20 years worldwide there have been lots of digital technology innovations...

2) Over the past 20 years the world has seen lots of...

3) The past 20 years has seen around the world lots of...

此例中，"今天""过去 20 年""世界范围内"等状语，及随后的名词短语"大量的数字，围绕数字技术的创新"都是意思明确、形式稳定的，可以译出。而"我们所有的"形式不稳定、意思不确定可以不处理，"无论是"这类关联词的信息可以后置，后面视具体情形决定是否译出（类似的还有"因为……所以""虽然……但是"等）。

而在这里我特别想讲一点，就是阿里巴巴 20 年的发展，我们最大的感受是这样的一个数字，这样的一个经济行为的数字化以后，给这个世界特别是中小企业和个人的创业者带来一种新的天地，就使得他们突破了原有经济秩序当中，原来我们一直把它称为一个树状的经济结构。

1) Here, I would like to highlight one point: Alibaba's 20 years of growth has impressed us that the economic behavior digitization has made the

world different, particularly for small and medium-sized enterprises, as well as individual entrepreneurs. They have been offered new space and been able to break through the traditional economic order, the hierarchical structure of it.

2) One point to note. Alibaba's 20 years of growth has shown us that the economic behavior digitization could offer small and medium-sized enterprises, and entrepreneurs a new world, so that they could go beyond the traditional economic order, the hierarchical structure of it.

3) Alibaba's 20 years of growth has shown the potential/power of the economic behaviour digitization. It has provided small and medium-sized enterprises and entrepreneurs with a new world and ability to transcend the traditional economic order, the hierarchical structure of it.

四、信息听辨

1. 讲解

(1) 语言、意义与信息

同传的根本目的是传递信息，促进交际。译员听到的同传源语包含语言形式、意义与信息。语言形式指语言结构形式，包括语音、词汇、短语、句型等；意义指语言结构形式所表达出的意思，意义基于静态语言结构形式；信息基于现场动态交际，指说话人要传达给听众的消息，是可以减少或消除听众某种不确定性的新内容。信息有时与意义重合，而有时是为了更好促进交际而被加工、提炼过的意义。从初学者成长为专业译员的过程中，听辨理解的层次一般会从语言结构和意义为主，逐步过渡到主题信息与交际信息为主。

受文化因素、教育程度、思维方式、语言能力、表达风格等影响，会议发言人表达信息的能力存在差异。有些发言的语言形式能够清晰、流利表达信息,有些则不够清晰、流利,或者语言形式、意义、信息间距离较远,或者言不达意。对译员听辨带来挑战的中文源语类型主要包括:抽象模糊的表达、繁复冗余的表达、迂回凌乱的表达和文化信息丰富的表达。可围绕这些源语类型进行针对性信息听辨训练,努力理解:发言人想表达什么、希望听众听到什么?听完源语后,尝试用与源语不同的、更为简洁的语言形式复述源语意思;也可以听后用简洁的译语复述源语意思,并且尽量避免译语和源语在词汇、短语(专有名词、数字、术语及有固定对应译语的除外)层面直接对应。由于同传听译同步、渐进加工的特征,信息听辨效果往往不如交传。因此,一般建议进行一定时间的交传训练后再学习同传。

(2) 信息结构/单位

根据信息结构理论,话语信息由命题信息与信息成分组成。命题信息是一种述谓关系(也可理解成一个包含主谓结构的独立句子),信息成分是构成述谓关系的词汇。词汇本身无法表达信息,其所构成的述谓关系才可表达信息。命题信息由预设命题与断言命题两部分组成,即发言人认为听众已知的信息,和发言人认为听众还不知道、希望告知的新信息(须由独立句子或可还原为独立句子的结构进行表达)。假设在一次会议上,发言人对听众说:

> 改革开放以来,中国经济实现了高速增长。

发言人通过该句向听众表达了一个断言命题。该命题是发言人对听众知识状态进行评估后表达出的。发言人认为该命题是听众听到句子之后才得知的,能够更新听众的知识状态。该命题的表达要基于一组预设命题,比如:"有个国家叫中国""中国进行了改革开放",等等。如果发言人认为听众并不了解"中国进行了改革开放",那么他一般会通过独立句子来表达这一内容,而不是将之置于句子的状语成分位置。他正是评估了听众的知识状态,认为听众知道"中国进行了改革开放",但是并不清楚"改革开放以来,中国经济发展状况如何"才说出这句话的。

进一步说,如果在特定语境中,发言人认为该句所表达的命题信息是听众已知的,那么他一般不会通过一个独立句子进行表达,因为这会影响听众获取信息的效率。此时，发言人可能会说：

  由于改革开放以来中国经济的高速增长……

  显然，这不是一个独立句子，只是组成句子的词汇语法成分。这些成分能够唤起一组预设命题："中国进行了改革开放""中国经济高速增长""改革开放以来的中国经济高速增长"等。然而，这些成分无法表达一个断言命题。或者说，这些成分仅能唤起旧信息，无法表达和传递发言人期望传递的新信息。发言人这么说，是因为他认为该结构表达的内容是听众已知的，无须通过独立句子或者断言命题告诉听众，以免影响信息传递效率。会议发言的目的是传递新信息，因此，发言人一般会在这些已知内容的基础上，表达出他认为听众尚不知道的内容，即表达一个断言命题，如：

  由于改革开放以来中国经济的高速增长，中国高净值家庭数量激增。

  发言人在预设命题基础上增加了"中国高净值家庭数量激增"，表达出一个断言命题，传递出他希望传递给听众的信息。

  当然，有时，"由于改革开放以来中国经济的高速增长"也能够表达信息，前提是该表达被置于一种语用关系中。比如，如果发言人设问或者听众中有人向发言人提问："为什么中国高净值家庭数量增加这么多？"此时，"由于改革开放以来中国经济的高速增长"便可表达一个断言命题——"中国高净值家庭数量增加这么多是由于改革开放以来中国经济的高速增长"，只是该断言命题的表达在语境中有所省略，但是听众一般可以基于语境还原出这一断言命题。

  根据以上分析，同传中，应以命题为同传的基本加工单位。同传中的信息听辨主要指对命题的深度理解，或者说同传源语听辨的本质就是专注于高效乃至自动化搜觅源语命题信息，同传过程是一个命题接一个命题滚动着进行理解、记忆、转换和译语发布。整个加工过程中多种技能与策略的运用往往也是以命题为单位，如断句和动态调节 EVS 以命题为操作单位；在认知负荷过重时，优先加工命题信息（而非信息成分）；源语命题密度过高时，可将多个命题压缩为一个命题，反之，源语语速过慢，信息过少时，可将命题成分变为命题，一个命题拆分为多个命题。命题质量影响译语可用性与听众理解效果，要确保命题表达完整，信息明晰、凸显，命题之间衔接、连贯。

当然，能够在高压力下瞬间理解源语命题信息，是同传最大挑战之一。要做到这一点，译员除了需具备良好的语言能力、灵活流畅的思维、快速反应与抗压等能力之外，还需具备丰富的领域知识（学科和行业知识等），会议知识（会议背景、交际目的、会议环节、会议常用语等），了解源语文化、思维及信息表达方式、常见口语特征，同时要有语境和情境意识，基于语境、情境和所听信息进行预测及信息有效整合。平时应加强信息听辨，培养听交际信息的习惯，边听辨边思考：发言人为什么说这些？想传递什么信息？话语明确表达了什么信息？哪些信息想表达但没有清晰表达出来？发言用语和想表达的信息为什么不对应？通常会有哪些语言与信息不对应情形？同时，加强中英语言对比，尤其是词语、句子和话语层面在信息表现方式上的异同对比。

2. 训练与点评

> 会议：联合国教科文组织国际工程教育中心理事会暨顾问委员会2019年会议，互动环节发言，清华大学前校长

> 4A：

源语：我来自清华大学，我的名字叫顾秉林（原来是清华大学校长）。首先我觉得这个袁驷代表 ICEE 的一个工作报告，内容很丰富，很充实。确实 ICEE 这一年多来，从成立到现在，其实不到两年，但是做了相当相当多的工作，包括教育和培训，包括咨询项目，包括组织学术会议和论坛，也包括了一些高层之间的交流和互访，我觉得这都是很难得的。同时我也认真地听了袁驷关于下一步的工作打算，未来的工作打算也还是很实事求是的。我想我相信他们肯定在启迪主任的领导下，一定能够把这个事情做得很好。这是我想第一个表达我参加会议

以后的第一个意思。

译语：I'm professor Gu from Tsinghua University. And my name is Gu Binglin (The president of Tsinghua University). First of all, I, I would like to say that the report of ICEE is very resourceful. Over the past year, ICEE has made a lot of work, including education, consultation, academic conferences and also corporations. I think it is very important. And I also told, I also heard their future plans. I think they can do a good job under the leadership of professor Gu.

源语：第二个意思就是说，刚才大家讨论听了听，都是讨论工程教育本身的一些问题。当然都是为了更好地改进工程教育。我在想提另一些问题，就是工程教育和社会的问题。就是原先我们在西方留学的时候，最聪明的学生，不太愿意学工程，对吧？最聪明的学生一般学医，学法律，学经济，金融，也有些学理，对吧。就是说这件事情，我们工程教育本身会出现什么问题？当然我们很多取得了很大很大成绩，但是不能够吸引最优秀的学生来学工程，我觉得肯定是出了点什么问题。相对说来，中国好一些，就是说最聪明的学生，还是有一部分人把工程学工程，作为他的第一选择。但是已经有越来越多的不像我们那个时代，那时候最好学生肯定学工。现在不一样，现在他选择是多样化，取向是多样化的，工程只是一部分学生。

译语：Second, I, we've just talked about engineering and the educational change reforms. I would like to focus on other aspects, the relationship between engineer education and society. When I studied abroad, the most excellent student didn't willing, are, weren't willing to study engineering. They were, they prefer more law, economy and so on. From this perspective, we can find that there are some problems in our engineering education. Despite the great achievements, we still need to attract all kinds of students. Compared with other countries, China faces a relatively better situation. We just, we have some excellent students who want to learn engineering, which is not, which is different from our times. Now there are some students who want to learn engineering.

教师点评：译语中各类语言错误比较多，译员自述因为同时学习两门外语，英语基础不够好。但除了英语资源有限外，中文源语信息听辨也有问题："我觉得这都是很难得的"应该是发言人赞赏 ICEE 的工作，可译为 Great work has been done；"同时我也认真地听了袁驷关于下一步的工作打算"中的前半截属典型中文发言习惯，不含主题信息，可不直接译为英语，译语可从 work plan 开始。此外，"讨论工程教育本身的一些问题""但是不能够吸引最优秀的学生来学工程""工程只是一部分学生"等处均有信息理解错误。同传中源语信息听辨问题的原因常常包括：语言能力不足、知识（百科、专业与会议知识等）储备欠缺、信息分析整合能力不足、认知精力饱和等多方面。

4B：

源语：其实中国传统上对工是非常重视的。因为大家知道工这个字，本身中国都说中国是象形字，你看他工字虽然很简单，上面一横代表天，下边一横代表地，中间是个人，所以做顶天立地的事情，这就是工。中国从古代从象形字开始，就对工给予了高度的重视。但是我们不说每个工都是能够做顶天立地，但是整个作为整体来讲，作一个学科整体来讲，它确实来讲是改造世界，这样的一件大的事业。而我们对这个方面强调，实际上越来越淡漠了，越来越淡漠了。过去从中国象形字来讲，中国的文字来讲，它都是把工和天连在一起的，天工开物，对吧？那把理和地点连一起，地理，把文和人连在一起的，人文。是这样的，天地……

译语：Traditionally, China places emphasis on engineering, because the Chinese character gong. It's simple yet represents a lot. The first line represents the sky, the secondary represents the land. And the people, the first line stands in the middle. So you can see the stress, the Chinese people places are engineering from the character itself. However, I'm not saying that every engineering can be like that, shouldering the whole sky. However, we are all engaging in a big experiment. If we address, I think the emphasis is fading out from the form of the character, we usually connect the character Gong with the character Tian the sky, or we connected with the land and outcome the geography. So we see a happening between the sky, the land and the the subject itself in the Chinese culture.

源语：所以这个工，是最高的。这件事情我觉得现在我们都淡漠了。为什么淡漠呢？我想举个例子，在我们当时就在中国，我说也发生了一些变化。在我们年轻的时候，那时候说科学家、工程师都是非常羡慕的。但现在取向是多元化以后，当然有什么有这个明星，这个那个有各种取向。但是就科学家和工程师而言，我觉得大家更重视科学家了，已经不重视工程师了。你要说科学家，大家心目当中还是很神圣的，但工程师大家心目当中就不是那么非常向往，望而生惧。这件事情说明了我们的教育，我们工程教育和社会之间关系是出现了一些问题的。如果我们现在不抓紧的话，我们以后越来越聪明的学生，可能不学工程了，而是把第二流的人才和第三流人才来学了。所以我觉得应当是敲醒这样的一个警钟。

译语：So why is it fading out? Why is this very fading out? I want to share with you an example. We have seen some changes in China. When we are younger, some engineers are the targets of people's admiration. However, now we have more choices for students. Yet for engineers and scientists, their focus are shifting from engineering itself. Of course science is still enshrined. However, the engineers are not placed at the same place. So we see a disconnect between engineering, the subject and society. If we do not catch up now, we will see a phenomenon that in the future students fall out of this major bright students. Now, some other students going to this major.

教师点评：(1) 译员的信息听辨与加工能力较差，较多地方的源语信息理解及表达存在问题，存在明显的字面对译，译语表达的语法及地道性问题较多，且衔接连贯性较弱，这些与汉语源语理解层次及英语资源丰富性、可用性和灵活性都有关。

(2) "中国传统上对工是非常重视的"可处理为 China has had a tradition of valuing engineering，原译语中的 emphasis 是字面对译。"工"字这段，需要把信息传递出来，可以译为 engineering in Chinese is Gong, a character consisting of three lines, upper horizontal line for heaven, lower horizontal line for earth, middle vertical line for people. "作一个学科整体来讲，它确实来讲是改造世界，这样的一件大的事业"：as a discipline/field of study, engineering transforms the world and plays a vital role.

(3) "我们对这个方面强调，实际上越来越淡漠了"指的是 we no longer value it that much as we did，emphasis is fading out，是字面对译，表达不地道，信息不清晰。"工程师都是非常羡慕的""科学家，大家心目当中还是很神圣的"可以处理为 engineers/scientists are highly respected and admired professionals. "我们会以后越来越聪明学生，可能不学工程了"可译为 we will lose top students/top students will increasingly stay away from engineering/be increasingly disinterested in pursuing engineering.

(4) 此外，译语的发音、语气、语调、节奏、流利性等音韵方面存在不足，导致译语的可听性、沟通感不强。

会议："文化走出去的价值应用与传播路径"论坛，问答环节，外交学院领导、《中国日报》周日版执行主编

5A：

源语：刚才您提到那个程抱一先生，我就现场搜了一下程抱一先生在网上的一些记录，然后因为今天咱们讨论的是文化走出去，我个人认为如

果要想让中国文化走出去,一定要深深地植根于中国这样一个文化的土壤当中。刚才我看到程抱一先生的简介的时候,注意到程抱一先生在1972年加入了法国国籍,我就想到另外一个挺严肃的话题,当我们鼓励中国文化走出去,那个中国的学生作为留学生出国的时候,往往大量的人才可能就留在了国外,我们怎样能够让我们的文化走出去,让我们的人才流回来呢,谢谢您。

译语: I have a question, Mr. Zhao, you have mentioned about François Cheng. So, I did some research. Now, our topic is "culture going out". I think if we want to promote cultural dissemination overseas, we need to based on the true Chinese culture situation. I noticed that François Cheng has become French. So, I have a question, when Chinese students are studying abroad, after the study, they just stay overseas, and what should we do to attract them back to China?

源语: 首先,程抱一先生他后来是定居在台湾。他虽然是出生在南京,但是后来呢,在家庭大概战后吧,就到了香港,最后定居在台湾。他是从台湾到法国去求学,最后加入到法国籍了。那么这种经历,就是中国的青年到国外学习,然后留在国外,例子很多,从我个人来讲,我是支持和赞赏这样的一种选择,因为什么呢?因为我们中国,特别是我们改革开放以后,我们来看,虽然我们发展得很快,很迅猛,但是我们在很多方面,特别是我们的基础设施的建设,包括在我们的一些学术,在我们的技术、科学、研究一些课题等等很多方面,我们还没有处在世界的高端的或者是最先进的水平。所以我们有一些青年要把他们要留在有一些氛围更好的一些环境当中,来进行他们自身的提升、研究。我觉得在那个诺贝尔的这个获得者当中有很多的华人,那么这些人我觉得他们把科学作为一种追求或者是自己的一个人生的目标,是很好的。

译语: Now, the first thing I want to say is that François Cheng is in Taiwan. So, he went from Taiwan to French to study. This experience is shared by many Chinese students overseas. From a personal level, I support them. I support this kind of experience. Why? Because after the reform and opening up in China, despite our rapid development, we still lag behind other countries in many areas, including infrastructure construction, scientific research, etc. We are still not the first rank of the world. If we want to so we need to send our talents to those better advanced countries for their own improvement. I see many Chinese people who have won Nobel prize, I think for them...it is good for them to study overseas to fulfill their goal.

教师点评：(1) 该译员也来自复语专业，英语基础有些薄弱，出现了不少语言错误。

(2) 从信息传递角度看，还存在不少问题。首先，信息不够完整、具体、清晰，如"赵进军大使"，单纯 Mr. Zhao，不仅不准确，而且也会引起误解——现场另外一个嘉宾也姓赵；"一定要深深地植根于中国这样一个文化的土壤当中"处为 we need to based on the true Chinese culture situation，即便没有语言错误，该译语的信息也不够清晰，译员没有理解源语信息，提问者可能是指，向外宣传中国文化的人，本身应该是植根于中国文化当中的人，因此可以处理为 people spreading/promoting Chinese culture overseas should be rooted in/have a strong foundation in Chinese culture themselves；"他后来是定居在台湾"是指 he settled down in Taiwan；This experience is shared by many Chinese students overseas 表达得也比较模糊，可以调整为 Chinese youngsters studied abroad and stayed there, as is not rare；"我是支持和赞赏这样的一种选择"的原译也不够准确清晰，可以调整为 their decision is understandable/reasonable/I think they made the right choice/decision/I understand and appreciate their choice/decision.

(3) 其次，译语中存在不少停顿填充，如 so, now，其中一些是受源语影响，中文发言里有一些填充语，并非逻辑连接词，听辨时要加以区分，另外一部分是译员不良发布习惯所致。

（4）此外，译语删减源语信息的地方较多，初学者应注意避免这一点。

（5）当然，译语的语音、语气、语调、节奏等尚可，内容连贯性和语言衔接方面总体也还可以，有些英语表达比较简洁、清晰。

5B：

源语：我记得我当年在法国的时候，有一次我们请一个国内的一个领导同志，也是我们的国务委员，研究负责科学的一位老同志。然后我就在问他，我说怎么看这个，就是现在这个科学家在想些什么，在做些什么，他告诉我，他说我们这个地球说现在有46亿年，目前的估计大概100亿年的寿命，那么也就是说已经到了它的中年了是吧？再过一半的时间，这个地球要毁灭。因为有了太阳才有了地球，太阳也比地球就是多了几亿年的寿命，将来太阳也会熄灭。因此他说现在高端的科学家研究什么，研究怎么样保障地球、人类这个精灵，他说这人类的产生绝对是世界的一个宇宙的一个奇迹。如果地球毁灭了，人类就毁灭了，不可想象。因此科学家想的是什么，地球、人类的一些问题，所以我觉得你刚才提到的这个问题呢就使我想起这个故事。有的时候我们思考问题的时候，可能更多的或者是愿意从我们自身，从我们的国家、我们的家乡和我们的家人，从我们自身角度来考虑，但是我们能不能跳出来一点，要从一个更宽阔的广阔的一个角度来思考问题。

译语：When I was in France, I invited a Chinese official, the State Councilor, who was responsible for science research. I asked him what's his take on the scientists' work. He answered: the earth is 4.6 billion years old. So it's in its middle age. It will die out someday. The sun gives the earth life. It is older than the sun, but it will also go out someday. In this context, scientists are trying to preserve the human beings, the miracle of the universe. If the sun dies out, the human beings will also disappear. These are what the scientists are studying, are doing. Your question reminds me this story. So maybe sometimes we need to think bigger, not only about ourselves, our families, our country, we should think beyond the context.

教师点评：（1）总体上，译语信息加工还不错，语言虽有少量错误，但是比较简洁清晰，发布也比较流利。

（2）其中有一处听辨理解错误："我说怎么看这个，就是现在这个科学家在想些什么，在做些什么"，这句话发言人说到一半又改口，实际不是问他的观点，不可译为"what's his take on the scientists' work"，他是想问"科学家在想些什么，在做些什么"，可以处理为"what scientists are thinking about and doing/working on"。对于即兴发言，尤其是互动性较强的环节，译员需要及时从发言人不规范、不流利的表达中，听辨出其想表达的信息，避免被不当语言形式干扰，去伪存真。具体方法就是在快速语流中不断搜寻、捕捉、理解命题（主谓结构）。

（3）另外，漏译了"目前的估计大概100亿年的寿命"，该句信息可以置于前句，处理为 the earth is currently 4.6 billion years old in its lifespan (habitable lifetime) of 10 billion，也可以和后一句整合，处理为 Its lifespan being 10 billion years, the earth is now middle-aged.

（4）it's in its 的问题一般是因为同传中译员认知精力不足，短期记忆饱和，也未有足够精力监控译语。有关地球和太阳这一段，译语把两者弄混了，也可能是因为记忆精力饱和所致。在即兴发言中举例子，讲故事或者罗列环节，往往有较多专有名词、时间、数字等，这些内容缺乏冗余性，不易记忆，因此建议译员缩短 EVS 或者适当记笔记，降低记忆负荷，减少因记忆问题导致的错译。

（5）最后一句，译员采用了预测策略，改变语序，先译出 think bigger，但是在同传中，译员应在可能的条件下尽量顺句加工，以减少记忆负荷。此句可顺句处理为：We tend to think more of ourselves/often prioritize ourselves, our country, our hometown and our family, but it's essential to think beyond these and consider the bigger/broader picture.

5C-1：

源语：非常非常激动，谢谢主持人给我这样一个机会。我今天参加这个论坛，我觉得非常有启发，非常有收获。在我看来啊就是文化创新最关键的还是要自觉和自信，文化传播……

译语：I'm very excited for this opportunity. I joined this forum today and it's very inspiring. For me, the critical thing of culture innovation is innovation.

源语：拜托稍微简短一点好吗？谢谢你，提给谁的问题，谢谢你。

译语：Please be brief, thank you.

源语：我主要想提的问题，主要向这个赵部长和三位媒体界的专业人士提。现在我们都在热讲"中国梦"。前不久有一部《中国合伙人》的电影创下了票房七个亿，那么在这部电影中就体现了我们中国年轻人的梦，也是我们中国的梦。我们中国梦包括哪些文化因素？在外国人看来，中国梦应该怎样为我们中华民族的伟大复兴提供一些文化支撑呢？谢谢！

译语：So my question is for Mr. Zhao and three professionals from the press. Now we are all talking about Chinese Dream, and a movie about this topic made 700 million yuan. And what's the cultural aspect of Chinese Dream, and as for foreigners, what they can do?

源语：好，谢谢你，你一下提问了四位是吧？还要听听外国朋友的见解是吗？那这个好吧，正好，除了赵大使，你把台上四位都提问到了，那能不能我们还请赵主任您最后做总结？我们先请三位专家看一看怎么回答他这个问题。中国梦当然是当下的一个热议的话题，而这个词也是每一个人做着每一个人的梦想，每一个人都有他自己的解读，那么Doctor 罗，您所理解的中国梦是什么呢？

译语：Thank you. So you have a question for four people? Ok. So your question...now let's have the three professionals to answer first. Chinese Dream is a heated topic now, and it involves everyone, and everyone has his or her interpretation, and what's your understanding?

教师点评：（1）译语的信息听辨与表达问题较多：第一句就是误译，应该是 thank you for taking my question。

（2）"我今天参加这个论坛"与之前会议材料中的"我也认真地听了"类似，属于一种发言习惯，不含主题信息，不可直接对译，可以和后面一起处理为 it is an informative forum；"提给谁的问题"是重要信息，不可漏译。

（3）同前面，"赵部长"不可简化为 Mr. Zhao，另外需注意此处是中文里常用的尊称，实际头衔是"赵主任"（全国政协外事委员会主任，正部级）；三位媒体界的专业人士也不应处理为 professionals，应该是 experts，或者直接说 three panelists from the media。

（4）"中国梦应该怎样为我们中华民族的伟大复兴提供一些文化支撑呢"可以处理为 How does the Chinese Dream contribute culturally to our national rejuvenation/What cultural significance does the Chinese Dream hold in our national rejuvenation/What is the cultural role of the Chinese Dream to the rejuvenation of the Chinese nation?

（5）最后一段漏译信息较多，"请赵主任您最后做总结"具有很强的现场互动功能，"Doctor 罗"也是，不可漏译，译员需要时刻意识到源语与译语信息的交际功能。

（6）总体看，译员听译协调、听辨理解与转换的效率以及英语表达资源尚需提高。

5C-2：

译语：Today, I attend this meeting. I am very inspired and fruitful. In my opinion, culture renovation lies in culture.

译语：Please, be brief, OK? Thank you. Please, indicate who your question is to. Thank you.

译语：I mainly want to ask to Minister Zhao and three professionals in media. Now, we are talking about China's Dream. A few days ago, *American Dreams in China* has made a 700 million tickets. This Chinese dream contains what kind of cultural elements. And in foreigners' eyes, how can China's Dream provide cultural support for China's great rejuvenation? Thank you.

译语：You've directly asked four experts, even foreign experts. Except Minister Zhao, you've also asked other experts on the stage. So, we would like to have foreign experts first, and then have Minister Zhao to give a brief conclusion. About China's Dream, every individual has their own dream, have their own explanation. Doctor Luo, what's your opinion on China's Dream?

教师点评：译语存在较多语言问题，这一点后文再谈。译语中有几处能够充分反映译员听辨信息能力不足：同上一例，译员直接对译了"我今天参加这个论坛"；"我主要想提的问题，主要向……"中的"主要想"是口语特征，不具有主题信息，不宜译为 I mainly want to；同样"赵部长""三位媒体界的专业人士"也不能直接简单对译；provide cultural support 也是字面简单对译的结果；有趣的是译员竟使用了 directly，译后访谈中得知，其是想翻译出"一下子"；此外"解读"也不是 explanation，"您所理解的中国梦"不是询问 opinion。这些细节都说明，译员听辨加工单位过小，过于关注源语语言细节，话语的信息听辨能力较弱。

五、信息加工

1. 讲解

由于中英语言、文化及表达习惯等差异较大，加上同传要求边听边译,译员的理解和表达常呈渐进式,时间压力大,中英同传时,译员需要通过具体操作策略,将源语语言所表达的信息在译语语言中重新配置,对源语信息在译语中的表达位置、方式及内容等进行加工、调整。调整总体有两大目的:减轻源语负荷,保证同传顺利进行,提升译语表达效率效果,促进交际。前者主要对应语言加工策略,即侧重从信息表达方式(语言结构位置及表达方式)方面进行调整,克服中英语言结构差异对同传的挑战,减轻译员信息加工负荷,具体包括信息前置、信息后置、信息分散、信息提取等;后者主要对应内容加工策略,即侧重对源语表达的内容进行调整,旨在增进译语交际效果,具体包括信息简缩、信息显化、信息修正、信息软化和信息过滤等。

(1) 信息前置

信息前置指通过预测将源语某些语言形式及其信息的位置在译语中往前调整。

中文发言中经常出现"长修饰语+中心词"的情形。由于英语的长修饰语多后置,在发言人还未说出中心词前,译员难以翻译修饰语,此时可采用等待或插入中性填充语等策略。但如果修饰语较长、信息较多或语速较慢,译员等待或拖延过长,会增加记忆和加工负荷,可能导致后面来不及译或者记不得,也影响译语可听性。此时,译员可以根据语境及时预测中心词,将之提前译出。如果预测有偏差,可以随后调整。

> 本次会议为我们提供了一次相互学习交流经验、共同应对未来挑战的机会。

此例中,译员可以视现场情况决定自己的开译点,可在听到"机会"时再开口翻译,也可在听到"提供了"处提前预测出"机会",产出译语:The conference offers us a chance to exchange best practices and address the challenges ahead. 如果预测出现偏差,比如发言人实际说的是"平台",可再追加 So it's a perfect platform 之类的表达。

> 我们将进一步贯彻创新、协调、绿色、开放的发展理念,将我市打造成创新之城、生态之城。

该例中,"……发展理念"结构中的修饰语所含信息点较多,若译员等待到"发展理念"说完再开口译,可能会因记忆负担重而错、漏译,也会影响译语流利性,还可能影响后面信息点的准确、完整翻译。此时,译员可在听到"贯彻创新"附近时,基于发言风格、语境和搭配习惯等及时预测,将"理念"这一信息提前译出。We will remain committed to the philosophy/principles of innovative, coordinated, green and open development, and build an innovative and eco-friendly city.

(2) 信息后置

信息后置指将源语某些语言形式及其信息的位置在译语中往后调整。

即兴发言中,有些不善表达的发言人,可能会使用较多关系词,如"因此""所以""虽然""即便"等,但这些词或许并未表达应有的逻辑关系,仅是口头禅或填充语。译员可根据发言风格和语境及时作出判断,暂时不译该类词语,若下句源语确实表明了这一逻辑关系,在该句的译语前添加关系词。

很高兴能有机会在这里和大家交流,这对我来说也是一个学习的机会,所以呢我要先和各位简单介绍下我们公司。虽然说我们公司去年才成立,我们的市场份额已经进入行业前十了。

此处的"所以"并未表示因果关系,无需翻译。当译员发现发言人有这种习惯后,需要谨慎对待接下来的一些关系词,因此"虽然"可先不译,先将事实译出,在听到后面半句存在转折关系时,将 but 加在后半句的译语前:Our company was set up last year, but it is now among top ten in this sector in terms of market share.

还有些发言人会出现类似口误的表达,歧义表达,或者译员当时不确信是否理解正确的表达,译员先不用急着译出这些信息,先译出确信的信息或先模糊处理,再根据后续源语决定是否译、如何译,如有必要,可在后面译语添加有关信息。

谢谢。对你刚才所讲的这个问题,我想讲两点我的看法。两点中的第一点……

"两点"可能表示概数"几点",也可能就表示两点。译员可先将两点处理为 a few/several,等听到"两点中的第一点"后,再添加 basically two points 之类的表达。

(3) 信息分散

信息分散和信息提取指在理解源语信息的基础上,放弃源语语言表达信息的主要构造方式,以新的译语结构配置表达源语信息。其中,信息分散是将源语有限结构内的密集信息疏解到较多的译语语言结构中去。

在比较正式的会议,或发言比较正式的环节,可能会碰到中文源语有限的语言结构凝结承载密集信息的情形,读稿发言中较为多见。尤其是中国政府治理的相关用语,往往表达凝练,内涵丰富。翻译时,可将密集信息分散到不同的英语结构中去。在发言语速较慢、译员有充分时间和精力时,此策略较为适用。

持续深入的"放管服"改革提高了人民群众办事的便利度。

"放管服"指"简政放权、放管结合、优化服务",若将源语主语处理为一个作主语的英语短语,可能会因为信息过于密集而影响英语听众理解。此时,可将该部分信息分散为一个独立句子进行表达,再顺接后面译语:We have been deepening reforms to streamline administrative procedures, delegate authority, improve regulation and improve services. By doing so, we have made government services more accessible to the public.

"兜底线、织密网、建机制"等工作,完善了社会救助体系。

同上例,译员可将"兜底线、织密网、建机制"部分的信息独立成句,再进行顺接处理:We have worked to help those most in need, build a tightly woven safety net, and build the necessary institutions. By doing so, we have improved the social assistance system. 该处理既可提高译语的可理解性,又能增进信息传递效果。

(4) 信息提取

信息提取指去除某些源语结构中的语言形式框架,提取凝练、清晰的信息进行表达。

同传首要任务是传递信息，信息是译员加工对象和听众理解对象。信息只能通过独立句子表达，从句或短语一般仅是信息成分，无法独立表达信息。因此，从译员传递信息和听众获取信息的效果、效率角度看，译语中应尽量安排独立短句表达重要信息。而中文发言，尤其是读稿发言，常用一些状语从句或长状语结构，如"为……""对……""在……""自……"等。如果按照源语结构进行对译，可能会使译语支离破碎，信息不凸显，影响译语可听性和可用性；如果采取等待和句式结构调整策略，则会耽误时间，增加译员记忆负担。此时，可去除此类表达的语言形式框架，提取出其要表达的信息，以简单独立句子将该信息及时译出。对于表达逻辑关系的一些框架结构，可先译出框架中的信息，将关系词适当后置译出。以上两种操作分别接近于前面所谈的信息前置和信息后置。

世界经济论坛为扩大中国与世界各国的对话，增进国际社会和中国的相互了解发挥了重要作用。

此例中的"为……发挥了重要作用"可看作是一个语言形式框架，该部分要表达的重要信息在框架里面。熟悉此类中文表达的译员，在听到"为"时，会很快识别出语言形式框架的存在，此时可及时去除框架，提取并译出信息：The World Economic Forum has helped China engage in broader global dialogue/wider global discussions, and has enhanced mutual understanding between China and the international community.

我公司自2005年向市场推出第一款产品以来，目前已经累计推出30多种产品。

可先将"自……以来"这一框架中的关键信息译出，再将该框架表达的逻辑关系译出，顺接到后面的译语上：In 2005 we launched the first product. Since then, we have launched over 30 products.

(5) 信息简缩

信息简缩是对源语中繁复、冗余、松散部分进行压缩、整合，实现译语精益化。

有的发言语速较快，表达或繁复、或松散，语言形式多，表达的信息少且分散，信息冗余度高。这一情形在读稿发言和即兴发言中都存在，但在即兴发言，尤其互动性较强的环节（如问答、讨论等）更常见。读稿中的繁复冗余表达主要体现在为加强语气、体现节奏和音韵而进行的排比、罗列、重复等上；即兴发言中的冗余分散表达主要受汉语语言特征、发言人的表达习惯和能力、话题熟悉状况及发言准备状况等因素影响，出现"简单信息复杂表达，单一信息反复表达，相同信息重复表达"等情形。若译员直接在语言层面寻求对应，则译语也会变得繁复臃肿，表达不地道，信息不清晰。此时，译员可适当拉长 EVS，增大加工单位，快速理解长句、复杂句、流水句等所表达的信息，将多个句子压缩、整合为一个句子，将较长的复杂句简缩为简单句，将简单句简缩为词组，将较长词组简缩为词。

最常用的策略是，通过英语中的 5 种简单句型——主谓、主谓宾、主系表、主谓双宾及主谓宾补，对源语信息进行简缩式表达。这些句型构造简单，形式灵活，易于凸显信息，不仅利于高效传递信息，减轻译员认知负荷，还能促进听众高效理解发言人的信息。

> 刚提出要把这个城镇化作为国家战略的时候，很多的最热闹的人群是谁？是房地产开发商，大家都觉得哇这个中国的房地产要迎来新一轮的繁荣了，所有的讨论都跑到那地方去了。

此例来自即兴发言，语速较快，表达松散，信息分散。如果按照源语结构逐句对译，时间上来不及，且会影响译语的可用性。通过整合压缩部分信息，译语可以更加简洁高效：When urbanization was first made a national strategy, real estate developers were among the most enthusiastic expecting new momentum in the sector.

> 李院士积极投身建筑设计，发表大量学术论文，在我国建筑领域学术论文高被引作者排名中位居第一。

此例中，主持人介绍发言人时读他的简历，语速较快，译员并未拿到相关材料，此时，顺句驱动显然不合适，可对源语信息进行压缩整合，再以简单译语表达：Academician Li's active role in architectural design made him China's most cited author in architecture.

  我们要感谢组委会的积极筹备，感谢志愿者的热情服务，正是因为他们的辛勤工作，我们的活动才能取得圆满成功。

此例来自闭幕致谢部分，语速较快，可通过一个简单句表达源语信息：We thank the organization committee and volunteers for making this event possible/happen/a big success.

此外，还可通过"合并同类项"方式，将排比表达中的部分重复信息合并译出。如，下例可处理为 gaps in infrastructure, management and human resources。

  基础设施不足，管理水平不高，人力资源有限

再如，下例选自读稿演讲，语速较快，可以合并重复信息：we are (doing) increasingly better at/we have increasingly better sources of students, quality of teaching and administration. 当然也可以将 sources of students, quality of teaching and administration 作为主语译出。

  生源也在逐步地优化，教学质量呢不断地提高，日常管理水平呢日益地规范。

简缩的另一思路是使用上位词、原型词，如 come, go, put, take 等，这些词汇通常是最早学习的基本词汇，用法灵活。下例可处理为：We need go green, live and think green. 该处理使得译语变得简洁高效。

  我们要推动绿色发展，生活方式、思维方式都要朝着绿色发展方向调整。

此外，也可以使用表达同类意思的较短音节的词，如用 cut 代替 decrease，reduce 等。

上述两种方法有时候可以结合起来使用。下例可处理为：Major

developed and emerging countries view international education as an edge-sharpener/enabler of/aid to/contributor to their national image, soft power, revenue and human resources. "塑造、集聚、拓展和延揽"的排比，在听辨时可以预测，之后合并通过一个上位词表达译出。

> 主要发达国家和新兴国家都把国际教育作为塑造国家形象，集聚软实力，拓展经济收益和延揽全球人才的重要手段。

上述策略可以根据语境综合选择使用。下例来自某投资研讨会的开幕致辞，发言人读稿，语速较快，可合并部分重复信息，将多个句子简缩表达为1个句子，将中文句子简缩表达为英语词组，中文长词组精简为较短英语词组，使用上位词、原型词进行表达：Chinese businesses have a hard time investing overseas./Chinese overseas investment is defined by challenges./Chinese investor's journey abroad is a bumpy one. Quality service provider can make a significant difference. Inexperienced investors put cost and personal connections before quality service and their brother company, inexperienced in project planning and management, costs them the project and even their corporate performance.

> 中国对外投资并非一帆风顺，而是充满了挑战和风险……此外，一个项目的成功与否，负责提供服务的专业团队的素质十分重要。举例而言，某些企业由于是首次尝试对外投资，一心只想节约成本以及照顾"关系户"，却忽略了服务质量实为成功的主要因素之一，而最终由于所谓的"兄弟"公司缺乏国际经验，导致项目在缺乏专业规划和管理的情况下无序进行，可想而知，不但项目失败，对企业自身的利益亦造成了极大的损害。

(6) 信息显化

信息显化是将源语中虚的表达实化，抽象的表达具体化，模糊的表达明晰化。

发言稿常常经过字斟句酌，语言华丽，内容务虚，空泛、抽象、模糊、口号式表达不少，典礼、仪式致辞、会议开闭幕致辞中较为常见。这类表达有的是口号性排比结构或对比结构，节奏感强，但信息不凸显；有的看似简单，实则抽象空泛；有的使用了缩略表达，从字面难以具体理解。此类表达如果字面对译，往往难以传达源语信息，导致听众理解困难，甚至误解。此时，译员应及时听辨分析这些表达的深层意义及其传达的信息，并以具体清晰的译语进行传译。

近年来，郑州市在省委、省政府的正确领导下，着眼于"全国找坐标、中部求超越、河南挑大梁"……

"全国找坐标、中部求超越、河南挑大梁"类表达常见于政府发言，对于中国人来说，这类表达意思不难理解，但不宜直译给英语听众，可将信息明晰为：lead the province, impress central China and influence the whole country 或者 be a leader/leading city of the province, a rising/an influential city in central China and the whole country。

2014年是中国LNG产业集体反思的一年，15年是LNG行业全面调整整顿的一年。

"集体反思""全面调整整顿"是比较典型的中国式表述，信息不够清晰，如果直译，英语听众或许难以理解，此时可分别处理为 identify problems and solutions、make corrections/adjustment，将信息显化。

(7) 信息修正

信息修正是对源语中明显的错误信息进行修正。有些发言人可能会出现口误，尤其数字、专有名词等。如果译员非常确信发言人出错，比如出现常识性错误，或者译员对某信息非常熟悉，或者后面信息与前文不符（要确保前面信息正确），或者某些信息与正式发言稿不符等情形时，译员可在译语中进行修正。此外，发言中政治不正确的表达，如涉及我国主权问题的某些表述，译员也应加以修正。当然，对于不确信是否错误的情形，译员最好按照发言人的说法进行翻译。

而我碰到这个东西，这个绩效技术大概是在93年，那个时候

×××和我在印第安纳大学……再后来就是2003年,我在名古屋大学,他们让我做一个邀请报告……所以这是93年的事情。

此例中,根据语境,发言人显然在最后一句误将"2003"说成"93",译员应在译语中加以修正。

(8) 信息软化

信息软化是通过对源语中过于情绪化的表达进行语气软化,以既保证交际信息的有效传递,又维持交际活动的顺利进行。有些发言人可能因过于情绪化或者出于标新立异等目的而说出一些语气或内容上不利交际的话、偏激的话、气话等,译员应根据语境和场景及时判断,这些表达中是否含有实质性信息,这些信息是否为听众所需,是否有利于增进现场交际效果。如果有,则可对表达的语气、内容进行软化、降调处理,如果没有,则可省去不译。

笔者曾多次碰到需要软化信息的情形。有一次论坛上,国家某部委领导演讲结束后,主持人请听众提问。有位听众站起来后,说出一长串有关化工厂技术改造的专业术语,主持人赶紧打断,提醒他因为时间不多,请简单提问。结果提问者仍坚持自己的提问方式,并表示自己不远千里来北京参会,就是为了向某领导咨询这一问题。主持人再次打断他,请他会后私下交流。此话似激怒了提问者,他开始批评指责主持人,越批评越激动,竟满口脏话。前面几排的外宾纷纷往后看,手按着耳边的接收机迫切地想了解发生了什么。笔者并未直接翻译,而是用比较平静的语气把提问者的提问愿望和主持人的打断理由详细解释了下,外宾们频频点头示意理解。

(9) 信息过滤

信息过滤指出于文化、社会及交际等因素考虑,对源语中某些不利交际的内容进行删除。

有些发言中可能存在从跨文化交际角度不必译出的内容,如发言人的过谦表达。中文发言开始部分的自我介绍中常存在此类表达。

我也是李教授的弟子,但我不学无术,碌碌无能,没能继续走学术道路,下海经商了。

该例中，译员根据语境不难判断，"不学无术、碌碌无能"属于发言人过于自谦的表达。此类表达对于身处中国文化的人来说很容易理解，但是若译成英语，则可能造成英语文化听众的误解，反而不利于交际，因此不必翻译：I was also once a student of professor Li, but I stopped pursuing an academic career and went into business.

有时发言中含有从社会与交际角度不宜译出的内容，如违反党的路线、方针、政策或侵害国家利益的表达，含有侮辱、诋毁、戏谑、攻击、色情用语的表达等，此类信息，译员也应进行过滤。

总之，译员应具备跨文化交际意识和能力，同时扮演好"守门人"角色，对不必和不宜译出的信息进行过滤，按照译语政治正确、促进交际的原则进行传译。

上述九种策略的使用和会议类型、目的、主题，源语发言特征及现场情境因素等紧密相关。上述策略在商务性、学术性会议中更为常用，对于政治、外交、法律类会议则要谨慎使用。例如，政治性会议中，发言人可能故意保持某种语言风格或者表达风格，译员一般不可随意加工调整。相比语言策略，内容策略的应用要更为谨慎，要综合考虑交际类型、目的等。比如，在谈判、庭审等情形中，说话人可能故意作出某类表达（如非流利表达，模糊表达等），以实现特定交际目的，译员不可随意调整更改，而需在译语中保留某些风格特征。源语特征，如语速、信息密度、语言结构复杂度、口音、专业性、表达流利性等也会影响具体策略的使用。信息密度较高、语言结构较为复杂的读稿发言中，可能更常使用信息前置、信息分散、信息提取、信息显化等策略；而发言流利性较差、口语特征较为明显的互动性发言中，信息后置、信息简缩等可能更为常用。另外，现场情境因素，如客户的特殊要求（比如客户要求译员对某些类型的话语进行过滤等），现场突发情况（比如译员配置不足）等也会影响策略的选择和使用。

从根本上说，译员能否及时从源语语言形式中理解其欲表达的信息，是否具备丰富可用的译语表达资源，是进行有效信息加工的关键。此外，译员须注意，在采用各种策略时，应确保译语不会对源语信息扭曲、减少或增加。

2. 训练与点评

> 会议："IEA 世界能源展望特别报告"发布会，嘉宾点评，生态环境部环境规划院领导

下面是两位译员同一材料的同传表现，我们对第一位的表现进行了较为详尽的点评，同时，将第二位译员经课堂教师点评后进行的译后反思呈现在这里。

6A-1：

源语：谢谢大家。我很高兴来参加这个发布会，但是我是第一次参加这种发布会，所以来之前我就问自己，我说我去干嘛呢？所以我就看了一下报告，感觉到还是有意义，第一个是感觉看到 IEA 在它的年度报告里面特别关注空气污染与能源这个话题，跟我现在关注的事情、从事的研究是完全吻合的，所以我就来了。

译语：Thank you. It's glad to be here. This is my first time to attend such a meeting. So I asked before I came: What's my task? So I read the report. And I think it's really meaningful. In its annual report, IEA focus on the air pollution and energy, and this is in line with my research. So I'm here.

教师点评：这一段，译员在准确理解源语信息，简洁、清晰表达源语信息上还有较大提升空间。

（1）要有"发布会"的交际场景感，会议发言一开始常常会交代出席背景，致谢主办方，其中常会提及会议名、主办方机构名、人名、头衔等，这些内容对于主办方来说比较重要，发布类的活动，主办方一般更重视和发布会有关的各种品牌信息的传播效果，因此此处建议显化活动相关信息，处理为 IEA's China Launch (of IEA World Energy Outlook)（按照客户所给日程中的说法）。

（2）What's my task? 有些生硬、模糊，建议处理为 what was I supposed

to do?

（3）发言人的"感觉到还是有意义"有歧义，可能指这个报告或者活动有意义，即 the report/event is relevant/significant，也可能表示他觉得来参会很值得，即 I am in the right place/event 或者 I made the right decision to come，即兴发言同传中，译员时常需要根据语境、情境等综合判断，但是由于同传中发言人与译员无法交流，有的歧义难以消除。

（4）可以提取"IEA 在它的年度报告里面特别关注"状语中的名词做主语，处理为 IEA annual report，这样做比译为状语再加主谓结构的表达信息效率更高，另外，"特别关注"没必要处理为 focus，处理为 looks closely/specifically at 更合适。

（5）this is in line with my research 也显得生硬、模糊，可以处理为 which/this is the very area of my interest/happens to be my research interest.

源语：第二个就是说中国现在正在实施大气污染防治行动计划，从这个层面上跟国际的层面上，应该有一种对话的这种机制。我看了这个报告以后也是简版，厚的也没有那么长时间去看就是了。有8个字的评论，那么第一个就是说，这个报告应该说体现了转型的特点，我们一般地认为，以前我IEA也去过一次，总觉得这个IEA是发达国家、市场经济国家一个能源俱乐部一样，为发达国家能源的安全各方面保障做很多事情。但站在国际世界这个舞台上，他们现在把自己的目标，尤其是他们其中第二条目标，就是转向这种可持续发展，转向这种环境保护、气候变化这个领域。那我想这也是随着这种国际的发展潮流，本身IEA做的一个转型的实践吧。

译语：Second, China is implementing the air pollution control measures. So we should have a communication, conversation with international communities. I don't have much time to read the entire book, so I read the short version. There are eight reports. First, the report reflects the transformation. I went to IEA once. I thought it's like an energy club for the advanced economies that provides secure and services for advanced economies. But now, in the international stage, it has provided the second goal which is to transform to sustainable development and environmental protection against climate change. And I think this is an international trend. And IEA has achieved this practice of transformation.

教师点评：(1) we should have a communication, conversation with international communities 可以改为 China need dialogue with the rest of the world，让表达更简洁，信息更明晰。

(2) "简版"指的是 executive summary，译员需要充分译前准备，同传中要有语境和情境感，不能完全根据语言进行字面对译。"厚的也没有那么长时间去看就是了"是比较典型的中文口语特征，可以不译。

(3) 发言人稍有方言，译员未听懂"评论"，"8 个字"一般情况下不用译出，可以概译为 the following comments。

(4) First, the report reflects the transformation 这句在寻求字面对译，信息不够准确、清晰，可以处理为 the first key word is transition，或者 first, the report calls for transition。

(5) it's like an energy club... 一句译员因为没有顺句，记忆负担过大，造成错译，可以顺句和简化为：IEA is for developed countries, market economies an energy club /IEA is developed countries', market economies' energy club/for their national energy security，或者断句处理 IEA is for developed countries, market economies. It is an energy club for their national energy security。

(6) it has provided the second goal... 这句译语的问题同上一句，译员的英语表达不够灵活，不够简洁，信息不够凸显，而且顺句加工上还需努力。可以提取介宾结构中的关键名词做主语，their target, particularly the second one, is in transition to sustainable growth/ sustainable transition。

(7) And IEA has achieved this practice of transformation. 同前面几句，字面对译，英语表达力不足，表达中式、生硬，信息不凸显，可以改

为 As part of a global trend, IEA is in transition.

源语：第二个评论就是担当。大家知道我们在国内过去可能讨论空气污染是谁造成的，那都是讨论得很激烈。在座的都很多是能源大腕。但我至少从这个报告里面，它已经承认这一点，可以说90%以上的这种大气污染物都是能源生产和使用产生的。所以从这点角度来看，告诉我们能源这个部门在给我们人类带来福利的同时，也是给我们公众的健康，给环境污染带来了巨大的影响。任何事物都是有正有负的，这种信息能不能正确地传递下去，传递到我们国内的能源部门里面去。我个人看法，这是报告的一个很积极的意义。

译语：Second, in China, we talked about who causes, what causes the air pollution, and we have a heated discussion. And everyone here are experts. From this report, there is acknowledgement that over 90% of air pollutant are attributable to energy production. Therefore, we know that energy is beneficial to human, human-being, but it's also harmful to public health and environmental protection. So it has both positive and negative influence. Can this message be sent to the domestic energy sector? I think this is what the report can do.

教师点评：（1）因为口音，未听出"担当"。

（2）"在座的都很多是能源大腕"有点令人费解，理解困难与发言人表达方式有关。虽然从字面上看，似乎是指参加今天会议的有很多能源大腕，但是做了译前准备就会知道，听众基本是媒体记者，而且该句意思与后面一句显然不连贯，因此该句意思应该是参加激烈讨论的很多都是能源大腕，可以顺句处理为 There were heated discussions among energy experts.

（3）"至少从这个报告里面，它已经承认这一点"同前面，将介宾结构中的名词"报告"提取出来做主语，处理为 the report says/admits that... 译员的 acknowledgement 过于正式、抽象，are attributable to 也是同样问题，可以简化为 are/come from.

(4)"所以从这点角度来看,告诉我们能源这个部门"直接提取关键名词"能源"做主语,不要受口语特征带来的语言形式干扰,处理为:energy benefits/brings benefit to people,后一句可以通过预测,处理为 and also poses health and environmental risk,或者将该句的介宾结构的主语提出,处理为 but public health and environment are also risked in energy use。

(5)"这种信息能不能正确地传递下去"可以处理为"can we get the message across.../can we effectively communicate the message...",也可以直接处理为陈述句:we need...

总体看,译员信息听辨理解与表达均存在不少问题,比较容易受源语语言形式影响,理解字面意思,寻求字面对译,抽取关键信息并顺句重组的能力不足,译语不够地道、灵活、简洁、清晰,中式词汇与句式较多,影响了译语可用性和交际效率、效果。同传三大关键技能中,译员的口齿伶俐性较好,语言资源丰富性、灵活性和可用性一般,信息加工能力较弱。

6A-2:

译语:It's my pleasure for this China Launch and it's my first time for such event. Before I came here, I asked myself, what am I going to do? So I watch this report. I think it's meaningful. First, in its annual report, it gives special focus on the air pollution. And it's the same for my work and research. So I'm here.

译语:China issued the plan for tackling the air pollution. And China should have the mechanism to have dialogues with the other countries in the world. I have some comments on the report. The first one is that this report indicates the characteristics of transition. We used to believe that the IEA is an energy clubs for the developed countries to ensure the energy security of these wealthy countries. But on any arena of the international community, they will focus on their second objective, which is the transition to environmental protection, climate change, and energy transition and its keep pace with the international trend.

译语：Second, as we know, we used to discuss who should be responsible for the air pollution. And there is a heated discussion. I know all of you are experts in this area. And in this report, it recognized that 90% of the air pollution come from the production of energy. So from this perspective, the energy sector, which brings benefits for humanity, also poses a threat for human's health. Whether this message can be transformed to China, it is a very important meaning of this report.

译员反思（1）：同传过程中反应速度较慢，不能迅速理解发言信息并摆脱源语结构束缚进行表达。

教师点评：译员加工节奏比较平稳，EVS总体合理，可能由于该发言语速较慢，所以译员能做到平稳且基本流利，但有些地方显得稍慢。译员需要思考：如果发言语速突然变快，自己能否切换成稍快的加工模式。在教学中会发现有些同学的加工模式更接近交传，这受听译协调、反应速度、思维灵活性、口齿伶俐性、语言资源丰富性、灵活性和可用性等多种因素影响。

译员反思（2）：译语更多是照着字面的意思走，很多时候选词并不准确，问题一方面在于摆脱源语结构束缚还不够，过于纠结其中文措辞并寻找英文对应表达，而不是从信息传达的角度来思考合适的英文表达；另一方面也因为语言资源的丰富性不够，容易因为无法迅速反应出英文表达而出现卡顿；这也会导致译语中式思维明显，僵化，不够灵活，需要多读英文平行文本，并多积累常用词的多样化英文表达。

教师点评：注重字面翻译而非信息传达的情形不少，如 this report indicates the characteristics of transition, it is a very important meaning of this report。语法问题和中式英语问题也比较明显，如 watch this report, message can be transformed to China 等搭配问题，issued, there is a heated discussion 时态错误，on any arena of the international community 表达中式，its keep pace with 基本语法错误，come from 数的错误等。英语表达问题是很多同学共同的问题，原因包括：英语是外语，高压力下，英语资源很容易捉襟见肘；过往学习中中式英语输入过多，地道英语输入不足；不正确的翻译观等。

译员反思（3）：句子的衔接较弱，最常用的连接表达是 and；很多时候跟着中文的表达走，导致如果单独听译语并不能很好地理解源语所要表达的含义。因此首先要理解源语逻辑关系，像中文中的"因为"和"所以"等连接词也不能直接对译，需要看前后是否有因果等逻辑关系；同时也要多积累并列、因果、转折等逻辑关系常用的连接词替换表达，在适当的时机进行补充。

教师点评：句子间的语言衔接和信息连贯的问题有些明显，译语给人支离破碎的感觉，信息的清晰性、可理解性有些弱。比如，in its annual report, it gives special focus on the air pollution. And it's the same for my work and research，第 2 个 it 可以明晰为 IEA，第 3 个 it 实际上是指 this area。同传中要加强源语信息和逻辑理解，转换和表达中需要加强监控和译语调整，确保译语衔接和连贯，做到心中有听众。

译员反思（4）：发布上，总体来说保持了比较平缓的语速，但是有时语速过慢，且在主谓和宾语之间有较长时间的停顿，听起来不够流利，存在 filler、重复和改口、句子结构不完整的情况。要避免等待时间过长而导致句子不流利，适当地对后文信息进行预测，把控好节奏。

教师点评：可通过提升听译协调能力，动态调节 EVS，加强译语监控，对具体流利性问题进行针对性的训练等方法加以改善。

会议："IEA 世界能源展望特别报告"发布会，嘉宾点评，国务院发展研究中心能源政策研究室领导

7A：

源语：好，谢谢大家。学习了这个报告，其实我觉得这个报告还是有别于

以往 IEA 的报告，更多地从一个能源消费的后果来包括环境影响有一个追溯，那么我觉得这些也是中国所关切的，就我们所感同身受的一些东西，可能中国现在面临的最大的一个资源环境的挑战，就是关于空气质量的一个问题，那么化石能源的这种燃烧和它的治理的不当，可能是导致了大气污染的一个主要原因。那么我们其实也是觉得是不是 IEA，包括以后 IEA 在中国开的合作中心，能对中国的一些特殊的情况进行一个跟进的一个研究，就所谓的拍个续集，因为中国现在也处于能源转型的过程中，也面临着很多不一样的情况。

译语：Thank you. After reading through the report, I think it is different from the past IEA report. And it's based on the results, and consequences and environmental hazards from the energy consumption. And I think these are the concerns for China. And it also strike a chord in Chinese people's heart. It's probably the biggest challenge for China, which is the air pollution, the fossil fuel combustion, and also under-regulation. And this has caused the air pollution. And in China, I think whether IEA and IEA cooperation center can have a follow-up research in China. Because China is now in energy transition, and it's facing different situation.

教师点评：（1）虽然该材料与前一个发言来自同一会议的点评环节，但是源语特征差异较大，本段发言的风格对同传挑战较大：语速快，信息密集，口语特征更加明显，流利性弱，条理性弱，表达不够明晰，发言后半段术语较多等，译员需要适当提升加工效率，动态调节 EVS，顺句驱动，同时注意避免紧跟发言节奏及其语言形式，以免误解误译，要尽量理解发言信息，过滤、省略冗余信息、非主题信息或干扰性表达，去粗取精，去伪存真。

（2）"学习了这个报告，其实我觉得……"，可以处理为 I read the report/The report is informative/insightful/makes for an interesting read. It/This report is different from... 同传基本是以句子（命题）为加工单位，有些相邻句子之间意义或逻辑关系不太紧密，可以分别独立处理，如果处理为一个句子，会给语言结构的安排带来挑战，影响意思连贯和译语可用性，也会造成记忆负担。但是如果几个句子的主题信息关系比较紧密，或者围绕同一主题但比较松散，信息量比较少，冗余性高，而且语速快，可以进行适当压缩合并。

（3）"更多地从一个能源消费的后果来包括环境影响有一个追溯"的处理不用颠倒语速，可以接前句顺句处理为 (different from IEA's previous reports) with a focus on energy use consequences, and environmental footprint/impact tracking.

（4）"就我们所感同身受的一些东西"的处理太贴字面。此句与前句意思冗余，且在语境中的信息作用不大，属于虚指而非实指，可以不译。如果译员觉得此句不译，造成译语空白较多，也可以接前句 This is also a concern for China, and a concern for the Chinese people.

（5）"我觉得""我认为"在汉语口语中很多时候只是填充语，不是实指，可以过滤，译员似乎有些急于保持翻译或说话状态，就像有的译员常用拖长发音的 and, and also, the 等填充语起句（该译语中也存在），来做等待，并保持说话状态，填补空白，这样做必要性不大，会影响译语流利性和可听性。

（6）It's probably the biggest challenge for China, which is the air pollution, the fossil fuel combustion, and also under-regulation. 译员在开译该句时，已经听到了"空气质量的一个问题"，意思已经相对完整，不用切割地这么碎，信息和语言这么松散，it is...which is...the fossil fuel...，可以处理为相对完整、表达紧凑、高效的英语句子，用关键名词做主语 the biggest environmental challenge is air pollution，后面的"化石能源的这种燃烧和它的治理的不当"和该句逻辑关系紧密，可以直接挂在该句后面，顺句译出 from fossil fuel use（"燃烧"不一定非要处理为 combustion）without proper treatment。

（7）"是不是 IEA……"这种问句的处理方法有多种，如处理为比较开放的结构 is it possible that IEA...，这样后面的语言表达回旋余地比较大，或者稍微等一下之后处理为 Can IEA，或直接处理为陈述句 IEA and its potential cooperation centers in China should/may/can...

（8）"it's facing different situation"较为中式，可以接前句处理为

in energy transition with different local conditions/stories/in a different context。

源语：下面我大概提几点感受，第一个是从结构上考虑，那么中国城乡差异比较大，那么我们农村还消费大量的非商品能，这部分可能是缺乏统计。从城市的角度来讲，咱们就讲老三样，工业、建筑、交通。工业的事情我不想多讲了，因为现在可能我们通过各种行政的这个手段，包括去产能也好，或者是监控也好，包括一些治理的手段，环保部门包括工信和能源部都做了很多工作，那么可能有比较快速的这种效果，那么工业的产能可能在未来的七八年内，尤其是制造业可能会达峰，那么它实际上增量是有限的，那么我们随着未来城镇化的进一步的潜力，那么建筑、交通这块可能增量还比较大，我们自己的预测光是交通用的成品油消费，那么在十三五期间可能要增加大概比15年大概增加 1/3 左右。那么这里面除了效率的改善和当然清洁的限值逐渐提高以外，这是一个减量，那么规模的增加包括建筑和交通燃油它是一个增量，那么最后我们的结果是什么呢？ 其实未来我觉得看好更应该增加治理，建筑和交通，就所谓社会用能的这一块，这是关于结构的这块。

译语: And I would like to promote my thinking. The first one is structure, with the big divide in the urban and rural areas, like some consumption products. And I will not elaborate on industrialization. From the administrative ways, from the de-overproduction, China's ministries have done a lot. And we also witness rapid results and good achievement. And industrialized capacity will reach peak in 7–8 years. And with the further urbanization, the building and transportation's increment will be a lot. And it is estimated to be about a third in the fuel consumption during the 13th five-year plan in the transportation sector. And apart from the clean energy usage, we will witness a result in the future that in the future, we need to improve the governance in the oil consumption in the society.

教师点评：(1) promote my thinking 反映了译员草率进行字面对译的加工模式，应该是 make/share a few points/comments/ideas.

(2) with the big divide in urban and rural areas, like some consumption products, 问题类似于上一段的第(1)点，可以处理为两个句子 China has a big urban-rural gap and rural areas rely heavily on non-commercial energy sources/in rural areas a lot of non-commercial energy sources are available. 也可以前句为主句，后面信息挂上，China has a big urban-rural gap with rural areas using a lot of non-commercial energy.

(3) "工业的事情我不想多讲了"在语境中不是实指，后面还在谈工业，因此可以不译。

(4) "通过各种行政的这个手段……"，可以直接提取关键名词，处理为 administrative measures/tools/approaches such as capacity reduction, monitoring/supervision, treatment, have been used/employed.

(5) "环保部门包括工信和能源部"需要根据当时的部委设置及对应英语名称译出，有时可视情形（如源语语速高、信息密度高的商务、学术性互动交流）合并处理为 regulators in charge of/administration of environmental protection, industry and information technology and energy。

(6) And we also witness rapid results and good achievement 与前句衔接不佳，可以直接挂在前句上：done a lot and their efforts may produce quick effects/pay off quickly/deliver immediate outcomes. And...also... 以连接词作填充语，有时会割裂、破坏原有逻辑关系。

(7) "工业产能"译作 industrial capacity，"达峰"可直接用动词 peak。

(8) And with the further urbanization, the building and transportation's increment will be a lot 该句比较贴字面，比较中式，要加强信息传达，可以调整为 as we/China urbanize(s), construction and transport sector will use much more energy.

(9) "我们自己的预测光是交通用的成品油消费，那么在十三五期间可能要增加大概比15年大概增加1/3左右"可顺句处理为 we estimate

transport fuel alone during the 13th five year plan period will rise over 2015 by 1/3.

（10）最后两句译员没有理解源语。"那么这里面除了效率的改善和当然清洁的限值逐渐提高以外"可以处理为 we will use cleaner and more efficient fuel."规模的增加包括建筑和交通燃油它是一个增量……"可处理为 expanding construction and transport sector will use more energy with more consequences/footprint. Ultimately we must face the consequences with more treatment.

译员反思（1）：感觉自己的知识面还是不够广，译前准备也不够充分，导致在翻译的时候知识背景和相关的表达无法很快地调动。

教师点评：确实要加强对行业内在逻辑，国际和国内，过去、现在和未来及各利益相关方情况的了解，熟悉行业故事和话语，并且积累双语行业术语、语块，学习使用简单清晰的语言讲述行业故事。

译员反思（2）：平时地道英文输入不够，尤其是对英语口语化的表达不太熟悉，听到一些中文词句时，需要反应很久才能找到对应表达，而且很多时候也不符合英文的表达习惯，甚至是错误的表达，导致后文无法跟上，无法将很多句子顺畅地连接在一起。

教师点评：译员口齿伶俐性较好，语言资源可用性尚可，但丰富性和灵活性欠佳，信息加工能力较弱。从总体风格看，译员有些急躁与随意，比如过于急着进行语言层面（尤其是词语、短语）对译，加工单位过小，过于急着保持翻译状态，语言使用过于随意，且对自己译语监控不足。建议译员加工过程更严谨，更平稳，适当增大加工单位，以完整命题（句子）为加工单位，以信息加工为目标，深度理解发言或交际信息，在较为完整理解信息基础上再进行转换和发布，要注重传达信息，注重译语的简洁明晰。同时要加强自我监控，提升译语句子间的衔接连贯性，减少非流利情形。

第二章 中英同声传译技能讲、练、评

> 会议：第五届中国国际液化天然气大会，开幕致辞，LNGCHINA 技术委员会主席

8A：

源语：第五届中国国际液化天然气大会 LNGCHINA 2015 今天如期开幕了！我谨代表大会主办单位和大会技术委员会，向参会的各位来宾表示热烈的欢迎，向热情参与本届大会的国内外朋友们，表示诚挚的感谢！

译语：The fifth China International LNG Conference LNGCHINA 2015 opens today. On behalf of the organizer and technical committee, I would like to extend my warm welcome to all the guests present today and also my sincere appreciation to friends both at home and abroad.

教师点评：（1）译员要有交际意识，做到心中有听众，不受语言形式干扰，把源语与所在语境、情境相结合进行听辨理解，传递重要交际信息；平常训练时，也要带着交际意识，有现场情境感。"opens today" 缺乏场景感和交际感，更像是媒体对会议的报道，可以调整为 is now open，或者 I declare + 会议名 (to be) open。

（2）2015 可以读作 twenty fifteen，比 two thousand fifteen 音节短，容易发音，省时省力。

（3）主办一般是 host，承办是 organizer，联合主办（承办）co-host (organizer)，协办 supporter，赞助 sponsor。

（4）"向……表示……"可顺句处理 to...I would like to extend...appreciation 可改为 gratitude，后面的 at 改为 from。

源语：本届中国国际液化天然气大会，是继 2011 年创办以来，连续第五次举办。五年来，LNGCHINA 大会见证了中国液化天然气工业的发展，同时也为国内外行业界同行提供了一个高端的技术和市场交流的平台，为 LNG 行业的发展做出了有益的贡献！近十年来，中国 LNG 产业发展很快，无论是 LNG 液化厂，还是 LNG 接收站，无论是 LNG 汽车、LNG 船舶，还是 LNG 加注站，至少在数量上都走在

了世界各国的前面。这十年，中国引领了世界 LNG 液化厂小型化的浪潮，引领了 LNG 交通能源产业化、规模化、网络化的浪潮，也推动了世界能源经济向天然气清洁能源经济转型的世界大潮。

译语：This year's conference since its inception in 2011 is the fifth consecutive event. Five years on, this conference witnessed the development of China LNG industry and provides a way for us to communicate of high-end technology and market for better LNG development. For the past decade, China's LNG industry has developed rapidly. For example, LNG plant, receiving station or LNG vehicles, ships and refilling station, we lead the world in terms of the scales. During the past decade, China has played a leading role in minimizing the LNG plant and shaping LNG transportation energy toward industrialized, large-scale and Internet-based and also for the transformation toward a cleaner economy.

教师点评：（1）This year's conference 可以调整为会议品牌名 LNGCHINA，对一些行业性或发布类会议，凸显和传播品牌常常是客户所期待和关注的。

（2）its inception 可省去，该句有多种处理方法：LNGCHINA since 2011 is in its fifth annual session/has been held for the past four consecutive years/This is LNG CHINA's fifth edition (annual event) since 2011.

（3）witnessed the development 过于正式，商务、行业会议往往比较务实，一般是以传递主题信息为目的，一些常常用于政治外交场合或书面语里的大词、正式表达不太合适，此处可用更为简洁清晰的语言，如 LNGCHINA has been part of China's LNG growth story/ has been growing alongside China's LNG sector.

（4）下一句可以完全顺句，且 provide 可以简化成 is/serves，即 it is for domestic and international market players a top technology and market information/exchange platform。

（5）develop 在商务、行业会议上较少用，可用 expand, grow 等替代。

（6）"无论是 LNG 液化厂……"可以处理为状语 as for/in terms of LNG

liquefaction plant..., China leads... 也可以全部处理为主语,后面接 by scale, lead/are among the top in the world.

(7) 下面的四个"化",要摆脱源语形式,传递出主要信息,"小型化" China is a leader in making liquefaction plant smaller/in liquefaction going smaller 或者直接处理为 leads in smaller... "产业化、规模化、网络化"也不建议全部用 -ization,可以解释出主要意思,其中网络化应该是指资源供应网络,这块可以处理为 China leads in industrializing LNG/scaling up LNG use as an alternative transport fuel with an expanding servicing network,或者简单处理为 Also in China, LNG is increasingly used to fuel/power its transport/increasingly ready as an alternative transport fuel/China is fueling more of its vehicles with LNG/China's transport system is increasingly LNG-driven/powered.

(8) 最后一句可处理为 making the world's energy cleaner with LNG, moving the world/aiding in/helping with the global transition to a LNG-driven/based cleaner economy。

源语:但是,从世界 LNG 工业半个多世纪的发展历程来看,中国 LNG 工业还很年轻。与世界 LNG 工艺技术发达国家比较,中国 LNG 工业规模还很小,前面的路还很长。近三年来,中国 LNG 产业经历了戏剧式的发展,几起几落,先是经受几次天然气上游价格大幅上调的压力,后是经受国际油价大幅下跌使天然气下游市场竞争乏力的影响。特别是近两年来,国内经济发展放缓的影响,使中国 LNG 工业遇到了一系列的新问题、新政策、新形势和新挑战。因此,如果说,2013 年下半年,是中国 LNG 产业发展开始停滞下滑的半年,那么 2014 年,是中国 LNG 产业集体反思的一年,15 年,就是 LNG 行业全面调整整顿的一年。

译语:However, the world LNG industry has experienced 50 years of development. China's LNG is still at its early stage with smaller industrial scales. We have a long way to go. During the last three years, China's LNG industry has experienced twists and turns, which is affected by the surge of the natural gas price and the drop of international oil price, making downstream natural gas market less competitive. Especially during the last two years, China's economy has slowed down. So it is faced with new questions and challenges. Therefore, during the second quarter second half of this 2013, China's LNG began to halt its decline. And 2014 was for self-examination of China's LNG industry. 2015 is for its readjustment.

教师点评：（1）第一句的处理有些过于贴字面，语言不够简洁地道，信息不够凸显，尤其是 experienced, development 等，可以调整为 However, global LNG industry being over half a century old/global LNG being an industry for over half a century, China's LNG sector is still immature/is still a market with big potential.

（2）第二句的问题同上。"中国 LNG 工业规模还很小"可以处理为 China has a much smaller LNG market/LNG in China is still quite a small market，"世界 LNG 工艺技术发达国家"可以处理为 global LNG technology leaders/leading players/countries，"发达国家"不可直接译为 developed countries。

（3）"经历了"未必一定对应 experienced，可以处理为 had，twists and turns 也可以调整为更为简洁的 ups and downs，此外，"先是经受……压力，后是经受……影响"也可以简单处理。在以传递信息为主的商务、学术交流场合，汉语的许多较为书面的动词（词组），如"开展……建设、强化……举措、加大……力度"等，可以去除框架，进行口语化/弱化处理（简译、略译等）。此处可顺句简单处理为 with several upstream price hikes/surges followed by global oil price plunges making downstream natural gas less competitive。当然，如果源语语速较慢，也可以处理为独立句子 there were/it met...followed by...

（4）根据语境，"新问题、新政策、新形势和新挑战"并非实指具体的问题、政策、形势和挑战，只是概指遇到了新的挑战/问题/形势，可以简洁处理，另外"国内经济发展放缓的影响"可以提取关键名词作主语，这一句可处理为 China's economic slowdown has presented the sector with new scenarios and challenges/has been redefining China's LNG sector/is putting China's LNG sector in a new/complex context.

（5）halt its decline 是译员误解为"停止下滑"，实为 stagnated and declined。

（6）"集体反思"不宜字面对译为 collective reflection, self-examination 的信息也不够凸显，可以明晰为 identify problems (and solutions)/problem-solving。

源语：但是中国 LNG 工业发展的总趋势是不会变的，中国液化天然气工业的发展，是清洁能源经济发展不可缺少的重要组成部分。LNG 作为新的清洁能源，将逐步取代传统煤炭石油能源的总趋势是不会变的。虽然艰难，这个困难时期总会过去的。近几年来，中国 LNG 工业发展遇到的问题，给我们留下了深刻的教训。一个教训是，一个健康的 LNG 工业的发展，应该是稳定、持续、渐进式的发展，不应该是爆发式、短平快式、急功近利式的发展。

译语：But the general trend of LNG will not change. It is important for clean energy development. As a clean energy resource, LNG will gradually replace traditional fossil fuel. That's will not change. Despite difficulties, we will get through it. For the past few years, China's LNG are encountered with problems, which left us with lessons. First, a sound LNG development should be stable, sustainable and gradual instead of explosive, reckless and short-term.

教师点评：（1）前两句的译语同样存在信息不凸显，语言不够清晰地道，术语或行话不准确等问题，两处"总趋势不会变"可以处理为 will continue to，两句可以调整为：China's LNG sector will continue to grow, contributing to a cleaner economy/as a key part of cleaner economy agenda. LNG as a clean alternative will continue to replace fossil fuel/ fuel oil and coal.

（2）Despite difficulties, we will get through it 不如简化为 The current difficulties/challenges are temporary. 汉英同传中，状语＋主谓的结构经常可以将状语中的关键名词提取出来做主语，形成信息更为密集、结构更简约、更省时省力的表达。

（3）encounter, problems 太贴源语字面，太实、太大，可以弱化为 were amid/had/came across challenges。

（4）最后一句的译语可以调整为 LNG growth is expected to be steady, sustainable and progressive rather than explosive/follow a steady...pattern rather than an explosive and quick-success/benefit-driven one.

源语：第二个教训是，一个健康 LNG 工业的发展需要一个稳定的上下游市场环境，和一个稳定的产业政策。LNG 工业项目的投资，通常都比较大，动辄数亿元的投资，而且，LNG 项目的投资，不同于房地产投资，也不同于互联网投资，更不是股票投资，LNG 项目的投资是能源装备制造的全产业链的实业投资，它不仅受能源装备制造由原材料到产品制造水平的限制，也受工业化生产本身自有规律的制约。

译语：And the second is a sound LNG industry development need a stable upper and downstream market environment and industrial policy. Its investment involves large amount of money, sometimes millions of yuan. Its investment is different from real estate, internet and stock market. Its investment covers all industrial chains of equipment manufacturing. It is affected by the production of raw materials and energy equipment manufacturing. It is also limited by industrial production.

教师点评：（1）第一句译语还是存在贴字面，中式，信息不凸显问题，可以调整为 a sound LNG industry is based on/ is about/means/what sustain LNG industry are/ healthy up- and downstream markets and consistent industrial policies. 有些汉语词汇在不同语境中有不同内涵，比如"稳定""科学"，需要根据语境明晰其具体意思，不可完全字面对译。

（2）译语多次使用 its/it 替代 LNG，不利于听众理解，替代、省略等需要根据语境适当使用。

（3）"LNG 工业项目的投资"可以直接处理为 LNG project，汉语很多较长名词词组都可以简译，译出其中信息最具体、最丰富的词汇即可，冗余部分可省。

（4）"能源装备制造的全产业链的实业投资"可处理为 A LNG project is/involves energy equipment manufacturing covering the entire industrial chain，"实业投资"是语境冗余的框架，可省略，也可以处理为...energy equipment manufacturing, a kind of whole industry chain investment。这类长定语，综合使用顺句、脱框架、顺句+追加（补充）、顺句+适当重复等策略，当然，这对译员英语资源丰富性、灵活性和可用性提出较大挑战。

（5）"不仅……也受……"可以处理为两个独立句子，it/which is affected/impacted/constrained by raw materials and technology, and also by the industry life cycle 或者一个句子 ...by raw materials, technology, and the industry life cycle，或两个并列词组 ...subject to...。如果前一句的译语不是以 equipment manufacturing 结尾，此处也可处理为 equipment manufacturing is constrained by/subject to...

译员总反思：自开学以来主要在训练边听边说，但是有时候会因为纠结某一个词语/术语的表达，或是句子结构的调整，而听漏一些句子，觉得根本原因还是语言资源丰富性不够，所以碰到定语状语过长的句子的时候，虽然知道要顺句，但是有时候还是想不出怎么架构句子，然后退而求其次，采用定语、状语后置的方法。另外，译语中会有大量中式表达，究其根源，是没听懂中文发言的内涵，没摆脱源语结构的束缚，尤其是即兴发言，这种情况会更明显，难以快速理解源语，摆脱源语形式影响，实现句子的精练化。

教师总点评：作为初学者，译员总体表现还不错，译语基本完整、准确，语言虽有一些错误，但总体比较通顺，可理解，发布也比较平稳流利。译员基本解决了边听边译的协调问题，EVS 较为合理，基本熟悉同传的顺句、等待、断句、拆分等基本操作策略。主要问题包括：1）受源语语言形式限制还较为明显，信息加工（源语信息准确理解、译语高效传递信息）还有较大提升空间，译语还不够清晰、简洁、地道；2）一些行业用语还不熟悉；3）一些地方存在漏译。

> 会议：第五届中国国际液化天然气大会，主旨演讲：我国天然气市场供需形势与展望，中国石油集团经济技术研究院天然气市场研究所领导

9A：

源语：尊敬的各位嘉宾，各位代表，上午好，非常高兴有机会能够在这里和诸位业内的专家共同地交流学习。今天我为大家做报告的题目是《我国天然气市场供需形势与展望》。首先我声明一点，我这个这个做的这个汇报的所有的内容，都是我们经济技术研究院，我们天然气市场研究团队的这个团队的研究成果，不代表中国石油天然气集团公司的这个观点。首先的话我觉得这个我们这个报告的话，这个强调一点，就说目前我们天然气行业是一个机遇与挑战并存的一个进入了一个阶段，对于这个三大石油公司这种签了长贸协议这个进退两难的三大石油公司来讲的话，是处于一个历史上前所未有一个挑战。但是对于我们这个下游用户，包括我们这个在夹缝中生存的中游企业来讲的话，我觉得更大的，更大地给我们提供的是一个机会。这个是我们在去年14年，实际上我们就已经提出了我们中国天然气市场正面临一个转折，很不幸的是这个这个转折的速度太快了，让我们没有没有办法在这么短的时间适应。

译语：Distinguished guest, ladies and gentlemen, good morning. It's my great pleasure to talk with you. Today my topic is "China Natural Gas Supply and Demand and Its Future Prospects". All of my presentation today is a collective effort from my team. We are not stand for our company. The report today emphasizes this point we're now facing both opportunities and challenges. For the three major corporations, we are facing great challenges. But as for the middle stream corporations and users, we have more opportunities. Last year in 2014, we proposed that we are facing a turning point, but the speed is quite high and which leads to a very short time for us to adapt.

译员反思（1）："共同交流学习"翻成 talk with you 有点过于随意，当时是在时间压力下就脱口而出这个简化表达，感觉自己还是对会议开场套话熟练程度不够，导致在这一句翻译时对应语块语言资源不够丰富。

教师点评：此处可处理为 to join you here/to be part of this conference。中文发言的一些客套话（如自谦、自损等），需要跨文化处理，不宜直接对译。会议常用语确实有必要学习，可以通过中英平行语料相互借鉴。

译员反思（2）：We are not stand for our company 这里是我的预测出现错误。我在听到"首先我声明一点……成果"的时候，觉得讲者的意图应该就是类似客套开场（先声明这个报告是他们整个团队通力合作的成果，而非讲者自己一人的功劳），所以才有了 All...team 这句。但听到后半部分"不代表……"，我就意识到前面的预测出现了偏差，信息重点应该是后半句，整体表达的应该是"本报告仅代表讲者团队的观点，不代表公司的官方观点"，因此后面再补了一句，匆忙之中犯了语法错误。

教师点评：预测是同传中常用策略，甚至是基本策略，对即将到来的源语语言的预测和信息内容的预测贯穿同传过程，能够有效降低译员认知负荷，提高加工效率。但是预测和调整（顺应）要共同使用，一旦预测不对，可以立即调整、顺应源语。译员此处在译 effort from my team 的时候，发言人已经在说下一句，因此译员实际上是有时间立即放弃原有预测，译出 I am not speaking on behalf of... 问题的主要原因或许还是初学同传，总精力不足，加之语言资源丰富性和灵活性还有限。

译员反思（3）："长贸协议"听到了，但是对这个概念不熟悉，感觉现场对译会浪费时间和精力，所以就直接省略了这个修饰语。

教师点评：long-term trade agreement 这类行业术语比较重要，需要多积累，对于技术性较强的内容，万不得已的时候如果听准了术语文字，也可以尝试字面对译。"对于这个三大石油公司这种签了长贸协议这个进退两难的三大石油公司"可以采用顺句+重复的方式 for the three major oil companies in long-term trade agreement, for these struggling companies，也可采用断句方式，将词语译为句子，并将后面半句信息融入 for the three...agreement, they are in an unprecedentedly tough time。另外，前面的"报告……强调一点……"不宜直接对译为 emphasize，可以将信息凸显，处理为 The key message of/takeaway from the report is that... 或者将谓语弱化为 the report basically says that... 还有一点要注意，同传中的代词使用要慎重，不是 we are facing，是 they，"我们下游用户"未必真的指"我们"，不宜译作 our，汉语发言常用"我们、咱们"等，未必总是实指，要清晰译出真实指代对象。

译员反思（4）：but the speed is quite high and which leads to a very short time for us to adapt 这里出错主要是因为 EVS 有点长了，听到这句的时候，还在忙于翻上一句，心里有点慌怕跟不上，节奏有点被打乱了，因此翻的时候就在赶，在搭句子的时候也花了点时间思考，导致译语紧贴字面并出现语法错误（时态、多加 and），最后部分的英语译语输出也为了赶时间而比较模糊，可听性大打折扣。

教师点评：源语语速较快时，通过选译最重要信息、脱离语言外壳提取最关键命题（主谓结构），合并压缩部分内容（如把多句压缩为一句，句子压缩为词组，词组压缩为词），选择最简表达等方式进行应对，此处可处理为 but it happened too quickly for us to adapt/it was too sharp for us to adapt.

译员反思（5）：这节出现了不少语法错误，如 be 动词＋动词原形、同位语从句漏掉引导词 that、代词误用、时态错误，还有习惯性添加 and。

教师点评：基本的语法问题常常是同传中监控译语产出的精力不足所致，训练中要合理分配自我监控精力，平时也要进行针对性刻意练习，提升监控意识和能力。当然，随着听译协调问题的解决，同传基本操作策略的娴熟，以及英语资源丰富性和灵活性的提升，明显语法问题会逐步减少。

源语：首先第一部分，我们从需求角度分析下中国天然气市场面临的一个主要形势。首先第一点，目前中国天然气需求增速已经逼近拐点，我们看我们从按照我们这个研究的角度讲来认识的话，我们认为全国性中国天然气市场的发展是从西气东输管道长输管道 2004 年投运开始，才有了这种全国性的天然气管道，那也就是说到现在中国全国性天然气市场发展只有不到 15 年的一个历史，可能是 12 年的一个历史。从 2000 年到 2004 年，我们中国天然气需求从 245 亿方增长到了去年的 1845 亿立方米，年均增速是接近 16%。但是我们从增量的角度看一下，年均增量只有 110 亿立方米。那么这样的话，我就说在 2000 年我们国家这个天然气需求只有 245 亿立方米的时候，那每年 100 亿立方米的增量，相同于我们增速 30% 到 20%，40%，但是现在我们天然气需求已经达到了 1800 亿立方米，那么在这种背景下的话我们每年 100 亿的增量的话，很显然我们的增速是不会再超过两位数这样一个增长。

译语：The first part is the overall picture of the natural gas. And first of all, the demand growth of the natural gas growth rate is approaching the turning point. The natural gas pipeline started in 2004. So we only has a history of like 12 years. From 2000 to 2014, China's natural gas demand has increased from 24.5 billion cubic meters to 184.5 billion cubic meters with an annual growth rate of 15.5%. But the annual average annual improvement was only 11.4 cubic meters. By 2020, we will only have 300 billion cubic meters. But now the demand is increasing. So in the future, our growth rate will not be over two-digit growth.

译员反思（1）：第一句中文有点绕，在听到这一句话的时候，还在翻上一段末尾，匆匆收尾，等跟上这一句的时候就忘掉了"需求"这个关键词，节奏导致核心信息缺失。

教师点评：发言人的说话方式，译员无法选择和影响，只能尽力适应，对于源语较快、口语特征特别明显的讲话，译员要提升加工速度，对于源语要去粗取精，去伪存真，迅速识别关键信息，并以简洁译语快捷处理：first, the demand side of China's natural gas market，甚至可以视情形处理为更加简洁的 first, current demand。

下一句，译员 the demand growth of the natural gas growth rate 中重复了 growth，这种情况在同传初学者中比较常见，有时候职业译员也可能因为认知精力不足出现这类问题，主要因为精力饱和，短期记忆容量下降，监控精力不足，前面所说内容转瞬即忘，同样的问题还可能包括：长主语译完后忘记谓语是单数还是复数，各类搭配不当等。

译员反思（2）："我们认为全国性……"一句主要因为"西气东输管道长输管道"不熟悉，占用了精力，加上源语语速快，未能听辨理解更为关键的信息"天然气市场的发展"。

教师点评：源语较快、信息较密集时，迅速识别关键信息特别重要，要搜觅听取命题（主谓结构），在相邻几个命题中加工更重要命题，相邻若干词组中加工最具体、信息最多、最不冗余的词组，舍弃一些虽具体但是加工困难明显，且不太影响命题信息的成分。此处关键命题是 the national natural gas market was formed/started in 2004，"西气东输长输管道"可以视译员当时的认知状况决定是否译出。

译员反思（3）：最后一部分是很典型的数据描述，且译前准备的 PPT 里面也有，但问题就在于处理的时候没有精简，句子虽然译出来了，但耗费太多时间精力，觉得我的数字转换速度需要提高。另外，这部分的数字我翻的和源语不完全相同，比如2014、15.5%、11.4（billion丢了）等，因为这些是译前准备的PPT里的，以为这一段讲话就是完全一致并不会有增减或变化，便一口气说完，结果讲完PPT上的内容之后才发现讲者中间还加了两三句话，此时再想跟上就很难了，只能进行一些大意的概括。

教师点评：首先，数字部分可以尽量合并、压缩、精简，搭建一个简单句后挂上多个数据信息，即句子（简单主谓）+数值+趋势，有些地方可以像呈现表格一样，根据语境省略重复部分或不必要的语言形式，或者使用最简洁的语言形式（如 go, come, be 动词等）。例如，"我们中国……110亿立方米"可以合并处理为 natural gas demand rose from 24.5 billion cubic meters to 184.5 billion, up by 16%, but just 11 billion annually；"但是现在我们天然气需求……两位数这样一个增长"可以简缩处理为 given the current demand of 180 billion, a yearly rise of 10 billion won't lead to/result in/translate into double-digit growth.

带讲稿/PPT同传时，译员需要以听辨源语为主，以视译、阅读手边材料为辅，不可完全放弃听而视译，这样会因为视觉加工速度慢而严重滞后于源语，也可能会因为讲者突然插入自己的补充或解释的话而陷入被动。遇到讲话内容和材料不一致时，一般是以材料为准，当然译员也要加以判断，比如有时材料上的数据是旧的，而发言人可能会在读稿时补充最新数据。

关于数字口译，首先是平时将差异较大的汉英数量级当作词汇对比识记，如万 ten thousand，十万 hundred thousand，千万 ten million，亿 hundred million，百亿 ten billion 等，再进行快速转换训练，做到高度自动化的即听即译；同传时准备好纸笔，根据语境预测即将出现数字时可快速缩短EVS，并且边记边译；数字记录和译出时，可采用只译数字加最高段位再移动小数点的方法将数字译为小数。如123亿9682万，听到数字时，先记下具体数字"1239682"，记的同时译出最高段位——百亿，即十个 billion，然后移动小数点到十位数"12"后面（10个 billion 就移动小数点到十位数后面），即12.39682

billion，即 twelve point three nine six eight two billion 而不是 twelve billion three hundred ninety six million eight hundred twenty thousand（过于复杂，容易出错）。

源语：那我们未来我们按简单的判断一下，即便未来按照年均增长 200 亿立方米每年这种这种增量计算的话，那么 2020 年我们国家天然气需求，也不会达到，也不会超过 3000 亿立方米，这是我们整个研究一个大的一个一个背景判断。因为我们看在 2010—2014 年，也就是我们国家天然气市场增长增速最快的时候，年均天然气需求增量也只有 180 亿立方米。那么未来如果我们要连续五年每年增量都超过 200 亿立方米，这是一种，这是什么样的一种，而且我们是在这个天然气市场整个发展环境都发生转变的情况下。因为过去十几年我们国家天然气发展，我们我之前也写过文章，在什么基础之下。首先是我们长输天然气管网的一个快速的一个发展，能够使我们西部、西南的这种低价的国产气资源可以快速到东部沿海地区。

译语：Even though in the past, in the future, we calculate it at the rate of 20 billion cubic meters per year, by 2020, the demand will only at 300 billion cubic meters. In 2014, the most rapid growth of natural gas in China... the overall natural gas market is changing. The rapid development of network is providing the gas from the west to the east, the east to west.

译员反思：这节讲者讲得比较乱，没有把自己的意思说清楚，受源语特征影响，自己没有完全理解讲话逻辑，很多内容没有翻出来。

教师点评：在大量数据出现时，意思往往不会太难理解，围绕数据变化趋势处理即可，即便真的一时理解不了，也要听辨理解命题，顺句，使用最简洁语言，并快速对译数字。"2010—2014 年……200 亿立方米"一句可以简单处理为：2010—2014 when demand was soaring, annual rise was only 18 billion.

下一句，讲话人没有把话讲完整。他意思是，未来五年每年增量都超过 200 亿，这是很难实现的，何况现在市场环境已经发生转变。

此处可将前半句压缩为词组，后面补充"不可能"：for the next five years, an annual rise of 20 billion is unlikely given the changing market conditions。

下面一句存在同样问题，话没讲完整，不过同样可以根据语境猜测出来：过去十几年飞速发展是有基础的（原因的）。译员可以把信息明晰出来，the previous explosive growth was driven by certain market factors。

最后一句可以简缩处理为long-distance pipelines moved southwest's cheaper gas fast to the eastern coastal areas。

译员总反思：(1) 同传过程中翻译的感觉就像是"接包袱—丢包袱"，我的习惯是听到一个相对完整的意群就会开始翻译，先把"包袱"丢出去，在听的过程中也会辨识是否为关键信息，将其优先翻出，遇到一些我认为的次要信息在没有时间的情况下就会丢掉。所以有时候感觉同传就像串珠子，中英同传中抓到一个中文的关键信息就优先翻出，紧接着又听到下一个分句的关键信息就想办法看看是否与前面的信息有逻辑关系从而联系起来，没有就单独成句，大概就是这样的感觉。(2) 本学期开始练习同传一段时间，感觉中英能够做到边听边说，特别是一些即兴发言＋信息密度不强＋话题比较熟悉的内容进行同传会感觉比较轻松，比如前几周练习的"文化走出去"那个论坛的讨论，里面很多口语即兴发言中的冗余表达，且内容也不难理解，同传起来是比较舒服的。但是这一篇对我来说，可能因为能源话题有些不太了解＋有很多数字且部分地方表述不清或信息较为密集，相对来说就会感觉有难度。(3) 从这篇练习中，感觉应该注意以下几点：同传预测出现偏差后，需要及时补救，但不要打乱节奏；加强背景知识（行业知识）积累和相关常见词块语料的学习；听辨中需要把握发言核心信息及逻辑关系，并有意识地进行信息整合；表达中注意简缩，用最少的话传递最多的信息，避免结构冗余复杂；提高数字转换速度，数值单位和变化趋势的表达要熟悉；加强自我语言质量监控，尽量减少基本语法问题；发布译语时，不要慌，尽量保持平稳的节奏，减少改口次数和填充语。

六、纵/横加工

1. 讲解

同传过程包括纵向加工与横向加工两种路径。纵向加工时，源语理解和译语转换各为独立单语加工体系/过程，源语经音、词、句、语义与语用分析及概念表征，经由概念中介后再进行译语转换；横向加工时，源语理解与译语转换属双语加工体系/过程，两者同时发生，不经概念中介，而是通过共享双语表征寻求横向词汇、分句对应。纵向加工的对象一般是命题信息，横向加工一般适用于信息成分（关于命题信息与信息成分，见"信息听辨"部分），如数字、术语、专有名词、文化负载词、中国特色话语（短语），以及有固定对应译语的中国特色话语和引语等。简单说，在同传命题（句子）时，一般需要经过脱离源语语言形式（"脱壳"）过程，深度听辨理解信息，再进行译语转换，但在理解信息成分时，一般不需要经过"脱壳"的深度听辨分析，而是依赖于长期记忆中已经存储的对应译语，直接进行字面对译（"记忆配对"），或者将手边已经准备好的译语读出（"视阅配对"）。两种路径也分别称作：释意/脱壳与转码、重构与转码、意义加工与形式加工等。前面"信息听辨""信息加工"两部分主要与纵向加工有关。

纵/横加工的差异见下例：

行业年会是行业发展状态的晴雨表。本届大会正是在中国 LNG 产业处于十分困难的发展阶段举办的。出席本届会议的代表，与往年有大幅减少。

纵向加工/释意/脱壳/重构/意义加工：

An annual industry conference tells how a particular sector currently looks like/attending an annual industry conference is the best way to know the current state of a particular sector. China's LNG sector is in a very difficult time when we are gathering here. We have far fewer attendees/fewer people joining us/we have lost much audience/we have seen a big drop in attendance this year.

横向加工/转码/形式加工：

An annual industry conference is the barometer/bellwether/indicator of the current status of a particular sector. This annual conference is being held when China's LNG sector is at particularly challenging developmental stage. The number of delegates attending this year's conference has significantly decreased.

同传中的纵向与横向加工可以看作一个连续统，具体运用哪种加工方式或者偏向哪种加工方式，要根据会议类型、主题、发言方式、源语特征等多种因素确定。多以横向加工为主的情形：政务会议，典礼仪式等程序性较强、庄重正式或务虚活动，纯学术性、技术性会议，如科技类、法律类会议，读稿致辞环节，尤其是谈政策、摆事实、讲故事、具体描述时，语速快，信息密度高，语言规范，结构复杂，数字、术语和专有名词、各种列举较多，口音较重；多以纵向加工为主的情形：行业性、商务性会议或形式较为轻松活泼的场合，即兴发言，尤其是互动性环节（如问答、讨论环节），表达观点或思想，口语特征明显，语速适中或较慢，信息冗余度高。

此外，译员认知状况也会影响加工路径的选择。从译员认知负荷角度看，纵向加工较为耗费脑力，横向加工比较节省精力。当译员认知精力不足时，当源语理解或转换挑战过大时，译员会倾向于增加横向加工，减少纵向加工来应对危机。但是对于该以纵向加工为主的源语（比如信息比较丰富的即兴发言）进行过多横向加工，会削弱译语质量，反之，该以横向加工为主的源语（比如技术性演讲、读稿发言等），因为各种原因（如译员无稿）进行过多纵向加工时，会增大译员认知负荷，进而影响译语质量，甚至导致同传失败。

较为合理的做法是，译员既要培养听辨理解命题信息、脱离语言外壳的能力，提升听辨效率和效果，也要强化对一些信息成分、特色话语及其译语的记忆储备和译前准备，加强这些词汇、语块的双语快速对译训练，提升实际翻译中处理这些内容的速度和准确性，通过多种类型源语的训练，在纵向和横向加工中找到平衡，并且能够根据会议情况、发言特征、个人认知状况等综合因素，动态调节，自动、灵活、无缝切换。从口译教学和自我训练角度看，纵向加工应是口译教学重点和优先内容，是口译能力的关键要素、专业译员的区别性能力，应该成为学员口译训练的主要内容和目标之一。

2. 训练与点评

> 会议：IBM 中国论坛，主旨演讲：用区块链技术重塑供应链，IBM 中国研究院行业与解决方案研发总监

> 10A：

源语：我叫任常锐，来自 IBM 中国研究院，欢迎各位来光临下午的这个 session。我本人也特别荣幸能够有这么一个机会跟各位来交流我们在区块链上的一些实践，尤其高兴的是我们有两位我们非常好的合作伙伴来和我一起来做这个 session。事实上大家知道，区块链它的核心的一个特质就是说，怎么样更好地合作，所以我们也是用合作的方式来跟大家来介绍这样一个话题。其实可能大家都知道，除了上午我们讲的很多 cognitive 人工智能相关的东西，区块链差不多是现在最炙手可热的技术话题。由于时间的原因，我觉得可能今天我们不会对区块链本身是什么做特别详细的讲解，但是我是希望能让大家记住一些关键词，希望通过分享我们和沃尔玛、清华大学，包括我们的一些合作伙伴，一起做的一些事情，给大家一个概念，区块链为什么这么火，它到底能有什么作用。回到我们今天的话题，它对我们整个的面向消费者的价值链到底有什么样的一些颠覆性的作用。所以，其实，我想大家可能就记住这一句话可能就可以了。这是我们的全球的 CEO 罗睿兰女士她经常讲的一句话，她就讲"区块链之于可信交易可类比于互联网之于信息"。大家回想过去二十几年，我们的互联网带给我们的信息处理和传统信息化的颠覆性的变化。可以讲，我们坚信区块链对于我们的商业交易所带来的变化，不会亚于互联网对我们现有的信息带来的变化。

译语: Thank you. My name is Ren Changrui from Chinese academy. Welcome you. I'm very honoured to be here to exchange my ideas with you on blockchain. I'm very happy to have invited two partners. The core of blockchain is about cooperation. So, we're going to cooperate and talk about this topic. I think you know we have talked a lot about the stuff related to artificial intelligence. Blockchain is a heated topic. I won't go into details of this. I just want to sound a few keywords. I want to talk about what we have done with our partners, and how what blockchain is and how blockchain works, and the disruptive effects of blockchain. Madam Luo Ruilan said, blockchain is comparable to the internet. You can think about the change that the internet has brought to us in the past few years. We're convinced blockchain will be more than uh more than the internet.

译员反思:（1）由于这段时间忙于其他事情，课前老师发的 PPT 没有看，所以翻译的时候全靠听，有些内容跟不上，有些 PPT 上有的内容出现错译、漏译：比如 IBM 中国研究院，应该是 IBM Research-China，再如看了会议日程和 PPT 就明白是三个人一起讲这个话题，不是 I'm honoured to have invited。

（2）感觉自己最需改进的两大问题是："反应不够快"和"听译不协调"，往往需要等到听到更多的信息单元才能进行翻译。

教师点评:（1）企业的活动常常会涉及较多人名、机构名、产品名、服务名、项目名、口号、理念、概念等，而且不少企业的双语说法并非字面对译，需要进行充分译前准备。

（2）如果因为客观原因未能进行充分译前准备，临场应对策略一般就是缩短 EVS 进行快速横向加工，即尽量顺着句子结构快速对译，而此例中译员一直试图进行纵向为主的加工，寻求深度听辨理解、脱壳、压缩、简洁表达等，导致跟不上发言，出现错译、漏译，译语不流利等。除了译前准备因素外，该译员之前练习中一直以纵向加工为主，这种加工模式需要根据源语情况和自己认知情况灵活调整。当然，如果经过充分译前准备，这一段由于专有名词和术语并不多，也并非完全需要横向加工。

部分源语的处理建议：

我叫任常锐，来自 IBM 中国研究院

Ren Changrui with IBM Research-China

区块链它的核心的一个特质就是说，怎么样更好地合作，所以我们也是用合作的方式来跟大家来介绍这样一个话题。

（纵向加工）Blockchain technology is about collaboration/Blockchain is a technology for collaboration,

（横向加工）One of the key features of Blockchain technology is collaboration,

so we co-present/present in collaboration.

区块链差不多是现在最炙手可热的技术话题。

（纵向加工）Blockchain is a buzzword today.

（横向加工）Blockchain nowadays is one of the hottest technical topics.

区块链为什么这么火，它到底能有什么作用。

（纵向加工）why blockchain and how?

（横向加工）why blockchain is so popular/what makes blockchain so popular and what the role it can play?

10B：

源语：其实关于区块链呢，可能大家虽然不见得对这个事情有特别深入的了解，但大家一定听说过。而且呢，应该绝大多数各位一定会对关于它是不是跟比特币等等这样一些词联系起来。所以呢，其实区块链它确实是脱身于比特币这样一个，我把它叫作区块链的一个特别成功的应用。但是呢，从 IBM 观点认为呢，我们把这样的一个技术应用到我们的商业领域，尤其是说甚至是跟金融本身已经没有太大关系的这样一个我们常规的企业业务里边，它到底怎么发挥作用呢。那我们认为呢，它其实需要有具备一定的特性，而且要经过相应地扩展。就是说，大家可能都知道，区块链是一个分布式的记账账本，在比特币里也是这么做的。但是呢，我们想想，如果在我们实际的商业环境里边，我们不太可能是一个完全的无中心的、不受控制的这样一个，而且还得挖矿呢，大家可能知道，区块链有挖矿，比特币要挖矿。这样的一个机制呢可能是并不现实的。

译语：About blockchain, some of you might, many of you might have heard of it. I believe that most of you uh will connect it with uh bitcoin. Blockchain indeed derived from bitcoin. It's a very successful application. But this technology can also be applied to business sector, to uh uh regular enterprise that's not even related to the financial sector. What role can blockchain play? Uh we need to make some adjustments to use blockchain in our enterprise. It's a distributed ledger. In a business environment, blockchain uh cannot be completely distributed. Uh the blockchain mechanism might not be applicable.

教师点评：本段前半部分，译语质量总体还可以，但是后半部分术语增多、信息密度增加后，译员的纵向加工模式明显跟不上节奏，尤其从"我们不太可能是一个完全的无中心……"开始，译员因为未能及时横向加工处理，EVS被拉大，导致后面的漏译。

译员反思：很明显遗漏了"具备一定特性"这一信息，而且也没有理解到"经过相应地扩展"指的就是 be enterprise-ready。明明在译前准备时注意到了 enterprise-ready，但是当时没有看平行文本找对应的表达，所以没能马上把中文表达对应到英文表达上。后面漏译"挖矿"，这里不是没听到，也不是不会表达，而是没有找到这句话和前文的联系而主动选择了漏译，但是事后想想，这种情况下应该选择直接对译。

教师点评：译员译前准备后，应该制定相关术语表，在正式翻译前进行快速双向互译训练，确保实际翻译时可以快速横向对译。"它其实需要有具备一定的特性，而且要经过相应地扩展"可处理为 it must possess certain features and be enterprise-ready。"我们不太可能是一个完全的无中心……"可以处理为 we cannot be fully decentralized and permissionless.

源语：所以呢，其实在 IBM 倡导下面呢，事实上我们做了很多工作，比如说我们在隐私保护方面，就是我们既要，大家要监督，大家要共享，还要分布，那同时呢我还要能保证一定程度隐私。我不希望人能看到的事情还是需要一定的保护，尤其在商业、供应链的环境里边，我们是有商业机密的。我是需要接受大家的监督，但是呢，有些事情不见得所有的都要共享，所以要 permission。第二个呢就是我需要灵活的这种合约。就是说我在商业的任何交易里边，背后一定是有合约的，它可以是简单的，也可以是复杂的。而且呢，我们现实的商业中，它这种合约一定是非常灵活的。所以你必须有一个特别好的一个机制，能够做到可插拔这样一个感觉的这样一个机制。

译语：So we've done a lot to uh adjust to this new model. We need supervision. We need sharing. And we need a lower level of distribution. And business environment in terms of supply chain, we need supervision and we need a certain level of privacy and permission. And second, we need flexible uh contracts. In any business transaction, we need contracts and they might be complex and flexible. So we need a good mechanism uh to make it, make the mechanism agile.

译员反思：前几句译语的逻辑不够清晰，是因为对源语的理解不清晰，归根结底其实是因为没听完原文的信息块就立即开始翻译，不可避免会有理解、记忆上的问题。在意识到一个信息块要花比较长的时间才能完成的时候，我就应该开始调整 EVS 了，马上改掉深度理解的模式，进入转码模式，先字对字地跟上。

教师点评：同前，译员仍然坚持纵向加工，例如，在处理第一句时，译员在 we've done a lot 后犹豫了一下，说出了源语中不存在直接对应的 adjust to this new model，显然是基于语境深加工的结果。而这一深加工模式消耗了较多时间，导致 EVS 过大，后面出现漏译、错译。对于这种高语速、高信息密度，且含有较多术语的源语，译员应该采用横向加工模式，尽量简化、合并、压缩除术语外的语言，并快速对译术语，即用"简洁语言+术语对译"的方式处理。例如，第一句可以处理为 we have done a lot on privacy protection. We need oversight/supervision, openness/sharing/transparency and distribution, but we also need privacy/confidentiality. 最后一句的处理也是与第一句类似的情形，因为在处理"在商业的任何交易里边，背后一定是有合约的，它可以是简单的，也可以是复杂的"时明显采用了纵向加工模式，消耗了较多时间，影响了下一句的听辨、记忆，未能译出"让合约灵活"：make the contract intelligent/flexible。如果前一句采用横向加工简洁处理为 in every business transaction there is always a contract, simple or complex，问题应该可以避免。

源语：更重要的是，大家知道，在比特币里面，我们是要挖矿。这样的一个机制事实上在现实的商业社会里面，你很难找到这样的应用场景。所以你在做无论是记账也好，还是让一件事情发生也好，一定是有一个很好的机制。所谓的共识机制就是来解决这样的一个事情。所以可能比较偏技术，但是希望大家能记住的一点，是说呢我们认为呢区块链它具备了非常多非常好的特性，类似于透明、灵活、安全、可信这样一些技术。这样的一些技术是需要在已经在比特币等等这样一些技术成功应用了之后，做很多的相应的扩展之后，它能变成企业级的应用。那同时，我个人的观点是说，基于区块链去构建一个企业的应用，其实跟我们基于传统的技术去构建一个企业应用，也有同样的要求和难点，它同样是需要有好的设计，同样要解决安全、可扩展、稳定等等一系列的问题。所以这是我们的一个观点。

译语：In terms of bitcoin, we also talk about mining, but it's not applicable in our situation. We need a good mechanism uh to make things happen. It's a very technical thing, but what we need to remember is that blockchain has many good strengths. for example, it's transparent. It's verifiable and so on. Since bitcoin since blockchain is applied to many technologies like bitcoin, it can also be applied to our business. How do we use blockchain to create a new business application? There are many challenges. We need a good plan. We need to solve problems like instability of the system.

译员反思：这里漏译了"共识机制"，也是译前准备不到位，明明学过这个表达，但是在听的时候没有敏锐地在原文捕捉到这个术语。而且由于思考加工过度后还是无法理解这句话的内容和思路，导致整个句子漏掉了很多信息。

教师点评：同前，译员还是应该采用"简洁语言 + 术语对译"方式，例如对于"具备了非常多非常好的特性，类似于透明、灵活、安全、可信这样一些技术"可以直接对译为 it has many good features such as transparency, flexibility, security and reliability，而非 it's transparent. It's verifiable。不难发现，译员出现不流利 uh 时，往往是不了解术语而无法横向对译，试图纵向处理，如 in our situation 是无法横向对译"现实商业社会"business reality，need a good mechanism 处是因为"记账"bookkeeping 不会处理，good uh strengths 处是不会处理"特性"features。

译员总反思：从听众的角度上看：虽然重点信息大部分都在，但是明显不够流利，卡顿和思考痕迹很明显。有几处重要信息遗漏，几处专业术语的翻译不准确，有几处语义逻辑不对。从译员的角度分析：重点信息基本都在，可能是因为在听的时候花了大量精力去理解讲者的话，理解了，自然重点就抓到了。但也正是因为花了太多时间思考，导致停顿时间过长，EVS 拉得太长而遗漏了信息。

无论是交传还是同传，自己确实喜欢进行思考和信息加工，不熟悉转码的方法。原因是自己一直知道中英文差距很大，不仅是语言，说话的思维差异也很大，所以基本不敢照着原来的句子翻译。在交传的时候，这样的处理方法会提高翻译质量，让一些语言出彩，但是在同传时确实需要注意权衡，要在转码和信息加工之间找到一个平衡。

教师总点评：总的来说，译员在不适用横向加工的部分表现总体不错，但是适用横向加工的地方，由于本身对 IT 有关术语不熟悉，译前准备又不充分，加上本来习惯于纵向加工模式，未能采用横向加工为主的模式，从而影响了译语质量。建议译员加强数字、术语、专有名词、中国特色话语等的快速双向转码训练，并有意识地寻找技术性、政策性源语（如学术会议、政治会议等）进行横向加工训练，逐步学会将纵向与横向加工融为一体，实现两者动态、无缝切换。

10C：

源语：那在这个讲到具体案例之前呢，其实回到今天我们的这个 topic 主题，就是说区块链到底能给我们这个供应链或者相关的我们这个企业应用领域带来什么样的一些变化？所以我总结了八个字。就是大家知道，可能讲区块链的话，因为它跟比特币一些千丝万缕的联系，可能通常我们会，或者讲得比较多的，都是金融行业的，或者说跟金融比较相关行业的，讲供应链可能更多，讲的也是供应链金融。但事实上呢，包括我们今天跟沃尔玛、清华大学合作的这个例子，包括很多的 IBM 和其他的这个行业从业者做的一些事情呢，在供应链领域的应用呢，我认为也是特别有前景的。它能解决至少这几个问题。

译语：Before moving to the some examples, I will still want to emphasize our topic: what blockchain can provide for our enterprises and sectors? I have a few keywords. As bitcoin is closely related to blockchain technologies, we focus more on the financial sector when talking about blockchain technology. But in fact, the as our cooperation with Tsinghua University and Walmart in supply chain, the application of blockchain technology is also promising as it can solve multiple problems.

源语：第一呢就是大家都容易理解，大家知道区块链它具备了一个分布式记账特性，记录的数据是不可篡改的，永久保存的等等这样一些特性。那同样地，那我们供应链中的很多的需要有安全性、可信性，那同时还要能接受审计、不可篡改这样的特性的数据呢，毫无疑问区块链可以进行这样的一个保存。第二个呢，关键是说效率，我刚才讲了，区块链一个关键是说呢，它有一个好的机制呢，保证多方协作的时候呢，能够最大限度地减少有意地或者无意地带来的错误或者是说 fraud。这些有意无意的，这样一些恶意的或者是无意的这样一些问题，减少了问题就提高了效率，降低了成本。

译语：For exa- the first is trustable. The data is secure and reliable and tamper-evident as well as audible. In our supply chains, we have many information that need to be secu-, that are, that need to be secured. It can be stored on the blockchain technology. And second, high efficiency. It can reduce the dutible durable efforts and frauds. Thus, it can improve our efficiency.

译员反思：(1) 理解有误。"因为它（区块链）跟比特币有一些千丝万缕的联系"，主语应该是区块链，As bitcoin is closely related to blockchain technologies 不太妥当，应该改为 As blockchain technology is closely related to bitcoin.

(2) 翻得很笼统，不细致。第二段在翻译的时候明显感觉有点手忙脚乱，因为感觉讲者讲到了下一页的 PPT，但是又不太确定，我的目光在上下两页 PPT 之间反复横跳，占用了一部分精力，所以一上来翻得非常笼统，说出来的都是译前准备 PPT 的内容，听上去也不是很流利。

(3) 语言资源不够。翻的时候在想应该用什么表达，精力又被占走了。It can reduce the durable efforts and frauds. 这句中的 durable 口误，应该改为 duplicable efforts，重复性的工作。

(4) 表达不流利，改口和重复较多。

(5) 未来，输出质量可以进一步提高，加强监听，规避一些比较明显的语法错误，同时在能力范围内提高加工颗粒度。还应调整语流，尽量保持平稳输出，而不是时断时续，尤其是在句子中间的地方尽量不要断。相关的专业术语还需要进一步加强训练，多输入平行文本。

教师点评：(1) 首先，虽然译语有不少问题，但是译员的加工方式与前面两位不同，总体是横向加工，这是值得肯定的。

（2）译语的问题主要源于三个方面：译前准备不充分、多来源信息整合加工能力不足、英语资源尤其是商务或行业英语资源匮乏。既然"说出来的都是译前准备 ppt 的内容"，足见英语术语准备得不够充分，"数据的安全、可信、不可篡改、可审计"在查询好双语后，流利产出 data are secure, reliable, tamper-proof and auditable 或者 data security, reliability, tamper-proofing and auditability，而不至于出现口误 audible 和流利性问题。多来源信息整合加工能力是指译员能够在同传中协调精力高效定位、摄取并整合多种来源的信息，如电脑屏幕文字、手边的术语表、会场大屏幕 PPT 文字等，服务于双语转换与译语表达，且不影响到译语流利性，这需要长期针对性训练。另外，译员的商务或行业性英语资源明显不足，例如"案例、企业应用领域、供应链金融"应是 cases, business applications, supply chain finance。当然英语基本功也需要加强，emphasize our topic, as our cooperation with Tsinghua University and Walmart in supply chain, The data is secure, many information 等语法错误或不地道表达也不少。

（3）"保证多方协作的时候呢，能够最大限度地减少有意地或者无意地带来的错误或者是说 fraud"可以处理为：while enabling collaboration, it minimizes intentional or unintentional fraud.

10D1- 10D2：

以下是译员课上训练（10D1）及与课后时隔六天后再次训练（10D2）的对比与反思。

源语：其实关于区块链呢，可能大家虽然不见得对这个事情有特别深入的了解，但大家一定听说过。而且呢，应该绝大多数各位一定会对关于它是不是跟比特币等等这样一些词联系起来。所以呢，其实区块链它确实是脱身于比特币这样一个，我把它叫作区块链的一个特别成功的应用。但是呢，从 IBM 观点认为呢，我们把这样的一个技术应用到我们的商业领域，尤其是说甚至是跟金融本身已经没有太大关系的这样一个我们常规的企业业务里边，它到底怎么发挥作用呢。那我们认为呢，它其实需要有具备一定的特性，而且要经过相应地扩展。就是说，大家可能都知道，区块链是一个分布式的记账账本，在比特币里也是这么做的。但是呢，我们想想，如果在我们实际的商业环境里边，我们不太可能是一个完全的无中心的、不受控制的这样一个，而且还得挖矿呢，大家可能知道，区块链有挖矿，比特币要挖矿。这样的一个机制呢可能是并不现实的。

10D1 译语：You may not have in-depth understanding of blockchain and you may have relevant practice. But I think you may have some understanding of its relevation of bitcoin. Indeed, blockchain comes from bitcoin, and its successful practition on bitcoin is well known. But now we are using this technology in business, especially the practice of it is not very relevant to the finance and business operation. Actually we think it should have some special properties. As you may know that blockchain is a distributed account book as it is applied in bitcoin. But actually in the business environment, we may not see it as a complete non-centered, uncontrollable blockchain. It's not like how it is applied in the mining in bitcoin.

10D2 译语：You may not be an expert of blockchain, but you must have heard of it. And in most cases, you may know its relevation to bitcoin. Bitcoin is an example for the successful application of blockchain. Now we are trying to use this technology in business, especially that is less related to financial and the traditional business. So how does it work? I think with its characteristics and further extension, it can work. We may know that blockchain is a distributed ledge. It is also used this way in bitcoin. However, in the actual business environment it is hard to use it as a decentralized, uncontrollable system that also mines. It's not too realistic.

源语：所以呢，其实在 IBM 倡导下面呢，事实上我们做了很多工作，比如说我们在隐私保护方面，就是我们既要，大家要监督，大家要共享，还要分布，那同时呢我还要能保证一定程度隐私。我不希望人能看到的事情还是需要一定的保护，尤其在商业、供应链的环境里边，我们是有商业机密的。我是需要接受大家的监督，但是呢，有些事情不见得所有的都要共享，所以要 permission。第二个呢就是我需要灵活的这种合约。就是说我在商业的任何交易里边，背后一定是有合约的，它可以是简单的，也可以是复杂的。而且呢，我们现实的商业中，它这种合约一定是非常灵活的。所以你必须有一个特别好的一个机制，能够做到可插拔这样一个感觉的这样一个机制。

10D1 译语：Actually innovated by IBM, we use it in privacy protection, in the mutual sharing and supervision. At the same time, we need to protect some privacy, especially on things that people don't want other people to see. And we need to protect business conficience, confidence. And we don't want to share everything. We need to protect protect our permission. Also, we want some flexible contract in all our business transactions. We need some contacts. Actually in business, the contract must be flexible, so we need a good mechanism to make sure that it happens.

10D2 译语：So in IBM, we have done a lot of work. For example, we use it to protect privacy. We use it to share, distribute the information. But at the same time, we protect privacy, especially for the things that you don't want others to see. We need confidence in business. We like to share, but not everything. So we need permission. Second we need flexible contract. Every business require contract be it simple or complex. And business must and the business contract must be flexible with good system that is pluggable.

译员反思：（1）首先，还是之前老师就指出过的"信息加工弱"。其实从上次点评后，就一直在努力练习"信息加工"，并在前面几周的材料里感受到了很大的不同和改善。但是从上周开始，有一些材料信息密度很大，语速很快，而我本身不擅长加工信息，很多时候又缺乏相关知识，所以要花费很多精力去留意，就会导致大量丢信息。我处在一个加工信息就跟不上，不加工就信息混乱的状态。但这次课老师说"信息加工不一定要脱壳，而是更清晰，更凸显，让听众更容易听懂"，我觉得这是个很好的启示，先从小处着手，先以比较简洁的语言形式来凸显信息。之后会继续朝这个方向尝试练习。

（2）另一个很严重的问题就是语言质量低。太多的单词、语法错误、奇怪的中式表达，听自己第一次的译文感觉触目惊心。中式表达需要慢慢积累来改正，单词、语法错误要注意加强监听。

（3）此外我的 EVS 较短，所以要继续练习切成短句，快速对应，以关键词为中心，弱化其他语言，提升跟住重点的能力。

教师点评：（1）之前的课上曾告知该译员，其口齿伶俐性不错，语言资源一般，信息加工能力比较弱。这种情况本身会导致译员不擅长纵向加工。

（2）虽然译员反应较快，口齿伶俐性不错，但是其横向加工表现并不好，除了语言错误外，内容上不忠实的问题比较严重。原因可能是其在以往的口译学习中养成了不良习惯——不重听辨重产出、没听懂就急于表达、不监听自己的表达，教学中发现不少口语相对比较流利的同学或多或少都存在这类情形。需要强调的是，横向加工是在听辨理解的基础上进行对应式的翻译，不意味着不需要听辨，而是听辨理解和转换表达的单位较小，比如字、词、词组层面，或者有直接对应译语的句子（如中国特色话语）时的直接转换。

（3）译员间隔一段时间后再次用同一材料训练，虽然内容准确性提高，语言质量也有所提升，整体译语可用性得以提升，但是从前后两次的语言问题——relevation, business conficence, confidence, confidence in business 可见，译员的英语基础有待加强。此外，distributed ledge 再次出错也反映其译前准备不够细心认真，也许不只是译前准备问题，而是与"急于表达而听辨理解和记忆薄弱"的加工方式有关。

（4）EVS 需要动态调节，一般在信息密度高，尤其是专有名词、术语、数字或罗列较多时保持较短 EVS；此外，并不是所有场合都需切成短句进行快速横向加工，只习惯于过短的 EVS，不利于纵向加工。译员应根据源语情况和自我认知状况，动态调节 EVS 和纵/横加工模式。

七、译语发布

1. 讲解

从听众接受或用户使用角度看，同传是"语音即服务"交际方式，即听众所获得的同传服务质量几乎完全依赖接收机里的语音流。这与交传不同，交传译员在现场进行多模态交际，听众可以利用译员的面部表情、手势、体态语，或者与译员现场交流，来增进对译语理解，而同传中，听众从译员那里获得的只是蕴含信息的语音流。因此，同传译语发布方式对于同传质量和交际效果非常重要，尤其是音韵、流利性与噪声管控。

从音韵角度看，译员应该充分利用多种音韵，如音高、音长、重音、停顿、语速、语气、语调等，有效包装和凸显源语信息，契合译语音韵规范，这样有利于提高听众对译语的理解效率和效果。译员可以通过不同的音高、音长和重音来凸显某些词或词组的信息，进而勾勒出话语信息的轻重主次、逻辑层次、感情色彩等；在命题间及命题内部小意群间恰当停顿；确保产出语速既契合源语节奏，又利于听众理解，尽量保持让听众感觉舒适的自然、平稳节奏，既要避免一个词一个词往外蹦，也要避免为赶时间语速飞快，同时要避免忽快忽慢。语气语调一般应与源语语调保持同向，程度可以比源语稍微平淡中性一些，既要避免机械式平淡语调，也要避免过于丰富夸张，还要避免高亢型、说教型、消沉型语调。另外还应注意避免形成不好的一些语调习惯，每到句尾"扬"或"抑"一下，或在译语中添加不必要的语气语调。

译语流利性对译语质量和用户使用效果影响也较大。在口译训练中，应养成良好的发布习惯，尽量减少或避免填充语、犹豫、折返、修正、断句、口头禅、非必要重复等各类非流利现象，确保译语流利、干净、高效。

在平时训练中，要加强译语流利性监控。首先，要管好嘴巴，不急于在并没有听到多少源语信息时为保持翻译状态，而强迫性地快速地自说自话，自加信息，或机械重复部分词、短语、短句，追加若干同义表达，或加一些无关痛痒的口头语；尽量说完整的一个句子，原则上不在起句后折返重说，或者还未说完一句又开启下一句，非关键处尽量不进行自我修正；尽量避免补白语、口头禅，如"这样，我们，一个，一些，一种，这里，这么，那么，然后，因此，实际上，事实上，可以说，大家知道""呢，啊，吧""嗯，呃，那，这个，可能，大概"，等等。

此外，由于同传设备系统对声音比较灵敏，译员还需要管控好各种噪声。要保持嘴巴与译员机话筒的恰当距离（10厘米左右），避免过近影响声音效果；管控好自己发布译语时可能伴随的噪声，比如换气声、嘴巴吧唧声、吸鼻子声等，如遇打喷嚏、咳嗽等可按静音键；管控好其他行为产生的噪声，保持手机静音，尽可能降低敲击键盘声，翻动纸质资料声，避免受发言影响发出笑声；在搭档工作时，也应配合保持安静，喝水、走动、翻找材料时尽可能降低声音。

最后，声音本身会影响译语可听性和听众舒适度，发声方式也会影响译员工作状态，因此，参加一定的发声训练课程有益于提升译语质量与效果，保护嗓子，提升职业可持续性。

2. 训练与点评

会议：第五届中国国际液化天然气大会的开幕致辞的开端部分

源语：女士们，先生们，大家好。第五届中国国际液化天然气大会LNGCHINA2015 今天如期开幕了！我谨代表大会主办单位和大会技术委员会，向参会的各位来宾表示热烈的欢迎，向热情支持本届大会的国内外朋友们，表示诚挚的感谢！本届中国国际液化天然气大会，是继 2011 年创办以来，连续第五次举办。五年来，LNGCHINA 大会见证了中国液化天然气工业的发展，同时也为国内外行业界同行提供了一个高端的技术和市场交流的平台,为 LNG 行业的发展作出了有益的贡献!近十年来,中国 LNG 产业发展很快,无论是 LNG 液化厂,还是 LNG 接收站,无论是 LNG 汽车、LNG 船舶,还是 LNG 加注站,至少在数量上都走在了世界各国的前面。这十年,中国引领了世界 LNG 液化厂小型化的浪潮,引领了 LNG 交通能源产业化、规模化、网络化的浪潮,也推动了世界能源经济向天然气清洁能源经济转型的世界大潮。

8B:

可能因为听辨与转换加工单位太小,加工过于谨慎、精细,也可能与平时表达习惯有关,译语可听性、可用性较低,主要问题包括:1)不少地方都是一个词一个词往外蹦,而且很多词听上去都像是一个意群,都在重读并停顿,未能根据译语意群恰当运用音韵,导致译语听上去不流利,意思不连贯,不明晰;2)有些句子间没有通过停顿、重读、语调等凸显其边界,削弱了意思的可理解性。

8C:

译语听上去有些"无力、苍白",语调比较单调、乏味,没有使用相应的音韵来凸显信息,此外,也一定程度上存在前例中的一个词一个词地发布问题。

8D:

译语同时存在上面两例的问题——一个词一个词地发布,语调过于单调、乏味,而且还给人在自己世界里自言自语的感觉,交际效果弱,此外一定程度上存在忽快忽慢情形。

8E:

译语发布总体较好,比较流利,音韵运用较好,但存在句子或短语尾部部分词汇语调上扬过多的问题,比如 conference, today, years, LNG in China, growth, cars, stations, LNG, scale 等。

8F：

译语音韵运用尚可，但流利性问题明显，犹豫、停顿等伴随的噪声明显，也一定程度存在节奏不平稳问题。

8G：

译语发布总体还可以，但是节奏可以稍微再快点、流利点，音韵稍微再丰富点。

8H：

听译协调还有些问题，句间停顿（等待）有些久，沉默时间有些长，句内的等待、犹豫、修正较为明显，流利性不佳；部分大、小意群有些孤立，即有的句子间或分句及词组间的停顿和语气语调不当，使译语不够连贯，另外节奏也忽快忽慢。

8I：

译语发布总体不错，有三点需注意：1）说完主语后等待过久；2）通过 the 进行缓冲、等待，这两点影响译语流利性和可听性；3）句内意群间停顿有些久，容易割裂意思。

八、英语提升

1. 讲解

与日常交流用语的能力相比，同传工作对语言能力的要求高许多。首先，同传工作语言是在诸多认知限制下使用，比如时间压力，多任务加工，渐进加工，源语挑战（如语速、信息密度、句式复杂度、口音等），源语不可重复等，这对高认知负荷下语言资源的丰富性、灵活性、可用性、精确性、交际效率等要求非常高。其次，使用同传的国际会议跨商务、科技、政务等领域，交流主题丰富多样，探讨内容具有相当广度、深度，这要求译员能用领域、行业专家的方式进行表达，能够正确使用各类术语、行话、表达习惯等。因此，同传工作语言要精准高效且饱含主题信息，与日常用语及影视剧话语差异较大，与文学创作或者学术研究用语也非常不同。

如前所述，由于多种原因，我国的同传学习与实践者中，英语为A语的极少，英语达到B语要求的不多，不少人仅是C（即英语理解没有问题），甚至达不到C（英语理解尚存在问题）。此外，一定程度上还存在以下问题：书面语不弱，但口头应用能力弱；中式表达多导致交际效率低；文学或学术用语资源丰富，但行业或领域表达资源匮乏等。在中英同传中，英语能力不足主要会导致以下问题：1）语言加工耗费较多精力，导致其他加工（如源语理解、自我监控等）精力不足，整体上影响译语质量；2）无法及时产出合适译语，导致同传部分中断或信息遗漏；3）译语比较啰唆、冗长，导致同传节奏慢，滞后，最终引起信息遗漏；4）译语存在语法等问题，或者语言不够地道，信息不够明晰、高效，削弱了交际功能。英语能力既影响同传技能学习效率，也影响同传技能发挥效果。长远看，英语能力/质量的上限可能会成为中英同传能力/质量的上限。

提升英语作为同传工作语言的能力，显得格外关键，具体有以下几点建议：1）如果条件允许，建议赴英语母语国家生活一年以上，或者沉浸在英语母语社区、工作环境；2）培养英语思维，多读、听自己有兴趣且较为了解的领域、产自英语母语者的话语，尤其是产自英语母语社会权威或知名媒体、机构的话语，以口头话语，特别是即兴讲话为主；3）警惕中式英语，除中国特色话语的英语译语外，建议少接触产自非英语母语者的话语；4）加强中英对比，选择自己熟知的领域，读、听平行话语，体会中英表达信息的差异；5）提升英语效率，多读商务性话语，如行业报告、企业年报、品牌故事、使命愿景等，多听商务、科技类即兴演讲、讨论、访谈等，体会英语基本词汇、简单句型的灵活、丰富用法，学习简洁高效表达；6）熟悉领域用语，读、听领域、行业材料，可从自己擅长领域开始，逐步拓展；7）强化双语转换，重点进行中文命题信息的多样、脱壳翻译，加强行业语汇的快速对应翻译，提升表达迅捷度、伶俐度、清晰度和准确度。

在同传训练时，可以围绕同一主题进行英中和中英双向练习，或者利用同一个会议的双向材料进行训练，以便能够相互借鉴语言表达，即英文发言中的大量词汇、语块、句式等可以为同一主题的中英同传提供参考，反之亦然。遇到具体转换困难时，可查询、参考英汉双语平行语料库或英语语料库中的检索结果，或者其他类型平行文本、音频，但一定要确保所参考英语产自英语母语者。也可以尝试将英语源语视译或听译为中文，再回译为英语，并将译语和英语源语进行对比。

2. 训练与点评

笔者将一段英语即兴发言音频转写成文稿后，即兴视译（尽量保留即兴发言特征，为减少同学困难，略去了嘉宾介绍部分，此外，个别地方视译后的意思与源语稍有出入）并录音，以此作为课堂中英同传训练的源语材料。教学中，让同学尝试做内容几乎相同的材料的英译中和中译英，鼓励同学将自己的译语与英语发言进行对比，并从语言正确性、地道性、交际效率等角度进行比较和反思。英语母语者的表达可以帮助译员发现自己的语言错误以及不规范、不地道问题，此外，虽然英语母语者未必总遵循简约表达原则，且部分口语表达可能存在一定的不规范或不流利，但是母语者的表达总体上还是值得译员参考的，有利于提升译语的明晰度与交际效率，也有益于译员提升脱壳能力。

> 会议：创新经济论坛午餐会，变革时代：增加能源供给，减少排放，主持人：阿布扎比国家石油公司（ADNOC）首席财务官

> 11A：

中文源语（视译转写）：主持人：我们经常在说，本世纪中叶要实现净零排放，只有这样我们才能把全球气温上升的目标限制在1.5摄氏度之内。许多人说我们不太可能，很难实现这个目标。当然我们现在谈很多，比如说可持续发展，城镇化，实现联合国千年发展目标，但所有的一切其实都要靠我们思考，如何更好地来利用能源来推动我们的增长，这个就是我们今天对话这个环节的主题。

译语：We all know our challenges. We always talk about the target of zero emission so that we can limit the 1.5℃ temperature rise. It's hard to achieve that goal. We talk about the urbanization, the Millennium Goals. All these goals depends on better utilization of energy. This is the theme of our discussion today.

英文源语：So I'm not going to set the context too much. I think you all know the challenges at hand. We're hearing that we need to get to net zero by the middle of this century with carbon emissions in order to stop the rise of this globe temperature to 1.5℃. Many people say it's difficult for us to get there, if not impossible. Everything from sustainability to urbanization meeting any of the SDGs will rely on how we're fueling our growth. And that's going to be the conversation we have today.

译员反思（1）：内容："可持续发展"有遗漏，原因是在翻译前一句话时没有协调好注意力的分配，除此之外，整段的意思基本上表达了。

教师点评：译员可能过高估计了译语的准确性，例如，talk more about，实际这是主持人的开场第一句话，不应该是 more，而是 much，再如 limit...rise 未能准确传达源语信息，"本世纪中叶、全球、净零"等信息没有译出，"许多人说"漏译，扭曲了源语信息。

译员反思（2）：语言：有一些 Chinglish 的表达，如"I will not talk more about the background"；有些语言可以更简洁，如"This is the theme of our discussion today"可以去掉"the theme of"。

教师点评：语言方面可以从如下角度评估：正确、规范、地道、明晰、简洁/效率。

从语言正确、规范角度看，基本只有 depends on 问题；从地道看，I will...background, All these...energy 两句有较大提升空间。

从是否明晰、简洁高效角度看，we talk about... 与后一句可以合并，中文发言的状语与短句中的关键名词常常可以提取为主语，与后面内容构成新句子。当然,有一点需要说明,本段材料由于是笔者即兴视译录音,语速较慢,因此译语简洁和效率可能不是重点,但是许多中文即兴发言语速都较快,保持译语简洁高效是基本策略。

从学习角度看,译员可将自己的有关表达与源语对比,体会自己译语与英语源语表达在地道性、明晰性等方面的差距:set the context/ challenges at hand/We're hearing/stop the rise/it's difficult for us to get there/if not impossible/Everything from...to.../fueling our growth/that's going to be the conversation we have today。平时可以多进行英中和中英回译与对比练习。

中文源语(视译转写):首先我给大家提个醒,我相信大家也都知道我们分会场的讨论是遵循查塔姆法则,也就是说我们可以自由谈论,而且我很快就会请在座的各位听众观众来提问题,发表自己的看法想法,因为我们还是希望我们这个环节能更多地互动,我们当然要尽力地让我们这个环节更互动一点,毕竟这个会议两天的议程很满,今天是第二天了,而且刚吃完午饭也不容易,所以让大家一直坐在这儿能参与并不容易。但不管怎么样,我们今天肯定会有一些很棒的想法,所以请大家积极参与。另外我们这里提供了同声传译的耳机,我们全程都用英语交流,有一些听不懂英语的嘉宾和听众可以到后面取一下同传耳机。好,我就废话不多说,请我们的几位讨论的嘉宾上台。

译语: I want to remind you that our discussion should abide by rules. We can talk about this topic freely. I will invite you to raise questions and share your thoughts. I hope this section could have more your participation, engage you more. Because this is the second day of the meeting, we just had our lunch. So I want all of you to participate in. But today we will definitely have some good thoughts. We hope your active participation. And we discuss in English. For those who don't understand English, you can put on your headphones. So next, I will invite our speaker.

英文源语: A reminder, I'm sure all of you are well aware these breakout sessions are Chatham house rules only, so we can have an open discussion. I am going to go quite early on and call on you all to ask your questions and your comments and thoughts, because we want this to be an engaging conversation. We're attempting to do this on day two of a filled conference and right after lunch. So the challenge is there to keep you entertained. If not, you have great views around you. There are headsets for those who need them. We will be speaking all in English. So but for those who need the headsets, please get them from the back. Okay. Without further ado, I want to call our speakers onto our stage.

译员反思（1）：语言：中式英语问题突出，如"提个醒 I want to remind you that"，"请在座的各位听众观众来提问题，发表自己的看法想法 invite you to raise questions and share your thoughts"，"请我们的几位讨论的嘉宾上台 I will invite our speaker"。

教师点评：如前，译员同样低估了译语问题。语言正确性、规范性的问题至少涉及：our discussion should abide by rules，I hope this section...more，So I want all of you to participate in，We hope your active participation，we'll discuss in English，此外，还有地道性问题：talk about this topic freely，we will definitely have some good thoughts，I will invite our speaker。也有不少内容准确性问题。

译员要多对比和体会自己的译语与英语源语的表达差异，尤其要学习以下表达：A reminder/these breakout sessions are Chatham house rules only/an open discussion/we want this to be an engaging conversation/a filled conference and right after lunch/So the challenge is there to keep you entertained/Without further ado, I want to call our speakers onto our stage 等。

译员反思（2）：交际方面："毕竟这个会议两天的议程很满……并不容易"这几句话的翻译很生硬且有遗漏，交际性弱，原因是听的时候没有迅速抓住讲者要传达的信息，而导致贴着字面翻译，且有些语句没有

109

听到。

教师点评：译员需要加强会议知识、用语的译前准备和学习，如会议的类型、主题、目的、参与者、主持人与演讲人、环节、流程、话语内容结构、常用句式和语块等，相应内容可以通过自建中英国际会议用语双语平行语料库学习。译员刚刚提到的这两句是会议主持常用语，类似的还包括致谢用语、自谦用语、会议室安全、餐饮等事项解释、演讲人介绍、串词、总结等。

译员反思（3）：流利性方面：口齿不够伶俐，语言资源不够丰富，本次讲话语速较慢且信息密度较低，导致我一直在等有效信息出现，而使译语停顿时间长，听起来不流利。可以采用的解决办法是预测、增加词句填补空白。

教师点评：当源语较慢时，译员可以通过以下方式提升译语流利性和可听性：适当降低译语语速；以句子或话语为加工单位，拉长 EVS，将译语表达尽量拉长（和简缩策略正好相反），比如 to 可拉长为 in order to 甚至 in order to make it possible to，a reminder 变成 to begin with, I will take the opportunity to remind you that...；尽量避免句内（尤其是主谓间，小意群内部）停顿过久；有足够精力监听自己译语的信息是否明晰、可用，视情况增加一些逻辑词等，提升句子间的衔接性和连贯性。

译员反思（4）：在紧张状态下或无意识会犯一些语法错误，要多听自己的录音，努力避免下次出现类似的错误。

教师点评：从根本上说，语言错误是语言基本功不够扎实所致，当然，同传的节奏和时间压力、多任务处理模式等会凸显语言问题。译员除了要不断提升语言资源丰富性，可用性和灵活性外，也要不断提升同传听译协调能力、动态调节 EVS 能力，学会各种语言转换策略，加强译语监管，并且有意识地针对语言方面进行反思性刻意练习。

11B：

中文源语（视译转写）：Mark，我先想问问你，因为我们现在想要了解这个行业究竟发生了一些什么。我们谈到行业颠覆性改变，我们也谈到这个行业都在说可持续发展，同时我们都在谈如何来进一步地满足发展所需要的能源。我想问问你 Mark，你们 ADNOC 公司是如何来应对这个挑战？也就是说另外你觉得这个行业是如何来应对这个来保障能够降低排放的呢？

译语：So Mark I want to ask you first. We want to know what are happening in the industry. There are disruptions, sustainability, and talks about how to further satisfy the needs of growth with energies. And as a company, how does ADNOC rise to the challenge? And what's your opinion on the industry's ways to cope with the climate change?

英语源语：Mark, I want to start with you first, because we want to understand what's happening in the industry. We've talked about disruption. We're talking about sustainability, but also the constant need for energy to fuel our development. So how are you tackling this, ADNOC, and how do you see the industry tackling the issue of lower emissions?

教师点评：（1）语言正确性、规范性、地道性方面：start with you, what is happening, need for energy to fuel our development 胜过 ask you, what are happening, satisfy the needs of growth with energies；此外 as a company 显得多余。

（2）简洁、明晰表达与交际效率与效果方面：how do you see the industry tackling the issue of lower emissions 要比 what's your opinion on the industry's ways to cope with the climate change 更简洁、明晰、准确。

中文源语（视译转写）：Mark：谢谢您的问题。首先从行业角度来谈一谈，我觉得对于行业来说，现在确实是非常的难，大家也都知道现在气候变化对世界的影响是非常的大，潜在的影响。当然大家有不同的视角来看这个问题。大家现在想一想，闭上眼睛一两秒想一想，如果你是一个石油和天然气公司的CEO，那么他会在想什么一些问题？首先他们肯定要去支付红利，准备足够的资金用于资本的投资，还有偿还债务等，因为现在市场其实不会再给企业太多的时间去思考了，对吧？

译语：Thank you for your question. I'll answer from the industry's point first. It's a tough period. Everyone knows the climate is changing, its huge impact on the world. Certainly people have different perspectives. Now just close your eyes and visualize if you're a CEO of a gas company, what will you be thinking about. First you need to pay dividends, and get enough cash for investment, and pay your debt. Now the market is...is not giving much time for enterprises for reflection.

英语源语：Mark: So thank you for that. Can you hear me? Thank you. So let's try to answer for the industry first. I think it's a difficult moment to say the least for the industry. You know the prospect of climate change, the potential devastation is enormous. And people are looking at it from different vantage point. But just close your eyes for a second and visualize what he or she, the CEO of an oil and gas company, is thinking about. First they have to pay their dividends. They have to fund their capex. They have to repay their debt. Because the marketplace is no longer giving them a moment for what they're doing. Right?

教师点评：（1）语言正确性、规范性、地道性方面：have to 胜过 need；
（2）简洁、明晰表达与交际效率、效果方面：thank you for that, answer for the industry, visualize what..., fund their capex 要分别比 thank you for your question, answer from the industry's point, visualize if ... what will..., get enough cash for investment 更简洁，the prospect of climate change, the potential devastation is enormous 比 climate is changing, its huge impact on the world 更明晰、准确。

中文源语（视译转写）：大家想一想油气公司的组成，10年之前油气公司占这个标准普尔占12%，今天只占了4%，所以实际上我们的市场已经重新评估这些企业，这是一个问题，这是我们日常所碰到的一个问题。那么除此之外，一个大的油气公司或者中型的油气公司的CEO，它还要考虑一下这公司怎么来应对气候变化。除此之外，他们还要想一想公司未来的发展定位，所以现在很多公司都在寻求多元化发展，他们要么可能定位成一个能源公司或者可再生能源公司，或者说去定位其他方向的发展。所以从整个行业来说，我不想用这个词说整个行业很混乱，但是我想说确实现在整个行业处于一个转型期，那么这是我想说的一个总的背景，宏观的背景。对我们来说，现在现实，我们不管是我们还是其他的一些大的公司，他们都能够提供非常便宜的成本非常低的原油。所以能源的消耗模式，消费模式还会其中一部分模式还会继续存在，也就是说石油还会继续地使用，最终的挑战是什么？比如说我们世界一天可能需要1亿桶，比如说我们这个世界一天需要5000万桶，不管怎么样，我们在还会在用，所以不管怎么样，我们公司还会继续做一个值得信赖的能源供应商。

译语：The composition of market of gas companies changed. In the past 10 years, it has 10% of the market share, now it only has 4% of the market share. So the market is reevaluating those gas and oil companies. They're happening on a daily basis. In addition, a big and medium gas and oil company's CEO needs to think on the company's approaches to climate change and their future directions. Now many companies are diversifying. They're either...identifying as a energy or renewable companies or other directions. So the whole industry, I don't want to say chaotic, but surely, is in a transitioning point. So that's a general background. For us, the reality is that no matter just us or other large companies are providing low cost, very cheap crude oil. So energy consumption pattern will continue to exist, which means petroleum will be used in the future. And the final challenge is that, for example, maybe the world may need 100mn or 50mn barrels of oil per day. Consumption of oil will persist. So our company will continue to be reliable.

英语源语：Think about the composition of oil and gas companies. Just from 10 years ago was 12% of S&P, today is 4%. So the marketplace has already re-rated these companies. So you have that problem, right? which is the day-to-day problem. On top of it, your CEO of your large IOC or mid-sized IOC has to figure out what are they gonna do about climate change. And then on top of it, they have to figure out what are they gonna become. So you now have companies that are bifurcating. They are going in the direction of being an energy company or renewables company or looking at other options. So in the industry, I don't want to say is in disarray, but I say they're in a transition moment. So that's kind of the background in general. For us, the reality is we have, if not us, maybe one other large group has the low cost barrels. So we're going to be around. And the ultimate challenge is if we stay in a world of a hundred million barrels a day, or let's say we stay in a world of 50 million barrels a day, we're gonna still be there. So notwithstanding, we need to be a reliable provider of energy.

教师点评：（1）语言正确、规范、地道方面：identifying...or other directions 不正确也不地道，而 going...looking at other options 好很多，ultimate 比 final 地道、准确；

（2）简洁、明晰表达与交际效率与效果方面：除了准确性问题外，...was 12% of S&P, today is 4% 远比 it has 10% of the market share, now it only has 4% of the market share 简洁，we have...low cost 要比 no matter...low cost, very cheap 简洁，figure out what are they gonna do about climate change...gonna become 比 think on the company's approaches to climate change and their future directions 明晰、准确，energy consumption pattern will continue to exist, Consumption of oil will persist 表达比较复杂、僵硬，we're going to be around...still be there 则更简洁、地道、明晰。

译员总反思：(1) 重复啰唆：主要是由于代词使用不熟练，且遇到容易翻的地方会忍不住先说出来，导致有理解难度的重要信息反而被靠边放。如"谢谢提问"可以用 that 指代，"应对这个挑战"可以用 tackling this，标普占比第二次说可以只说数字，便宜的原油用 low cost barrels 就足够，后文紧跟着说未来的需求，反复重复 barrels of oil 更加没必要，中文习惯性的 filler 也翻了出来，比如"当然"。还有 low cost 就是 very cheap，不能强迫性地翻自己会翻的无用话。

(2) 模糊残缺：主要是因为精力顾不过来，说了下句忘了上句，且没法灵活使用英语的动词，导致说不了简短的主谓句。比如"这个行业都在说可持续发展"，上面翻了 there are disruptions，紧跟着又说 sustainability，出现错误，还有"对世界的影响是非常的大"its huge impact on the world 也是一个没有谓语的成分，这里预测错误，把介词结构翻成了整个主语，但下文却没有别的谓语衔接，再加上英语资源不丰富，这句话就接不下去了，其实可以补充 are clear/evident。"去定位其他方向的发展"同样没有谓语，因为被"定位"这个大词困住，听中文的时候应该把重点放在听名词上，再去寻找英文里与之搭配的动词，而不是死磕中文动词的英文对应表达。

(3) 表达中式，通过练习，自己能够积累更为地道的一些表达：start with you/want to understand/on top of that/fuel our development/how do you see/let's try to answer for the industry/look at it from different vantage point/fund their capex/give them a moment for what they're doing/day-to-day problem/figure out/you now have.../you know/if not...maybe.../go in the direction of/going to be around/still be there/if we stay in a world...

教师点评：作为初学者，译员同传的内容准确性与发布流利性还行，也运用了一些同传加工策略，如顺句、断句、简缩等，但是译语的语言问题比较多，既有基本语法问题，又有中式英语问题，还有表达繁复、模糊、低效问题。鉴于中英同传是在刚刚做完同样材料的英中同传之后所做，译语获得了英语源语的提示，英语提升的空间较大。

11C:

中文源语（视译转写）：除此之外，我们还需要去开拓。开拓什么？就是我们如何来采取措施来应对气候变化问题，因为我们也相信气候变化这个问题很重要，也是牵涉面很多，也是很严肃的一些问题。所以不管是技术还是碳捕获的技术，还是一些其他东西，我们现在其实都在努力地去开发一些新的技术，在技术领域里做一些探索，看看如何通过技术来应对技术变化，所以我觉得我们也意识到了还有很多要去做的工作。

译语：Besides that, we need to take more measures to tackle climate change because we believe climate change is important, it's serious. Technologies such as carbon capture, we are trying to research and develop more technologies and how we can tackle climate change through technologies. We have realized there's a lot to be done.

英语译语：And on top of it, we need to be in the forefront of a lot of what needs to be done to confront climate change because we accept that there are important, big seminal issues around climate change. So whether it's technology, whether it's carbon capture, we have a whole array of things that we're working on the technology sphere to address this. But a lot more has to be done. We realize it.

译员反思：（1）译员由于转换困难，未译第一句，有的译员此处译为 make further exploration，但是对比英语源语 be in the forefront of a lot of... 显然后者更为地道、明晰，这种对比能让译员更深刻意识到，用丰富、灵活的语言资源去传递信息而非字面对译对同传质量的重要性。

（2）climate change is important 是受汉语形式影响，是不正确、不准确表达，应该是 around climate change (there) are important/seminal issues。

（3）Technologies such as carbon capture, we are trying to... 译员认为，

此处变换主语是因为讲者说话时主语很长，不太愿意冒险等得太久到完整命题出现才开始翻译，等发现主语不一样时，当时心里是能明白自己犯了错误，很后悔，但是为了后面信息连贯就用了后出现的主语。此处可以抽取关键名词做主语 technologies such as carbon capture and other ones are what we trying to develop/work on；或者保持状语 in terms of/as for technologies such as..., we are working...

（4）How can we tackle... 也不准确，应该是 to see how/if we can... 这应该是译员精力不足所致。

（5）将译语与英语源语对比，不难看出译员英语资源丰富性、灵活性和可用性有很大提升空间，译员可以思考是否会在以后同传中使用 on top of/be in the forefront/a lot of what needs to be done/we accept/seminal issues around/a whole array of/be working on 等表达。

（6）除语言问题外，还存在听译协调（EVS 调节）、精力不足、加工单位过小等问题，影响了译语准确性、衔接性、连贯性、流利性等。

九、质量监控

1. 讲解

自我监控是言语产出的重要环节。同传中，译员除需要边理解源语、边产出译语，还要兼顾监控译语质量。监控内容除了"译语发布"部分所谈的译语音韵、流利性与噪声管控外，还包括译语内容质量、语言质量以及可用性。

内容上，确保译语准确、完整译出源语信息，不增添、删减、扭曲源语信息（不宜译出信息除外），确保客观中立，不加入个人观点、评价等。语言上，首先要确保语法正确，英语译语常见的语法问题包括：单复数错误、时态、语态、情态错误，冠词错误，主谓、动宾、介宾搭配错误，句式杂糅等。此外，要监控译语是否符合英语表达习惯，是否存在不恰当的字面对译、中式英语。除了语言正确和地道，还要确保语言是否衔接及其表达的信息是否连贯、明晰，表达是否简洁、高效、易理解。

自我质量监控需要从口译训练一开始就培养意识，养成习惯。并且通过持续的反思性刻意练习（reflective deliberate practice）加以强化，提升译语总体质量。反思性刻意练习指口译学员在口译训练中，将源语与译语录音转写为文字并对齐，根据录音和文字，从译语发布、语言、内容及整体可用性质量等方面发现问题，反思原因，并制定具体计划加以克服。刻意练习可按照发布、语言、内容质量的顺序，确定阶段性目标，循序渐进，持之以恒。

表3、表4、表5分别是译语发布、语言与内容及整体可用性质量检查表，供刻意练习参考，具体检查内容可根据自身情况丰富、调整。

表3 译语发布质量检查表

检查对象 \ 周次	1	2	3	4	5	6	7	……
音量、音高、音长								
发音准确、清晰度								
重音								
停顿								
语气、语调								
节奏								
流利性								
噪声管控								
是否有不良习惯								

表4　译语语言质量检查表

检查对象 \ 周次	1	2	3	4	5	6	7	……
正确性——数的一致								
正确性——时态								
正确性——语态、情态								
正确性——搭配								
正确性——句法								
地道性								
明晰性								
简洁、高效性								

表5　译语内容及整体可用性质量检查表

检查对象 \ 周次	1	2	3	4	5	6	7	……
准确性								
完整性								
衔接性								
连贯性								
可理解性								
交际效率、效果								

2. 训练与点评

会议：天津论坛，圆桌会议："城市再造与宜居城市建设"，城镇化新思维，凤凰城市与旅游研究院领导

12A:

源语： 谢谢！其实我不用话筒，在这个房间里面应该也能大家听得见，但是我为了省点我的这个力量，这个原来的我们的题目呢叫重新发现城市以社会的视角。那么这个题目呢其实它的所谓的新思维新在哪里就是我们的题目的那句话，那句话可能更有吸引力一些。那么为什么提这样的一个新思维的概念呢，因为在整个中国，现在最火的一个国家的一个战略可能就是新型城镇化，这个大家应该感觉到这几年应该是在舆论里面也好，还是在企业也好，还是在政府也好，包括我们的学术界可能都在讨论中国的城镇化到底怎么去做。那么提出新型，那么就应该有一个新的思维，那么新的思维在哪里，可能就今天我希望给大家分享的。

译语： Thank you. Actually, without a microphone, you can hear my voice, but for my convenience, I'll use it. Our original topic is to rediscover the city from a social view. And now you can see a new mindset in our title. Why do we have such a concept? Because now in China, a major nation national strategy is new urbanization, whether in public opinion, in companies or in academic areas, you can find people discussing how China will do urbanization. I think we should have a new mindset. And I want to share with you how to do it.

源语： 因为我们这个机构呢它是来源于媒体，那么媒体呢大家都知道它原来是做报道的。报道呢我们后来发现在媒体的碎片化以后呢，我们转向了研究性报道。那么在研究性的报道的基础上呢，按照这个全球的媒体发展态势，我们走向了一个媒体型的智库这样的一个概念。那么它的职能是多元的，那么其中它的一项我们说基于我们的客户也好，还是基于我们的发展实践也好，给出一些新的建议或者是新的宏观的意识，这个可能也是我们的努力方向之一。

译语： We come from media which does reports. But after the fragmented media, we turned to research-oriented reports. Based on the new trend, we turn to media think tank with diverse functions, one of which is based on our customers or our practices, we want to give some advice and macro awareness. That's what we are working at.

源语：我们说提新思维，那么在我们从去年应该说是201-，现在说应该是前年了，在2013年的下半年，我们当时在凤凰的体系内，我是正式提出两个概念。第一个概念叫城市中国，第二个叫文旅中国。城市中国呢可能是主要是基于定居的人或者说持续住在某个城市的这样一个人口的一个思考。还有一个叫文旅中国，文旅大家知道它其实和文化旅游，因为文旅天然不分家。那么旅游的概念是什么呢，它里边是有是一个移动的一个人群，那么怎么样在我们的城镇化过程中去考量移动的人群，它应该怎么去和它们之间发生一种关系，包括它怎么能够推动落地层面的城市的建设，这个也是一个需要思考的。所以说我今天的两个大的我把它理解为是两个大的时代洞察：一个是城市中国，一个是文旅中国。

译语：In terms of the new mindset, from the in the second half of 2013, we are within the IFeng system, I proposed two concepts, urbanizing China and cultural and tourism China. Urbanizing China is about the permanent population. And for the latter, we know that culture and tourism are closely related. It involves mobile population. Then for urbanization, how should we consider such population? And how such population can help build our cities? Therefore, I think they they are two insights of our era.

教师点评：（1）发布：译语发布总体较为平稳、清晰，语速、语气、语调与流利性尚可，但重音、停顿有一定问题。

重音是对信息价值的提示，译员要恰当运用重音凸显信息，以便于听众更好理解译语。但是此例中，译员似乎有在意群或句子最后一个词重读的倾向，不少地方没有能够根据信息轻重主次安排重音，导致重音位置和信息重点匹配不佳，例如 from a social view 的重音应在 social 而非 view 上，a new mindset 的重音在 new 而非 mindset

上，share with you 的 you 无需重读，how 可重读，research-oriented reports、mobile population、two insights of our era 等处存在类似问题。停顿问题主要包括两方面：一是有些停顿没有按意群进行，结果如同重音问题，未能有效凸显源语信息，不利于听众理解；另一方面是有些句子句内停顿稍长，影响了表达流利性。此外，还存在一定的犹豫、修正、重复问题。

（2）语言：基本语法问题包括 in public opinion, you can find people discussing, we are within the IFeng system, I proposed, after the fragmented media 等；贴字面翻译、不地道、中式英语包括 you can hear my voice, original topic, macro awareness, do urbanization；衔接、连贯、明晰方面问题，如 Therefore, I think they they are two insights of our era，they 指代不明；译语不够简洁高效，如 Why do we have such a concept 表达可以凸显为 Why a new concept。

（3）内容问题：第一段中主要有两处：那么这个题目呢，其实它的所谓的新思维新在哪里就是我们的题目的那句话，那句话可能更有吸引力一些 And now you can see a new mindset in our title，译语未能凸显"新思维这个提法让题目更有吸引力"这一信息；那么新的思维在哪里，可能就今天我希望给大家分享的 And I want to share with you how to do it 未能传递出"新思维新在哪儿"信息。第二段的问题更多，既有理解导致的问题，比如 give some advice and macro awareness，也有英语表达能力不足原因，比如 turn to 的错误使用等。

译员反思：关于 And now you can see a new mindset in our title 一处的问题，译员进行了反思这里是信息预测失误引起，当时对着PPT，认为讲者会先说新的题目，但讲者直接开始说"那么这个题目……更有吸引力一些"，翻译的时候没能及时纠正过来。另外，由于之前预测失误，当时关注点在怎么把前面的句子补完整，没有反应过来"更有吸引力"在说新的题目。

教师点评：预测是同传的重要策略，发现预测错误要及时调整、修正。另外，该发言的口语化特征比较明显，对于此类发言风格，译员在非数字、术语、罗列等部分应注意保持相对较长 EVS，避免跟源语太紧，同时需集中注意力，利用语境脱离语言形式、理解和传递信息而非贴着字面翻译，而在遇到数字等非冗余成分时，需要迅速缩短 EVS，并适当记笔记。

另外，部分源语可处理如下：

那么这个题目呢，其实它的所谓的新思维新在哪里就是我们的题目的那句话，那句话可能更有吸引力一些。The idea/concept of a new mindset makes the current title more compelling.

在舆论里面也好，还是在企业也好，还是在政府也好，包括我们的学术界可能都在讨论中国的城镇化到底怎么去做。可以提取状语中的名词做主语，处理为：The general public, businesses, government agencies and academia are discussing what the new form of urbanization means/entails and how to do it.

我们走向了一个媒体型的智库这样的一个概念。那么它的职能是多元的，那么其中它的一项我们说基于我们的客户也好，还是基于我们的发展实践也好，给出一些新的建议或者是新的宏观的意识，处理为：we have functioned as both a media company and a think-tank with various functions/providing various services, one of which is client insights- or our own practices-based/informed advisory services/to leverage client insights and our own practices to offer advisory services.

旅游的概念是什么呢，它里边是有是一个移动的一个人群，那么怎么样在我们的城镇化过程中去考量移动的人群，它应该怎么去和它们之间发生一种关系，包括它怎么能够推动落地层面的城市的建设，Tourism is about/involves a mobile population, and how it is related/its relationship to urbanization and how it helps build a city/its contribution to city building.

12B：

源语：那么我今天主要的讲的两个角度，第一呢，我把它把城市或城镇化理解为是一个综合的社会变迁的过程，这是我的第一个，就是我们一直在主张的或者一直在诠释的。第二个呢，就是我们需要从人口迁徙的角度来去看我们的城镇化，来去看我们的城市，来去看我们的城市的很多的一些项目，包括这些项目将来能不能成功。可能这两个维度是目前从开发商到城市的决策者到我们的媒体，到舆论，包括到当地的居民或者我们说的公众，都在关心的一个问题。

译语：So I tend to describe it as two perspective of my modern time: Cities in China, Tourism in China. So first, I'd like to point out that urbanization is a natural process or transition in our country. And second, from the perspective of migration, I'd like to see how cities changing change, and how the projects in city could succeed. From these two dimensions, we'd like to research on the role of developers to media and the residents. And this question is of public concern.

源语：首先说为什么会有一个城市中国的概念。这张图呢是来自于中国城镇化的规划里边，那么大家可以看到一个什么概念呢，就是一条线呢是中国的城镇人口，还有一条线呢是世界的城镇化率，一个是中国的城镇化率，那么什么意思？到这个地方大概是在2010年和2011年的时候，两者相交了。这是一个非常有意思的一个现象，因为我们做研究很多时候是要看关键性的时机或者说关键性的历史节点。那么这个在2010年、2012年或者说换句话说叫什么呢，叫21世纪的第二个十年开始的时候，那么这个历史性的节点发生了。也就是说全球的城镇化率第一次达到50%。意味着什么，意味着在全球的范围内有超过一半的人口开始居住在城市，这个以前是没有发生的。大家会不会觉得挺有意思的，因为我们以前生活在中国可能还很好理解，但是如果说在欧洲的话，我们在一些发达国家可能觉得那到处是城市是吧，但是这个节点其实在今天才发生。

译语：So why do we propose a concept of Cities in China? This graph shows our planning of cities. This line show the urban urban population in China and the other line show the degree of urbanization in the world. What does that mean? In 2010 and 2011, two lines are cross with each other. This is what makes things interesting, because researchers always focus on the crossroads, or the key junctures. At that time, the 20- the year of 2012, or the second decade of the twenty-first century, we are we were in the juncture. That is, the global urbanization reached more than 50%. Hal- That is to say, half of the world's population lived in urban areas, which was unprecedented. In the past we lived in China, and we can understand it better. But some of the developed coun- economies may think unbelievable because in their countries, cities are everywhere.

源语：那么另外一个呢，就是在中国就是2011年的时候，其实中国的常住人口的城镇化率第一次达到50%，就是我们老是讲说，莫言在西方的诺贝尔文学奖获奖，当时大家在思考说莫言的他的文学更多的是代表乡土文学，那么为什么会有这样的一个获奖呢？我想它里边很重要的一块就是，它的这种乡土文学反映的东西完全符合西方社会对我们中国的想象，什么想象，就是乡土中国的想象。

译语：But in 2011, the residential population of China was over 50%. We said that Mo Yan wa become the Nobel Laureate laureate in literature, and his literature was about the lives in rural areas. And we often said that his literature is in accordance with the imagination of Western media. That is to say, about the rural areas.

教师点评：（1）发布问题：一些音不够标准，一些音未充分发出，一些音不够清晰，如 from, the, graph, other, world, on 等；发布方式稍有些急躁，节奏不够平稳，有些地方存在一突一突、忽快忽慢和紧赶慢赶的问题，如 this question is of public concern, concept of Cities in China 等；修正和犹豫有些多；此外，同前例，译员也有在意群或句末最后一个词重读的倾向，不少重音位置错配，未能凸显重要信息，如 two perspective of my modern time 重读放在了 perspective 和 time 上，实际应是 two 和 modern，类似情形还有 Tourism in China, each other, At that time, global urbanization, residential population, Western media 等。

（2）语言问题：单复数问题如 two perspective, This line show, the other line show，表达不当如 are cross with each other, crossroads，中式、不地道表达如 his literature is in accordance with the imagination。

（3）内容问题：准确性问题较多，第一段大部分内容没有准确译出。译员没有理解源语信息而进行语言层面转换，比较明显的地方包括：from the perspective of migration, I'd like to see how cities changing change, From these two dimensions, we'd like to research on the role of developers to media and the residents, researchers always focus on the crossroads, or the key junctures, In the past we lived in China, and we can understand it better.

以下是部分源语的处理建议：

我把它把城市或城镇化理解为是一个综合的社会变迁的过程，可处理为 urbanization as social transformation。

从人口迁徙的角度来去看我们的城镇化，来去看我们的城市，来去看我们的城市的很多的一些项目，包括这些项目将来能不能成功，可以处理为 urbanization as migration, how migration is relevant/related to city building and urban projects operation。

可能这两个维度是目前从开发商到城市的决策者到我们的媒体，到舆论，包括到当地的居民或者我们说的公众，都在关心的一个问题，可以处理为 These two perspectives are what developers, urban decision-makers, media, local residents and general public are all concerned about。

我们做研究很多时候是要看关键性的时机或者说关键性的历史节点，可以处理为 researchers are interested in critical or historic turning points。

因为我们以前生活在中国可能还很好理解，可以处理为 It's easily understandable for Chinese people。

这种乡土文学反映的东西完全符合西方社会对我们中国的想象，什么想象，就是乡土中国的想象，可以处理为 his novel depicts/presents/portrays the very China that Westerners often envision/have in mind, a rural China。

译员反思：（1）自我监控：没有自我监控语音语调、语法等，相对差劲的口语水平在对原文理解不到位的情况下更加凸显；单复数、时态和介词搭配上都出现语法错误；重复和改口的情况很多，有些是无意义的重复，有些是说到一半发现有语法/单词错误临时改口。解决方法及未来努力改善的方向：一方面，要牢记"Never Backtrack"的原则；另一方面，要加强口语练习，通过视译等方式多训练口语表达。

（2）信息处理：经过前几周的课堂学习，已经意识到要对原文进行一定的分析取舍，翻译必要信息，省去填充性无意义表达。但在实际运用中可能会删减过多，反而漏掉了应当翻译的部分，对可整合、压缩的信息也并未进行适当处理。

（3）遣词造句：英文水平低，遣词造句僵硬别扭。有时试图不照字面意思对应翻译，但容易精力不足。部分词句选择不准确，出现与原文的明显偏差。未来要多看"原汁原味"英文并尝试积累和学习相应的词句搭配。

（4）句子衔接：句子衔接较差，逻辑不清晰、不连贯。部分地方加工单位太小，句子显得破碎，前句与后句缺乏有效连接，多以 and 开头加新的短主句。未来应学习使用更多的表达方式，尝试一句多翻，提升表达灵活性。

（5）译前准备：在译前材料的基础上准备了相关词汇，也尝试听、读英文平行文本，对所谈主题有了一定的了解。但在翻译时未打开幻灯片，同传时缺乏参考材料，在翻译标题、图表等信息的时候遇到了一定的障碍。

教师总建议：（1）自我监控非常重要，从节奏、修正、基本语法错误、贴字面翻译等可判断，译员的质量监控不足，这一点需要及时加以纠正。

（2）理解应优先于转换与发表，译员应集中精力加强对源语命题信息和话语逻辑的理解，尤其对口语特征比较明显的发言，更要学会去伪存真，听懂源语信息。

（3）译员对于动态调节 EVS、顺句驱动、断句顺接、去除框架、精简压缩等策略尚不够娴熟，需要加强即兴发言中信息与语言加工策略的运用。

（4）译员在英语基本功，语言资源的可用性、灵活性，表达的简洁高效性，衔接连贯等方面都有较大提升空间。

（5）译员可让发布语速更加均匀，节奏更加平稳，发音更清晰，减少修正和犹豫，同时通过重音凸显信息，整体上提升译语可听性和可理解性。

12C：

源语：但是今天从 2011 年开始，中国开始进入一个城市国家。什么意思？有一半以上的人口开始长期生活在城市。这是在中国历史上从来没有发生过的。所以说呢，基于此，我们说两个时间节点的实现，那么到目前为止，这个节点来了以后，我们说按照全球的城镇化的规律来讲，超过 50% 到 30% 到 70% 的时候，会是一个继续快速的城市化的一个过程。那么在此情况下呢也就是说从人口从农村到城市的迁徙不但没有放慢，而且会越来越快，当然它的这种冲突性会越来越多。所以说我们有一个基本的判断或者基本的洞察，也就是说，无论是在国际上还是在中国，那么城市已经成为中国最具代表性的国家的镜像。而且我们在看待很多的问题，包括中国的整体性变革的时候，就必须用城市这个维度来去重新思考我们的未来怎么办，包括我们的农村地区的改革都需要置入到一个城市的背景下来去看，这时候它俩之间的关系变得更为复杂，同时呢可能让我们思考更多的东西。

译语：But starting from 2011, China has become an urbanized country. That is to say, half of our population now are urban. This is a new thing for China. So based on this, we have reached a new stage. And 50 to 70% of the people living in cities will be the future trend. That is to say, the speed of our people moving from rural areas to urban areas has become even faster. No matter for the international community or for China alone, this is an irresistible trend. And when we are talking about China's comprehensive revolution, we have to think about urbanization and how this will impact our future. For example, we can connect urbanization process with the reform of our rural areas.

源语：提到城市中国，在这种情况下，我们现在这个判断呢，是我们官方在这一次的城镇化的大讨论中间最后沉淀下来的一些基本判断。这个是我在大家看一下城镇化规划里边的官方文本里面是有的。那么这里面呢更多的是问题，问题里边其中有一块就是我们的说的管理服务也好还是更多的是人口城镇化的问题，其实跟人都是有关系的。我觉得这一次的就是发生在这两年的关于中国城市和城镇化的讨论一个最大的成果，我个人认为最大的成果就是开始越来越多的人真的用以人为本就是用人的角度可以思考城市了。

译语：So, talking about urban China, we identify that this is a judgment that we have agreed after a series of discussion. And when we are talking about management, service, or more people moving to urban areas, there are a lot of things to do. The biggest outcome we have from those discussions is that we are being people oriented.

教师点评：（1）发布：音韵、流利性与噪音管控等都较好，音高、重音、语速、语调、语气等音韵方面都不错，流利性方面，除了一些地方因EVS调节、顺句与断句等策略不够娴熟造成句间等待过久外，译语比较流利，噪声管控也不错，因此总体上发布监管较好。

（2）语言：除了 comprehensive revolution, connect urbanization process with, we identify...discussion 一句中 identify, agreed 等处存在语言问题外，其他译语的语法与地道性、语言资源丰富性与灵活性等总体不错，但表达简洁性和信息凸显度方面还有提升空间，具体见下面的源语处理建议。

（3）内容：内容问题较多，译员的加工模式偏向于交传式的深层加工，顺句驱动、断句顺接方面表现不佳，部分地方等待过长、开口过晚，导致出现比较多的概译、漏译、偏译甚至错译。

部分源语的处理建议：

这是在中国历史上从来没有发生过的，可以接前句处理为 which is unprecedented 或者 unprecedentedly。

这个节点来了以后，我们说按照全球的城镇化的规律来讲，超过50%到30%到70%的时候，会是一个继续快速的城市化的一个过程，可以处理为 at this point, as global trends indicate, between the rate of 30% and 70% urbanization will be faster.

从人口从农村到城市的迁徙不但没有放慢，而且会越来越快，当然它的这种冲突性会越来越多，可以处理为 people will move faster into cities causing more conflicts.

就必须用城市这个维度来去重新思考我们的未来怎么办，包括我们的农村地区的改革都需要置入到一个城市的背景下来去看，可以处理为 we need consider urbanization/have an urban perspective while redefining our future, and put the rural reform in an urban context.

我们现在这个判断呢，是我们官方在这一次的城镇化的大讨论中间最后沉淀下来的一些基本判断，可以处理（结合 PPT 内容）为 these are some of our conclusions. The Chinese government had much discussion on/extensively discussed urbanization and reached/come to some conclusions. 或 these conclusions are reached by Chinese government following extensive discussion on urbanization.

其实跟人都是有关系的，可以处理为 there is always the human factor/ The human element is always present.

总体建议：译员在现有口齿伶俐性、语言资源丰富和灵活性、表达流利性等优势基础上，首先重新反思、调整同传的加工模式，加强对源语信息的深度理解，以源语命题为加工单位，顺句（命题）加工，适当断句，听到长句或信息不明晰的句子时，不用等待太久，综合运用预测+调整、顺句、断句、占位等多种策略；同时要更尊重源语信息，警惕在转换和表达中过于自由导致扭曲改变源语信息。

十、译员意识

1. 讲解

初学同传时,应了解职业译员应坚持的一些基本原则,培养良好的职业译员意识,以提升同传译语可用性和交际效果。

①译前准备。口译前,利用各种材料与渠道(客户提供的资料、互联网检索的材料、自我整理的语料与术语表等,领域专家、会议海报、展示屏、宣传册、宣传录像等),进行充分的知识与双语词汇等准备,熟悉会议主题及各议题的知识框架,了解发言的交际意图和主要思路,理解涉及的部分关键理论、流程、概念等,备好双语版专有名词、术语、政策性话语,并能够做到快速转换。

②理解第一,听辨理解源语意义、信息、交际目的,不理解的部分尽量不翻译。

③听、译同步,节奏平稳,不建议听一段抢译一段的交替式同传,也不建议跟源语太近,产出碎片化译语,能够根据源语特征动态调节 EVS。

④交际意识,译员始终以弥合发言人和听众的信息差为目标,既尊重发言源语,理解源语已说、欲说内容,又要时刻心中有听众,确保译语对听众有用、可用。

⑤信息凸显,通过简洁、地道、清晰的语言,合理运用音韵,适当兼顾语言衔接与信息连贯,使译语信息明晰易懂。

⑥表达流利,加强译语监听,尽量减少或避免填充语、修正、犹豫、折返、口头禅等。

⑦角色意识,保持译员中立角色意识,例如,在话筒中提醒主办方或发言人有关事项,或者告知设备或声音质量问题时,应以"翻译/译员/同传(translator/interpreter/simultaneous interpreters)"开头,而不是以"我(I)"开头,不和听众一样笑场、鼓掌等,不将自己观点加进译语。

⑧团队合作,与搭档做好有关工作分工,相互协助,准点轮换,共同

完成同传任务。

此外，也要摒弃一些不良习惯。

①重译不重听，急着翻译，不听也译，不懂也译。

②翻译读稿或PPT发言时，放弃源语听辨，完全视译。

③对源语内容随意进行删减、添加、更改、编造。

④追求快速字面对译，不深入理解源语信息，不考虑译语是否规范、可用。

⑤追求译语越快越好，越多越好。

⑥译语节奏不够平稳，受源语节奏影响，翻译节奏忽慢忽快。

⑦缺乏自我监听，译语语言与音韵随意。

⑧工作中伴有不必要或不得体的动作、体态等。

建议译员多通过转写、分析同传录音，对照以上内容反思同传过程，也可邀请老师、同学、朋友从同传用户角度评价自己的译语，发现问题及原因机制，并制定计划进行改正。

2. 训练与点评

> 会议："积极应对人口老龄化：共同责任"国际研讨会，主旨演讲：国际视野下人口老龄化的形势与挑战，北京大学教授

> 13-1A：

源语：各位嘉宾，各位领导，大家上午好。非常高兴今天能够受会议组织者邀请做一个简单的汇报。我这个汇报应该是咱们会议组织的一个命题作文，让我讲一下国际视野下人口老龄化的形势与挑战。刚才郝司长重点介绍了中国应对老龄化，那么我的一些PPT的东西跟他有些东西好像我们也没有做沟通，但是不谋而合，不谋而合的部分我就少讲，我讲一些重点。我个人觉得不论是中国还是加拿大，还是其他国家，我们在应对人口老龄化，在关注国际在做什么，尤其像加拿大、日本、新加坡包括韩国。我们实际上中国在应对老龄化，在探索中国

的方案,这是我们下一步未来几十年所要做的一件事情。

译语: Distinguished guests, dear friends, good morning. I'm happy to be invited for this presentation. My topic is about the picture and challenges of ageing society—an international perspective. The previous speaker talked about ageing population. My PowerPoint and my presentation is in line with his presentation. Be it China or Canada or other countries, we focus on other countries' experience such as Canada, Japan, South Korea, Singapore. China has its own plans. That's what we will do in the future.

译员反思: (1) 信息缺失或错误

"我这个汇报应该是咱们会议组织的一个命题作文"这句话是听到了,但是不知道该怎么组织语言,而且觉得句子的重要信息是汇报的主题;"中国应对老龄化"中的"中国应对"漏译;"我的一些PPT……我讲一些重点"这句话主要是脱壳和语言丰富性的问题,翻译成in line with,是没有跳出源语结构,后半段做了省略,因为觉得信息不重要。

(2) 状语过长

"我个人觉得不论是中国还是加拿大,还是其他国家……"这部分的问题还是出在一听到状语就会直接译为状语,状语过长会让人遗忘前面讲了什么内容,其实可以直接提取状语中的名词——"国家"作主语。

(3) 时态错误,意思也偏离

"实际上中国在应对老龄化,在探索中国的方案",此处要用完成进行时或进行时,用现在时的话意思偏离了,此外没有表达出"探索"。

源语: 那么中国应对老龄化,我觉得我个人的思路应该有这样12个字,第一个4个字,要考虑近虑和远忧,就是我们现在面临的一些问题,和我们将来面对的一些问题。第二个我觉得要左顾右盼,我们要看看其他国家,看看加拿大,看看韩国,看看日本,包括美国,他们是怎么去应对?因为他们比我们走的早。还有一个很重要,我们要瞻前顾后，瞻前顾后呢，我们要考虑中国的国情，我们要考虑我们的文化底蕴，包括我们刚才郝司长说的孝道。

译语：China's efforts to address ageing society have several challenges. We should identify our current and future challenges. Second, we should learn from other countries such as Japan, South Korea, America, Canada because they have entered they aged earlier than China. Third, we should consider our culture and our tradition.

译员反思：（1）错译

第一句出现错译，因为听的时候没听懂"个人的思路"是要表达什么意思，就下意识翻译成了 challenges，其实应该是 suggestions。

（2）漏译

最后一句漏译"国情"，因为上一句改口，导致时间拖延到这一句，回过头来就听到"文化底蕴"了，没听到"国情"。"孝道"也没有翻译，是因为知道不能翻译成 filial piety，但是一时之间想不到好的翻译，就省了，还是语言资源太匮乏。这一句还有一个重大的问题，就是译语过短。这是因为上一句改口了三次，EVS 拉得太长了，所以导致这一句时间压缩。

（3）改口

we should learn from 一句中改口三次，其实第一次直接用 they have entered ageing society earlier than China 就可以了，不知道当时为什么非要用 aged，本意是想简洁，最后适得其反，还压缩了下一句的时间。

源语：所以今天我跟大家分享这样几个方面的内容，六个方面内容，第一个我们重点介绍一下世界的老龄化，它的一个变化的新的动向。第二和第三部分刚才郝司长讲了一些，重复的内容我不重复。我重点讲一下他没有涉及的内容，我谈一谈中国老龄化的新的形势和我们面临的新的挑战。第四部分我们介绍一下几个国家应对老龄化的一些经验和风险，重点介绍一下美国、日本这些国家应对老龄化，他们做了哪些事情，有哪些主要的模式。第五个方面就是回应我们这个题目，中国积极应对老龄化它所面临的机遇。我们的确应该认识到老龄化给我们引发了一些挑战，这个挑战重点是在于过去我们缺少一个老龄社会的一种思维方式，去设计，我们去应对。所以我更多地重点讲我们怎么积极应对，中国应对有哪些机遇和优势，最后谈一些应对老龄化的主要思路和政策框架。

译语：So my topic is about six perspectives. First, trend of global ageing society. Second, as the previous speaker talked about, the current picture of China's ageing society and new challenges. Fourthly, experiences of global efforts to address this issue, especially from the perspective of America and Japan. What can we learn from these countries? Fifthly, the opportunities and benefits of our efforts to address this issue. Certainly, there are challenges. We don't have this mindset to design for this issue. So how do we cope with this and what are the opportunities for coping this? And lastly is about policy framework.

译员反思：语言不地道或字对字翻译

例如，So my topic is about six perspectives. 太僵硬了，walk you through six points 比较好。the opportunities and benefits of our efforts to address this issue，这样翻是因为看到幻灯片上写的是"机遇与优势"，这种译法过于直接，应该用 What we have... 更能体现源语的意义。

译员总结：（1）这篇突出的问题，就是译语和源语长度不匹配，留白时间太多，听感较差，需要根据讲者语速和风格调整译语长短；

（2）改口次数较多，究其原因是语言丰富性低，一旦起句错误，就会下意识改口；

（3）脱壳有待提升，重要的是听信息，而非听字词；

（4）状语处理不当，导致句子结构混乱。其实大部分的状语都可以提取名词作主语。

教师点评：（1）译员的问题分析过于简单，译语问题远不止这些，尤其第

三段,建议更加深入、全面地评估译语,反思过程。

(2)译员这三段最突出的问题是不少内容的漏译、错译,可能既有理解问题原因,也有英语资源不足原因。译员没有将理解放在第一位,且过度干预、不够尊重源语内容,建议译员对这一加工模式和习惯加以反思和调整。

(3)译员另一比较明显的问题是译语不够流利、圆润,句子间的孤立、割裂感明显,如译员自己反思所言"留白太多、听感较差",而且句子间的语言不够衔接,造成译语可用性较弱,影响交际效果。这些可能主要和 EVS 不当、加工单位过小、自我监管不足等有关。建议译员提升听译协调能力,动态 EVS 调节能力,增大加工单位,加强对源语命题信息的理解,增进译语音韵的交际效果,改善句间衔接和连贯。

(4)译员口齿伶俐性不错,但语言资源丰富性、灵活性与信息理解和表达能力有待加强。

部分源语的处理建议:

我这个汇报应该是咱们会议组织的一个命题作文

I was asked by the organizer to speak on...

我的一些 PPT 的东西跟他有些东西好像我们也没有做沟通,但是不谋而合

Some of my slides happen to be similar to his/have been covered by him

那么中国应对老龄化,我觉得我个人的思路应该有这样 12 个字

China's responses/approaches to population ageing, as I propose, could be as follows/As I prose, China could respond to population ageing with the following approaches

考虑近虑和远忧 assess challenges at hand and those that lie ahead

左顾右盼 learn from other countries' best practices/draw upon other countries' experience

瞻前顾后 look to the past and to the future

这个挑战重点是在于过去我们缺少一个老龄社会的一种思维方式,去设计,我们去应对。

The challenge is that we didn't have in mind an ageing society and design our response to it/we did not think, design and act from an ageing society perspective/we were not ageing society-minded and ready.

13-1B：

源语：那么首先我们看一下全球老龄化的新的动向。我们说老龄化不是一个新的事件，但是事件发生了新的变化，老龄化，很重要，刚才司长也说了，和公共卫生改善、社会经济发展、平均预期寿命进步密切相关。大家可以看，世界不同区域平均预期寿命在不断地延长，不光是发达国家，包括发展中国家和欠发达、发展中国家。这条线是我们到2018年这样的变化。我们可以看到我们是根据联合国的中方案的变化，过去是一个分叉的，我们逐渐地在未来无论是发达国家、发展中国家，它的平均预期寿命逐步地在缩小。那么很重要是一个老龄化，就是预期寿命的延长是一个方面，还有一个方面是生育率下降，老龄化。那么特别是到大家可以看到2100年按照联合国，我们不论发达国家发展中国家，生育率水平都在下降，这个是世界的趋势。中国生育率下降不是一花独放。当然我们的生育率下降有很多行政的因素，计划生育，那么我们在思考老龄化究竟是什么样带来的？我记得1999年世界国际老人年，当时安南，上个月去世了，安南作为秘书长，在国际老人年说了一句话，他说population ageing is a silent revolution，就是人口老龄化是一场静悄悄的革命。这个革命其实是一件好事，但为什么带来了挑战呢？主要是我们缺少一种老龄社会的思维，我们缺少了用制度的安排去应对老龄化。

译语：First of all, new trends in global ageing. Ageing is not a new topic, a new issue. But there are some new trends. Ageing problem is closely related to uh better health care and rise in average life expectancy. Ageing is expanding from developed countries to developing countries. We can see in this graphic the situation from 1950 to today. And the situation is still changing. The median age is declining, because of the rise in average life expectancy and decline in birth rate. According to the UN, the birth rate in all countries are declining. This is not the only case in China. This is well spread in all countries. Next question is, what are the causes of ageing? I remember uh the General Secretary, the previous General Secretary, Annan, said that population is a silent evolution. This is a good evolution, actually. But it brings us new challenges, because we lack systems, we lack actions responding to it.

译员反思：(1) 发布方式有问题。音高、语音、语调有戏剧表演感觉。回听之前的翻译音频进行对比，问题没有这一篇这么集中，过去的音频在发布方式上接受度更高。我也采访了身边的同学，大家普遍觉得我就是那天问题比较集中。综合身边老师、同学的评价，得出的结论是这段音频是一个极端情况。但是无论如何，问题确实存在，如果不是老师点评我可能根本发现不了自己有时会有这个问题。个人分析可能的原因为：① 自己的译语监听不够，几乎是忘了监听；② 心态不稳，同时对自己声音控制不够，导致声音也不沉稳；③ 用嗓过度，每当我用嗓过度，就会出现声音变高变尖的情况。以后每次开口做翻译前要做深呼吸，让自己情绪和心态沉稳下来，注意控制自己的声音输出。

(2) 有很多地方意思和原文有较大出入。这段话的关键信息是以下内容：老龄化在全世界范围内有新的变化，体现在两点：全球范围内平均预期寿命延长和全球范围内生育率下降（重点强调了全球范围内）。就关键信息而言，信息点很模糊，信息之间的逻辑关系和层次结构不清晰。两块变化，第一块在讲平均寿命延长那里，信息完全没有凸显，还把"中方案"听成了年龄的"中位数"。除了关键信息以外的次要信息也有所遗漏，比如第二块讲到生育率下降，一方面主要强调全世界都有这样一个共同趋势，但另一方面也讲到了中国生育率下降的特殊因素——计划生育。这里就完全遗漏了。

(3) 语言错误，存在单复数问题、搭配问题。语言资源的丰富性和瞬时可用性低下影响关键信息的表达，是一个系统性的问题。比如说 This is not the only case in China, 意思表达就不明确，听众需要听到后面一句 This is well spread in all countries. 才能知道是什么意思，这就增加了听众的认知负荷。还有最后一句话，我当时一时之间想不到对应的表达，只能用了 system、action 这种在意思上跟原文有偏差，并且传递信息也不高效的词语，听起来就像我根本没抓住核心意思。

教师点评：（1）译语音韵过于丰富使得信息不够明晰凸显，影响交际效果。译员翻译所用音韵有些接近于演讲，抑扬顿挫等过于丰富。同传与演讲不同，译员服务于演讲，译语传递演讲的主题信息（不是传递讲话风格信息），而不是自我创造信息。一般情况下译员的音韵不应比讲者更丰富，很多时候应稍淡于讲者。此例中，译员音韵远比发言丰富，不仅不利于包装凸显源语信息，影响听众理解效果，也会消耗自身精力，减慢加工速度，影响 EVS 和流利性（实际本段中译员发布显得有些慢），从而影响整个同传表现。此外，不少地方的重读没能与源语信息的轻重主次匹配。

（2）EVS 稍微有些长，在源语没有大量数字、专有名词和列举等情形时，EVS 一般为一个命题，但是译员 EVS 基本为 1.5-2 个命题，好在此处发言语速和信息密度不高，否则可能导致译员工作记忆负荷过重、精力不足，造成漏译、错译（本段较多）、译语表达不准确、不明晰（既和英语资源有关，也与 EVS 长导致记忆模糊有关），如果该工作模式时间较长，易致译员精力不济，跟不上发言。

（3）内容的漏译和错译不少，原因既有前面两点，也和译前准备不足有关，不管是发言整体逻辑理解不到位，还是具体细节理解错误，例如"中方案"，都可通过译前仔细阅读发言 PPT 加以避免。Next question is 处译员有意识增加了凸显逻辑的表达，这个意识是好的，但是此处不合适，因为此处发言的音韵特征并未提示（没有明显停顿、句首重读等）发言人要开启新的话题。

（4）语言问题不少，如 This is not the only case in China 的主要问题并非如同学所说意思不明确，而是意思完全偏离源语，另外秘书长错译为 General Secretary，还有基本语法错误。这些问题除了与语言基础有关外，与译员精力不足、缺乏译语监管有关。

部分译语的处理建议：

老龄化不是一个新的事件，但是事件发生了新的变化

Population ageing is not a new thing/recent phenomenon but there are new/recent developments.

老龄化，很重要，刚才司长也说了，和公共卫生改善、社会经济发展、平均预期寿命进步密切相关

Population ageing, as the Deputy Director General said, is closely tied/linked to better public health, social and economic progress and longer lifespans./Population ageing, as the Deputy Director General said, is a result/consequence of...

过去是一个分叉的

Countries differed a lot./There were gaps among different countries.

中国生育率下降不是一花独放

China is not alone in birthrate decline./China is not the only country with birthrate decline./China's birthrate decline is not an isolated incident.

我们缺少了用制度的安排去应对老龄化

We lacked institutional arrangements to tackle population ageing./Institutional arrangements are not in place to tackle population ageing./We did not respond to population ageing with institutional arrangements.

会议："积极应对人口老龄化：共同责任"国际研讨会，主旨演讲：积极应对人口老龄化的战略思考和政策取向，国家发改委社会发展司副司长

13-2A：

源语：各位嘉宾，女士们先生们，大家上午好！谢谢，谢谢大家对我的鼓励。非常开心，非常高兴在今天的研讨会见到很多老朋友，特别是不远万里来到中国的加拿大朋友。我们作为会议的主办方，安排我是第一个发言，我的主要作用是抛砖引玉。我也注意到今天的研讨会来了

很多的记者，所以我虽然来自国家发改委，但我的观点不代表国家发改委，尤其是有争议的时候，因为人口老龄化确实是一个非常大的一个课题。我今天的题目是顺应大势，积极作为，从容应对。我想今天从三个方面跟大家做个交流。一个是全面评估我国人口老龄化的形势和影响。第二要乐观地来看待我国的人口老龄化。第三个就是把人口老龄化应对人口老龄化，融入经济社会发展的全局来统筹考虑。

译语：Distinguished guests, ladies and gentlemen, good morning. Thank you. Thank you for your warm applaud. It's my great pleasure to be here and see so many familiar faces, especially those Canadian guests. As the part of the organizer, I was asked to make the first speech. And I also notice we have a lot of friends from the media, but a kind reminder for you. Today, my speech is only on behalf of myself, not on behalf of the NDRC because population ageing is a very big issue, and my topic today is to follow the trend and tackle ageing population. I'd like to share my point of view from the following three aspects. First, the overall picture and influence of China's ageing population. Second, stay positive. Third, integrate the ageing population into the overall planning of the social economic development.

译员反思（1）：升调过多

简单将本段升调进行标记，短短一段中就出现了10处升调，仔细来看，一般都出现在同传自然停顿断句之处（包括句子结尾）。升调问题以前没有这么突出，这次老师课上指出之后，我特意再回听了一下自己这两周中英交传和同传的练习录音，发现确实是这段时间升调问题比较严重，但再回听日常的朗读练习录音却并未发现这种问题，说明其实对语调的基本语用规则是了解的，只是在这段时间口译中出了问题。究其原因，我认为是升调从语调语用功能来看是表达说话者"疑问"或"话未说完"的意思，而在同传和交传（特别是同传）的过程中，因为信息一直在不断输入，所以在同传断句停顿的时候，哪怕是该意群其实已经停顿结束，自己听着不断输入的源语信息，潜意识中还是认为"话未说完"，所以情不自禁用多了升调。这个主要是意识问题，相信此次认识到这个问题后，后面练习中多加注意，应该会有所改善。

译员反思（2）：源语发言逻辑不清

源语：我们作为会议的主办方，安排我是第一个发言，我的主要作用是抛砖引玉。

译语：As the part of the organizer, I was asked to make the first speech.

这句话当时听到的时候觉得有点奇怪，特别是前两个分句，导致在处理的时候英语第一个分句也翻译得很奇怪。

译员反思（3）：定冠词的读法混用

这是一个比较小的点，一般来说定冠词后面如果是元音开头的单词要用其强读式，如果是辅音开头的单词则定冠词用弱读式（强调时也需要用强读式）。但在回听自己的译语时发现这一篇很多地方都是混用的，这个后面也需要注意。

译员反思（4）：语法错误——词性误用

译语：Thank you for your warm applaud.

此处应用其名词形式 applause。

教师点评：(1) 升调的确过多，基本都是不必要的，建议训练中有意识避免。

(2) 部分译语存在不必要的概译、简译，比如 follow the trend and tackle ageing population, stay positive 等，没有能够充分表达源语信息，同传入门阶段一定要养成充分尊重源语信息的习惯。

(3) 译语可用性一般，其正确性、准确性、地道性尚有较大提升空间，除了 applaud，还有 part of the organizer, speech, my speech is on

behalf of... 等。

部分源语的处理建议：

我们作为会议的主办方，安排我是第一个发言，我的主要作用是抛砖引玉

On behalf of the host, I will be the first to speak to set a bit of the context.

顺应大势，积极作为，从容应对。

A more adaptive and proactive approach to tackling population ageing.

把人口老龄化应对人口老龄化，融入经济社会发展的全局来统筹考虑。

put population ageing in a broader/wider social and economic context/framework

源语：那么第一个方面是全面评估我国人口老龄化的形势和影响。那么大家知道，其实我国人口老龄化的特点非常鲜明，三大特点，就是总量大，速度快，不平衡。我考虑因为时间有限，我把尽可能的文字放在屏幕上，你们的眼睛总比我的嘴巴快。第一个是总量大，就是我们去年年底老龄人口已经是两亿四了，当我说老龄人口的时候是 60 岁以上的人口，那么占比已经值得达到了 17.3%。那么老龄化的进程是很快的，到本世纪中叶的时候将会翻番达到四亿八左右。那么老龄化将伴随我们国家现代化的整个进程。第二就是速度快。那么实际上在世纪之交的时候，中国跟世界实际上同步进入老龄化的。当时就是进入老龄化，大家知道是 10% 了，那么到 17 年的时候，大家看看，右边的柱子世界的平均水平是达到 13%，我们是 17.3，那么我们的速度应该是世界平均水平的两倍还要多。再一个就是不平衡，两个不平衡体现在，我们是区域不平衡首先是，那么最早的省份是上海，是我们直辖市了，然后晚一点是西藏自治区，差了接近快小 40 年了。再有一个就是城乡的不平衡，几乎是倒挂，是吧？就是农村的老龄化程度要高于城镇。那么我们也不妨看看做一个简单做个比较，因为下午还有同志专门做国际比较。我简单用了一个片子，大家看一看，就用的是联合国的经济社会人口司的一个去年的统计。大家看到实际上

看2017年吧,那么我们的实际我们的水平是17.3,但是很多国家是什么概念?前十个都是26以上,最高的是日本33%,1/3的老年人。那么我们展望一下,到2050年的时候,这是因为,这个数据是联合国的数据,我们国内也有很多的预测,大家可能看法不一样,但是水平上也就差也就几个点,一两个点估计是。到了中世纪,到了本世纪中叶的时候,我们的水平35左右。那大家看看主要发达国家都是40以上了。

译语: First of all, the overall picture and its influence. In China, we have three very featuring characteristics. Due to limited time, I have put the text on my PowerPoint. So you can see that here. The first one is the large in scale. Last year we have reached the ageing population has reached 240 million, which has already accounted for over 10 uh 17%. By the middle of this century, it was raised to 408 million. This will further develop as we urbanize. Secondly, the fast speed. By 2017, on the right, we have reached 17.3%. That is basically 2 times of the world's average. The third one is imbalance in two aspects. One is imbalance among different regions. Shanghai is the oldest ageing population and the latest one is the Tibet. So there is a huge gap in between. Then the second aspect is the rural and urban imbalance. The ageing population is much severe than that in the cities. So I have made one slide to made a simple comparison. It's statistics from the UN. In 2017, we are at 17.3. And top ten countries are over 16% with Japan at highest. These statistics is from the UN and we have different statistics in China. But those statistics are quite similar. By the middle of this century, we will reach about 35.1, and most developed countries will reach over 40%.

译员反思: (1) linguistic padding 和 filler 较多

有声停顿多,也有口头禅和滥用,还有两三处句子重启或是话没说完,这些对译语的听感影响很大。出现这些的原因是本段数字较多,要听到具体数值＋对应单位＋具体描述对象三个要素,同传的时候容易跟不上，导致犹豫，从而会出现很多有声停顿。信息密集、数字多的材料口译练习还是要重点强化。

（2）数字信息密集，译出率不高

主要问题包括：数值对但是会犹豫卡顿（240 million）；同传持续输入，短时记忆混乱，数值不精确或译错（10 uh 17%；408 million）；数据正确但是描述对象错误（<u>速度</u>应该是世界平均水平的两倍还要多）；一边听源语，一边看手边的 PPT，还在找对应 PPT 的哪个位置，精力分配协调不足，导致跟不上源语，信息丢失。

（3）语法问题

①搭配不当

词语搭配：three very featuring characteristics

主宾搭配：Shanghai is the oldest ageing population...

②比较级少 more

The ageing population is much severe than that in the cities.

③时态

一般现在时错用为一般过去时。

教师点评：（1）本段最大的问题是数字信息损耗严重，同传中数字、专有名词、术语往往都是比较重要的信息成分，尤其是行业、学术会议，此类信息成分较多。这类信息成分的损耗会严重削弱听众对发言的理解，影响交流效果。分析 EVS 和加工节奏会发现，译员还是延续前段的纵向深度加工的模式，这一模式对于信息成分较为密集的源语不适用，会造成译员严重滞后，信息成分漏译、错译。译员应根据源语特征灵活调整加工模式，对于数字、专有名词、术语、列举较多的源语，可快速缩短 EVS，跟紧发言，尽量降低源语深度理解和译语地道明晰表达等方面的精力付出，以字面对译的横向加工为主，对数字等信息成分在笔记配合下快速对译，尽量压缩、简化除数字、术语等之外的语言表达，可在一个主句挂较多数字，或者尝试音韵（停顿、重读等）+ 表格法（即利用语境省略冗余句子结构及部分词汇，仅译出数字相关内容）进行处理。

例如：

就是我们去年年底老龄人口已经是两亿四了，当我说老龄人口的时候是 60 岁以上的人口，那么占比已经值得达到了 17.3%。

By the end of last year, aged population in China, those over 60, hit 240 million, 17.3% of the total.

那么到 17 年的时候，大家看看，右边的柱子世界的平均水平是达到 13%，我们是 17.3%，那么我们的速度应该是世界平均水平的两倍还要多。

In 2017, world's average 13%, China 17.3%, over two times faster than world's average.

需要注意的是，在 PPT 上也有这些信息成分时，应以听译为主，以补充 PPT 漏掉的成分，尽量不完全视译 PPT（视译效率往往低于听译）以免译语严重滞后。此外，平时需要加强双语数字快速转换训练。

（2）语言问题多，如 the overall picture and its influence, three very featuring characteristics, Shanghai is the oldest ageing population, much severe than, These statistics is, to made 等，因为源语语速过快，数字较多，引起译员加工精力与自我监控精力不足所致，这也导致了较多的修正、填充停顿和犹豫等非流利情形，整体上削弱了译语的可用性。建议译员以后训练中注意根据源语特征调节 EVS 及加工模式，并加强译语监听；此外加强商务、行业性地道英语材料的听读、口译训练，将其中简洁、高效、地道的表达与行业性用语内化为自己中英口译用语。

部分源语的处理建议：

我国人口老龄化的特点非常鲜明，三大特点，就是总量大，速度快，不平衡。

Population ageing in China is extensive, fast and uneven.

我考虑因为时间有限，我把尽可能的文字放在屏幕上，你们的眼睛总比我的嘴巴快。

To save time, I will be brief and let you read the facts on the slide.

老龄化将伴随我们国家现代化的整个进程。
China will be ageing as it modernizes.
最早的省份是上海,是我们直辖市了,然后晚一点是西藏自治区,差了接近快小40年了。
Shanghai aged the earliest, Tibet the latest, a gap of nearly 40 years.
农村的老龄化程度要高于城镇。
Rural ages more than urban.

第三章 中英同声传译实战

一、译前准备

1. 了解口译项目

译员在接受口译任务前，应充分了解口译项目的基本信息，包括活动时间、地点、类型、主题、规模、主办承办单位、大致日程安排、翻译方式（是否有陪同口译、交传需求）、同传搭档安排、同传设备情况等，大致了解客户需求，评估自己能否胜任，确定服务报价，协助客户改善口译项目安排（例如，工作强度大的活动可建议安排3名译员）。

2. 获取相关资料

译员接受口译任务后，尽可能向客户方索取下列资料或了解以下信息：

活动日程与活动概况，包括会议名称、时间、地点、目的、主题、详细议程等；活动的主办方、承办方、协办方和赞助方情况等；发言人简介，包括国籍、头衔、工作语言、教育和职业背景等；听众的情况，如职业、行业、参会目的等；活动邀请函、预告等；既往活动情况、既往活动音频、视频或其他资料。发言人发言稿、PPT或发言摘要；

重大活动或政府性活动的嘉宾名单与头衔、主持词等；

学术性会议的学术论文集、论文摘要；

培训会的培训教材、培训用光盘（含若干视频或音频教学素材）、学员练习手册、练习答案及其他培训用材料；

行业或企业、机构的英汉对照宣传手册、英汉对照专业术语等。

上述材料或信息，需保持更新。

3. 熟悉发言材料

译员主要围绕以下几方面进行发言材料的译前准备：

（1）理解发言材料所涉及的重要理论、技术、概念等，如有必要，就有关内容编制双语平行文本；

（2）编制双语术语/话语表，包含人名、机构名、头衔等专有名词（尤其注意日语名的英译，取中文名的外国嘉宾外文名及取外文名的中国嘉宾中文名）、各类科技和行业术语、中国特色话语等；

（3）检查发言材料原有翻译是否恰当，是否需要修改；

（4）按照口译工作方式要求准备材料中某些内容的译语；

（5）在部分材料中补充双语背景材料；

（6）发言人的过往发言内容，外国嘉宾可查询有关音视频，提前熟悉口音。

不建议译员与搭档按照日程分工准备，以免日程变更造成被动。

4. 利用网络资源

（1）机构网站

主办、承办、协办、赞助机构及主旨演讲或其他演讲人所在单位的网站。涉及产品或服务介绍的会议，如 IT 会议、工程技术会议、新科技新材料会议、医药会议、金融服务会议等，译员可到相关机构网站阅读、观看、下载产品、服务或技术介绍、用户手册等资料。可以查询中国及英语国家同类机构的平行网站。

（2）中国知网

可以通过知网查询有关论文，尤其是权威期刊的综述性文章，了解行业、学科及领域趋势，关键技术、工艺与概念等。

（3）网络文档或图片

可以检索 PPT、PDF 格式的网络文档，了解有关概念、机制、工艺、技术、制度、约定、规则、标准、条文等；也可通过一些关键词检索相关图片，直观、高效了解工艺流程、技术路线、设备体系、硬件架构、软件系统等。

（4）语料库

可以查询英语单语语料库、英汉双语平行语料库，也可自建语料库，如中国特色话语语料库，此外，历次译前准备的电子材料可累加丰富为语料库。

此外，还可查询各类电子词典、在线翻译平台、行业术语库等。

5. 现场译前准备

译员一般要在活动开始前半小时至一小时到达工作现场，对于提供资料较少的活动，可以更早些到场，具体准备包括：

①确认同传工作间安放位置合理（与主席台距离合理，主席台、电子屏在工作间完全可视），检查同传设备声音效果，确认工作间的显示屏（如果有的话）与主席台同步；②到签到处领取纸质材料，如会议手册、主办、协办、赞助单位宣传材料等；③到会议宣传板、电子屏前记录会议名、主办、协办、赞助单位等双语信息；④在发言席向组织者、主持人或发言人索取更新的资料，如最新日程、主持词、嘉宾名单、发言稿、PPT 等，有时也可从负责播放演讲材料的设备人员处获取最新材料；⑤关注现场的宣传海报、标语以及会场播放的各种宣传录像或幻灯片等；留意客户方通过邮件、微信等发来的更新资料；⑥现场条件允许时，可就译前准备中碰到的问题请教现场嘉宾或听众；⑦朗读或视译与会议有关的专有名词、术语、发言稿等进行热身；⑧与同传搭档交流，约定轮次和轮换时间；⑨将各种电子和纸质材料按照使用的时间先后进行适当标记，合理摆放，以便需要时能够高效便捷利用；⑩会议开始后，在搭档工作时，熟悉搭档

对一些专有名词、术语的译法，尽量与之统一，同时在搭档工作期间可根据需要继续进行各种准备。

6. 资源整合加工

同传是多任务加工，也是对多种来源信息的整合加工，译员需要在线整合各种来源信息和资源，服务于源语理解与译语表达。除了边听边译边监听边看（主席台、电子屏、发言人等）外，还要能够快速定位、高效视阅、无缝流利低噪调用译前准备及现场可视资源，例如，边听源语边参考PPT及手边纸质材料边转换和发布译语，尽量避免调用外部资源时影响翻译加工效率和流利性，尽量降低翻找材料时的噪音。

译员工作状态可以比作一台正在运作的电脑，总认知精力与工作记忆如同内存，用于听辨、记忆、转换、产出及总协调，内存的大小主要取决于同传各分项技能的能力及分项技能综合运用的能力、效率与同传任务难度（源语变量与工作负荷），译员长期记忆（知识储备、可用语言资源等）犹如电脑硬盘，不少内容需要译前准备加以激活，译前准备的另一些内容（电子或纸质形式外部存储的内容）及现场可视信息（如电子屏、发言人等）如同外接硬盘。若要电脑高效运转，内存要足够大，自带硬盘和外接硬盘容量都要足够大且读取数据流利、迅捷。同传就是译员在较大认知和时间压力下，运用各种同传技能和策略，不断将源语输入信息与通过译前准备激活的长期记忆、难以进入长期记忆而进行外部存储的内容进行快速高效匹配、整合、分析的加工过程。

二、会议类型与同传策略

会议类型会影响发言方式（读稿、腹稿、即兴，单向发布、互动讨论）与源语特征（语速、信息密度、专业性、语言结构复杂度、发布方式、音韵特征等），发言方式与源语特征是影响译员同传认知过程和质量的主要因素。此外，不同类型会议的用户往往对同传质量维度（内容、语言、发布）有着不同的期待侧重。不同的源语特征与不同的质量期待，要求译员采用不同的同传策略。总体上，设置同传的会议可以分为商务、政务和学术三大类，政务会议、政务典礼仪式、商业典礼仪式、发布会、推介会、媒体招待会、行业会议、企业会议、学术会议、咨询会等若干小类。

1. 政务会议、政务典礼仪式

政务会议指主要由党中央及地方党组织、全国人大及地方人大、国务院组成部门及地方政府、全国政协及地方政协、各事业单位、人民团体等举办，以政治、外交、经济、社会、文化、环境等治理为主题的会议；政务典礼仪式主要指由上述机构举办的各种庆典、仪式，包括会议开幕式与闭幕式、签约仪式等。此类活动的发言一般以读稿为主，发言稿字斟句酌，语言或华丽或凝练，内容程式化，书面结构多，信息密度高。源语往往包含较多中国特色政治话语，涉及国家的价值观念、政治理论、政治制度、发展道路、内外政策等内容。这类话语既包括治理概念（名词词组）、治理举措（动词词组）和领导人讲话引语等，也包括各类专有名词，如人名，职务、机构名，会议（报告）、规划、倡议名，政策、法律、法规名，区域、地区名，项目、活动名等。

2. 商业典礼仪式

商业典礼仪式包括企业周年庆典、开业或落成庆典，机构、部门或项目的启运／启动、完结仪式，各类签约仪式等。此类活动既有读稿，也有腹稿发言（如专业主持人担任主持），发言一般较有文采，修辞较多，表达清晰流利，信息密度高，包含与企业人员、职务、部门、理念、项目、产品和服务等相关的各种专有名词、术语、数字等。

3. 发布会、推介会、媒体招待会

发布会是机构为发布新政策、新项目、新产品、新技术、新服务、新理念等而举办的会议；推介会是机构为了宣传推广新项目、新技术、新产品、新服务、新理念，介绍特定地区和领域等而举办的会议；媒体招待会与发布会、推介会功能类似，一般只面向新闻媒体人士。三类活动的宗旨主要是"广而告之"。此类活动一般也以读稿为主，语言经精心打磨，表达凝练、内涵丰富，较多使用修辞，文采较好，表达清晰流利。

以上三类会议的程序性、程式化特征明显，会议往往经过精心筹备、甚至经过排练，环节、内容、语言、发布方式等往往都经过认真设计，反复打磨，发言呈现自动化加工特征。从质量期待看，三类会议的内容质量、语言质量与发布质量都很重要，具体看，内容上要充分尊重源语意思，不随意改变源语内容，特色话语、专有名词、数字、术语翻译要精准，语言要正确、地道、明晰，发布要声音悦耳、语音标准、语气语调节奏契合场景、表达流利。

译员需要提前获取有关材料，精心准备，会议开始前与主持人等积极沟通，了解嘉宾名单、头衔等信息的更新情况，确保同传时能够接近发言人的自动化产出方式，至少保证半自动化加工。译员一般是基于发言纸质或电子材料等多信息来源，进行顺句快速横向加工为主。

对于政务会议、政务典礼仪式，译员要加强政治学习，熟悉国家路线、方针、政策，维护国家利益，避免翻译源语中的不当言论，避免在译语中使用不当表达，多学习积累党政文献文件（《习近平谈治国理政》、党代会报告、政府工作报告等）英文版、权威媒体发布的国家领导人讲话英译版、"中国特色话语对外翻译标准化术语库"及机构英文网站中有关译法，确保采用权威译法，不擅自改动和发挥。对于典礼仪式，译员应多了解机构、部门或项目缘起、内容、参与方人员名单及头衔、发展历程、阶段性成果、意义等。对于发布会、推介会和媒体招待会，译员要重点关注发布和推介对象及其特点、价值、意义，熟悉机构围绕理念、产品、技术、服务等所独创的一些词语、口号、标识等的双语表达。新产品、技术和服务的理论基础、技术思路、工艺流程、基本架构等方面的专业术语、专业名词也应关注。此外，对于以媒体人士为主的会议，译员最好能够获取双语版的参会媒体代表姓名、机构、拟提问题，被采访人姓名、头衔等。

4. 行业会议

行业会议是行业协会或行业重要企业围绕某个具体行业（如医药、化工、能源、电力、冶金、汽车、IT、电信、金融等）所举行的定期会议，行业年会比较多见。当下，行业交叉趋势不断增加，行业边界日趋模糊，行业主题不断细分，行业链条与参与者日趋增多，行业的生态体系日趋复杂。以IT行业为例，硬件、服务器、数据中心、应用软件、移动互联网、云计算、智能城市、智能交通、智慧生活等细分领域的会议较多，议题可能涉及环保、能源、交通、城建、金融等领域。行业会议以主旨演讲、圆桌讨论、互动问答等交流形式为主，也可能包括典礼仪式、发布推介等。发言形式多样，既有读稿致辞，也有带PPT的演讲，以及即兴互动讨论。发言内容可能包括国家有关政策解读，宏观经济形势分析，行业的过去、当下与趋势，行业监管机构，行业协会/学会的角色，行业上中下游市场分析与展望，行业技术的突破与工艺的演进，行业重要企业的发展等。

行业会议对译语内容、语言要求较高，译员要以地道、简洁、明晰的行业或领域语言，准确译出行业用语、专业术语、数字等。译员应熟知行业的价值链、行业的生态体系及各利益相关方角色、行业代表性企业或品牌、行业的交叉领域、行业当下热点领域与发展趋势等。

5. 学术会议

学术会议包括学术报告会、学术研讨会。学术报告会是围绕某个主题或领域，介绍科技发展动态，发布学术研究成果的会议，由一名或几名报告人进行演讲，听众较少参与互动。学术研讨会也是围绕一定主题或领域，但演讲人较多，互动研讨较多。学术研讨会一般围绕一个大的主题，设置若干具体议题。发言形式一般包括主旨演讲、圆桌讨论与问答互动环节。

学术研讨会涉及的领域一般窄而深，问答与讨论较多，对译员挑战较大。译员在接受任务时，应评估自己能否胜任，对于从未接触过的主题，尤其医学、法律、金融等，应谨慎。学术研讨会对内容质量要求较高，尤其期待译语能够精准译出专业术语。译员要熟悉学术领域的关键理论框架和重要概念、主要研究问题、主要流派与观点、研究趋势等。同传中可适当简化语言表达，集中精力传达学术相关信息。

6. 企业会议（年会、客户会、销售会、采购会、环境健康安全会、培训会、董事会会议等）

企业一般都会举办年会，此外也会围绕其具体运营举办多种会议，如客户会、销售会、采购会、环境健康安全会、培训会等。年会一般是总结过去、展望未来；客户会、销售会一般用以答谢客户，分析销售形势，确定销售任务；采购会、供应商大会等是管理供应商、确保采购质量的重要途径；环境健康安全的会议在化工、能源、医药、机械等行业比较多见，强调从原料采购，到产品生产、销售、回收等全生命周期的健康、安全和可持续性管理。培训会一般是跨国企业扩大商业版图后，从企业总部派员给新并购企业的员工、分公司或代表处的新员工做的培训，或聘请专业咨询机构给企业内部员工做的培训。

企业会议通常议题比较专业，信息量大，行话多，企业内部使用的缩略语多。另外，这类会议一般都涉及企业业务链条或产业链条上诸多部门、机构或企业，会出现较多的企业名、品牌名、产品或服务名、项目名等。也就是说，企业会议中可能涉及很多属于特定行业、企业的特有内容与表述方式。这类会议对内容和语言质量要求都较高，有些会议对译语发布也有较高要求。译员需要用正确、地道、简洁、高效的语言，准确、完整讲述企业的故事。

以上三种会议，源语比较常见的挑战是：市场分析人士、科技人员等在做大宗商品市场分析、金融期货行情、产品研发或项目管理介绍时，快速读稿，数字、专有名词、术语多。译员应尽量提前获取发言稿，标出、译出重要数字、专有名词、术语。同传中，译员需缩短 EVS，提高横向加工速度。此外，译员需留心发言人读稿中间歇性跳开稿子发挥，或改动、添加稿中数字，随时做好数字记录准备。若源语语速过快，译员可采用前面所提的表格法策略，即简化或省略一些语言形式，译出专有名词、术语和数字，并通过适当音韵（重读、停顿等）凸显重要信息。另外，有时源语中会出现需要深度加工或脱壳处理的内容，此时译员需要透过语言形式译出重要信息。总之，译员一般以横向加工为主，并根据源语特征在横向加工和纵向加工间灵活切换，动态调节 EVS，综合采用简译、概译、句子融合、压缩合并、解释增补等多种策略。

7. 咨询会

咨询会大致包括两种。一种是国家或地方政府及有关机构召开的有外方相关专家参与的就政策、技术、方法、理念、经验等进行咨询探讨的会议，内容多涉及城市规划、建设与管理、环境保护、园区与产业发展、人才战略、新科技等。另一种是由跨国企业聘请咨询机构就某种产品或服务在某市场的具体情况进行调查分析的小型讨论会，又称市场调查会。会议由一名主持和五六名讨论嘉宾参加，一般每节持续 1–1.5 个小时。主持人有预先设计的问题，按照固定程序提问各位嘉宾，内容主要涉及嘉宾对产品或服务的体验、感受与评论等。前一种咨询会，多是圆桌会议，互动比较多，嘉宾轮番发言，译员需要经常在译员机上切换中英频道，在讨论者未打开话筒或远离话筒说话时需提醒。后一种，发言语速常常较快，音效一般（尤其是到产品现场体验的时候，比如汽车类的咨询会，嘉宾要评论和体验汽车，有时候麦克风效果一般），话语比较松散随便，而且会出现多人同时发言的情况。

咨询会发言的口语特征常常较为明显，比如语言破碎凌乱，断句多，折返多，重复多，口头语多，语言形式多，思想和信息不够凸显等。咨询会主要是分享交流信息，译语的内容质量要求较高。译员要集中精力，提高加工速度和能力，抓住发言主题和思维脉络，帮助发言人补充欲表达却未表达出的信息，修补已表达但未表达好的话语，省去过多语言形式与不当表达，整合压缩松散的源语，即去粗取精，去伪存真。

除了上述各类会议，还可能使用同传的活动有餐会、参观等。餐会主要包括早餐会和午餐会,指一边用餐一边探讨问题、交流思想的会议。餐会在大型国际会议、跨国企业举办的会议上比较多见。餐会形式既可能是小组讨论,也可能是主旨演讲。参观包括对场馆、车间、景点的参观,译员边走边通过无线导览发布译语。另外,有些会议还可能播放视频、安排文艺表演等,这些内容有时也需要提供同传。

会议类型与环节常常相互交叉,有时一个大型行业会议可能涉及多种会议类型与环节,如开幕式(含视频播放、文艺表演)、项目启动或签约仪式、餐会、媒体招待会、学术报告会、学术研讨会、咨询会,小组讨论或圆桌讨论,等等。

上述会议类型,从源语特征看,总体可以分为四类:商务话语、学术、技术话语、互动话语与政务话语。

从口译训练选材角度看,建议先从一般性商务话语(一般性的行业会议)的即兴演讲开始,逐步过渡到具有一定专业性的商务话语(有一定专业性的行业会议、企业会议)与一般性学术话语,再到商务、学术、技术性互动话语(如小组讨论、圆桌会、问答等),之后进阶到纯互动话语(如咨询会、圆桌会等),再到读稿发言(商务发布、推介类会议)或较为专业的行业和学术话语,最后是政务话语。

上述顺序安排主要考虑到源语挑战大小、口译能力学习优先顺序、用户质量期待侧重等,一般从源语挑战较小(如单向发布、语速低、信息密度低、语言结构简单、专业性低、无口音、语言规范、表达清晰流利等)过渡到源语挑战较大的材料;从需要纵向加工(脱壳)为主的材料,过渡到纵向与横向加工(转码)相结合的材料,再到横向加工为主的材料;从更关注译语内容质量的材料,过渡到既关注内容又关注语言和发布质量的材料。然而,每位学员口译学习能力(语言、知识、认知等)与口译能力、翻译风格可能不同,如有些学员源语听辨优势更显著,商务或学科领域知识丰富,可从行业、企业或学术、技术性互动发言开始练习,有些产出优势更显著,政务类语言资源丰富,可从政务会议、典礼仪式读稿发言开始。总之,根据一般规律和自己实际情况,从易到难,循序渐进。

初入市场接受口译任务时,也可参照上述顺序。

三、商务话语同传

会议：猎豹移动全球年会，猎豹移动首席执行官

源语：请大家回到座位，我要开始，他们都讲够了，得我开始讲，我要征求一下总导演黄鸣的意见，我到底还有多少时间？他说，如果要超时了，他就以死相要！我还是很激动的，虽然其实我现在站在这么多人面前，已经开始不紧张了，但是这个变化之快，叫年年岁岁花相似，虽然岁岁年年人也同，但是每天的场景却完全不一样。

14A：

14A 译语：Please return to seat, I am about to start. But I want to ask for your advice, how many time I left. He said, if I surpass the time, he will kill me. I am very thrilled. I am no longer nervous in front of so many people. But the change is so fast. Every year we have a different view. Although we have same people every day, yet different days have different views.

译员反思：(1)"我到底还有多少时间？"我直接字对字翻译的"how many time I left"并不符合现场交际目的。这里可以直接省略不翻，翻出后面"不要超时"的意思即可。在注意力高度紧张的时候，同时多任务处理会导致不能迅速转换思维，我认为这里还是中式思维过重的原因，以及还是习惯自下而上（关注字词）地处理源语，如果从一个宏观角度的话，这里完全可以省略不译，但是因为太抓底层的细节，所以导致还是字对字地直译了。

(2) 源语中的"以死相要"是一个调侃、玩笑的语气，英文不能直接翻译成"kill you"，这太不合理了，可以处理成"If I speak for too long time, I will be removed from the stage."这里还是中英文思维转换的问题，没有做到脱壳。我觉得是日常没有接触过这样的情景所致。

第三章 中英同声传译实战

14B：

14B 译语：Please go back to your seat and I'll start my presentation. I want to ask how much time I've left. I'm very excited although I'm not nervous in front of such a huge crowd. We have experienced such great changes over the years, although all of you here are familiar faces, but we have experienced great changes.

译员反思：（1）"我要征求……他就以死相要！"这句话没有翻译，导致译文停顿较长。翻译时我不知道该怎么表达他的意思，因为"以死相要"明显是夸张的开玩笑的说法。

（2）"年年岁岁花相似，虽然岁岁年年人也同"，although 后面等了一下子，因为这句话肯定不能直译，直译会很复杂，后面肯定跟不上了。

（3）这段话里我说了两次 although，我注意到自己有时候会陷入一个怪圈，会不自觉重复同一个词，虽然不一定是错的，但从表达上来说丰富性不够。

教师点评：（1）开场这段话或者说这一说话方式和内容，很多同学都不熟悉或不习惯。发言中有调侃，也有因为紧张导致的不流利、表达不当、逻辑不清问题，给译员造成了困难。译员 A 明显在进行字对字翻译，但这段源语并不具备需要进行横向加工的特征（并没有术语、专有名词、大量列举、叙述等），此外译员 A 的语言问题较多，如 return to seat，应该是 to your seats，many time 搭配错误，if I surpass the time 不地道，different days have different view 语法不正确；译员 B 采用了纵向加工，总体质量不错，但是出现了几处语言问题，可能是因为纵向加工消耗了过多精力，影响了译语监听。

（2）"我要征求……他就以死相要！"

两位译员缺乏对会议场景和语境的认知。这时会议刚开始，刚开始主旨发言，因此不太可能是 how much time left 的意思。这场会议的会议流程已经提供，译员要对活动背景、参与人员、流程等有充分准备、清晰认识，在翻译时要有交际意识。

这是一场企业年会，"导演"可能指策划组织年会的负责人。由于客户没有提供相关资料，此处无法确认，因此可以对人名拟音后，根据语境译出主要意思：I want to ask Huang Ming how long I can talk，后面"以死想要"部分可以不译，也可处理为：If I talk longer than expected, he would stop me/remove me from the stage.

（3）接下来几句话的逻辑是：不紧张了——所以变化快——但是人没变——但场景不同，这一节可能与发言人的紧张有关，表达不够清晰，误用了一些连接词，其中有些也许只是停顿填充词。此种情形下，译员可以先省译这些词，译出句子本身意思，听听后面的逻辑再决定是否译出或增加连接词。这里可处理为：Facing such a large audience, I am no longer nervous. The change is fast/Things change quickly. Every year people stay the same, but the scenarios on each day/the situations we encounter each day are always different.

源语：在想这个年会主题的时候，我花了很多时间去思考，我说了dream，我说了要努力，我说每个人都值得去奋斗，但是，是怎样一个主题才能真正代表我今天的心情。有一天在车上的时候，我突然想起了一个词，两个词，叫Hello World。我记得这是我翻开第一本程序书上它写的那句话——Hello World，是一个被你创造出来的小程序和这个世界打的第一声招呼，和这个世界产生了第一次关联。

14A 译语：When thinking about the theme, I spent a lot of time. I thought about dream, hard work, about individual's dreams. But what theme can represent our mood today? One day when driving, I suddenly came with "Hello World". I remember it was written on my first programming book. Hello World, is also the first greeting of the program I created, and its first connection made to the world.

译员反思："什么样的主题可以代表今天的心情"字对字直译就会翻译出

160

"represent"，显得非常生硬。我觉得这里还是加工单位的问题，和我上一次"我主要想问"译成"I mainly want to ask..."的问题是一样的，听到一个词就急于翻译出来，而没有从更宏观的"传达信息"角度来理解和翻译。

14B 译语：Before this annual meeting, I was thinking a lot. I was talking about hard working, dilequent... What's our subject today that can better represent my mind, my idea. "Hello, world" is the topic I chose, which was seen in the programming book.... This is the program that first known by the world.

译员反思：(1)"我说了"不应该翻译成"I was talking"，至少要和上面的一致翻译为"I was thinking"。"dilequent"不是个词，口误了，应该是 diligence。

(2)"但是，是怎样一个主题才能真正代表我今天的心情"当时突然不知道该怎么表达，在这里卡了一下，还改口了。

(3)"是一个被你创造……产生了第一次关联"这句话卡顿了主要是突然没想起"问候"怎么说，当然最终也没想起来，只能乱七八糟说了一个。

教师点评：这一节，译员 A 表现好于译员 B。这节源语除了最后一句话外，几乎都是叙述。由于译员 A 习惯于自下而上、字词驱动进行翻译，而且语速快、口齿伶俐，因此对于需要横向加工的部分往往表现不错。译员 A 译语中也有几处需要调整，如 When thinking about the theme 应该加上 of this annual meeting；最后的 its first association made to the world 不恰当，首先该句和前一句意思差不多，可以不译，如果要译，可以处理为 With hello world, a new program was born。可以看出，需要横向加工的时候，译员 A 比较擅长，一旦出现不需或不能横向加工的时候，似乎就容易出现问题。

源语：我记得有一次我们在盘山开了一次会，一些同事开了一次会，那次会议长达十几个小时。我本来只想讨论一个庸俗的话题，我们如何从一家20亿美金的公司变成100亿，结果话题过半，大部分小伙伴开始主动谈起内心的梦想，人生的挑战，经历过的困难，在那一刻我自己反而被感染了。后来我跟大家说，我说你们知道吗？这个世界在我36岁这一年，突然向我展开了。我以前总是觉得世界就是我看到的那个样子，就是身边的几个人，旁边的几棵树，住的那个小房子，父母的教导，老师的教诲。可是当有一天我走出这个小小的环境的时候，我才发现世界是这么的广阔。这个世界上有着这么多有梦想的人，有这么多为了梦想不顾一切的人，我才知道以前我根本不知道这个世界是什么样子。直到了36岁这年，这个世界才从一个点开始展开成一个面，从一个面展开成一个巨大的立体，从一个巨大的立体，甚至变成了一个恢宏的宇宙。我突然发现，我的一点点努力真的可以让这个世界开始变得不一样的时候，我才知道hello world是一个多么有深意的词！

14A 译语：I remember once we had a meeting in Panshan. It lasts for more than ten hours. We were about to discuss a cliché topic, how to go from a 2 billion company into a 10 billion company. But halfway through the discussion, many started to talk about their dreams, challenges and difficulties. That moment, I was touched. Then I said, you know what? The world suddenly opened up to me when I turned 36. I used to think that the world is what I see, a few people around me, a few trees around me, the small house I live in, parents' teaching, teachers' teaching. But one day when I walked out of this small environment, and I found the world is so big, so many people with dreams, so many people fighting for their dreams. I realized I didn't know the world at all. Until I turned the age of 36, the world expanded from a point into a face, from a face into a huge object, and even into a grand universe. I suddenly realized that a little of my efforts can make the world different. I know that "Hello World" is such a profound word.

译员反思：(1)"有一次我们在盘山开了一次会"这里应该先把状语择出来，直接先说"in Panshan"，这样后面就可以独立起句，且不会因为一直记着状语而给自己增加过重的脑力负担。我觉得这个问题的根源在于从小到大接受的"笔译式"中英翻译教学，很多时候我们学到的都是"中文先说状语，而英文后说状语；中文喜欢把重要的东西往后说，英文则是把重要的东西提到前面"。在笔译当中也确实大多数情况都是如此，但是在顺句驱动的同传中，是有和笔译完全不同的处理策略的。

(2)"长达十几个小时"可以处理成"meeting"后的一个补语，译为"we had a meeting of dozen of hours"，这样比重新起一个句子省时省力。同传中英文译语可以减少谓语动词的使用，但这就对加工单位有较高的要求，一定要从"传递信息"这个角度处理译文，只有脱壳做得好才能摆脱中式思维和字对字直译的束缚。

(3) 源语中"我以前总是觉得世界就是我看到的那个样子"这句话如果直译就会变成一个从句，风险就是出现时态错误。

教师点评：对于这段叙述为主的源语，译语内容、发布等总体表现不错，但有少量语言问题。叙述型话语的同传，要特别注意时态，比如 it lasts 应该是 lasted，后面还有多处类似问题。此外，a little of my efforts 应该是 a little of my effort 或者 some of my efforts。"父母的教导"可以处理为 parents' kind words。the world is so big 也可处理为 the world is much broader/richer than that。the world expanded from a point into a face, from a face into a huge object, and even into a grand universe. 可改为：The world expanded from a single point into a vast horizon, then into a massive object, and even into the grand universe. "hello world 是一个多么有深意的词"也可处理为 how much hello world means/implies。

14B 译语：In Panshan, we had a conference of over ten hours. I was initially going to talk about, how can we become a company with value over 10 billion dollars? But after that, people started talking about their dreams, the challenges they met, and I was deeply affected by their emotions. When I was 36 years old, the world started to unfold in front of me. I've always thought the world is what I see. The world is people around me, the house I lived, my parents, my teachers, and after I walked out of my comfort zone, I found that the world is very broad. There are many people with great dreams. They will give everything they got to pursue their dreams. And I realized I didn't know what the world was like before until I was 36 years old. The world has unfolded from a point to a great universe, and my little efforts can make the world for the better, and I realized "Hello World" is such a deep phrase.

译员反思：（1）第二句话有两处卡顿，都是因为数字转换太慢了。第一处直接转换不出来，第二处转换了一会儿还是说出来了。之前老师说同传时听到数字时可以在纸上写一下，但目前真的兼顾不来。

（2）"在那一刻我自己反而被感染了"，这里当时翻译的时候就觉得自己说得特别荒谬。

（3）"这个世界才从……恢弘的宇宙"这句话在讲"点到面到立体到宇宙"时，我中间有较长的停顿，首先是我觉得他在说一些怪话，其次是我即使想对译，也不知道怎么说"面"和"立体"，所以就直接从点跳到宇宙了，但这样说其实也并没有什么道理。我感觉中间的空白可以说些 my world gets bigger and bigger 什么的。

（4）Make the world for the better 有点奇怪，change the world for the better 比较合理；"有深意的词"翻译成 such a deep phrase 有点荒谬，inspiring 之类的感觉更好一些。

教师点评：译语时态、单复数、搭配不当等语言问题较多，而且如译员反思所说，似乎目前不太擅长快速横向加工。

源语：也许正是从今天开始，从今年开始，一家真正从中国发迹，从通州的一个一百平米的小民居里面几个人开始，想做一家能够养活自己的小公司，结果却不经意地变成了一个可以去影响世界的大公司。虽然这条路我们才刚刚开始，但是我知道它就像一次裂变，就像一次成长，就像一次飞跃。只要它一旦开始这个趋势就不可停止，这个未来的恢宏就不可限量。无论在遇到任何困难的时候，我都不停地提醒我自己，你才刚刚开始。无论有多少人告诉我说，傅盛你这么年轻，做出这么多事情，你很了不起的时候，我都告诉我自己：我只是睁开眼，刚刚看到那个世界的那个孩子，我才刚刚地知道这个世界是什么样，了解了她的一点点的美好。其实我什么也不是，无非是有这么一个好的机会，有一群跟着我一起努力的伙伴，有一些一直相信我，不怕痛苦，不怕折磨的人，所以我们才开始了我们过去的这几年所做出的种种结果。让我们先回顾一下，在过去的 2014 年，我们究竟做了哪些事情？

14A 译语：Perhaps from today, from this year, a company started in China, in a 100-square-meter small room in Tongzhou, a few people originated to create a company to support lives, become a large one that can influence the world. Although we have just started, but yet I know, it is like a change, like a growth, like a leap. Once it started, it is unstoppable, and there's no limitation in its future glory. No matter what difficulties I encounter, I keep reminding myself, you are just getting started. No matter how many people said to me, "Fu Sheng, you are so young, you have done so many things, you are so remarkable." I told myself, I just opened my eyes to see the world as a child. I just began to know what the world is like and understand a little bit of its beauty. I am nothing actually. It's no more than a good chance, a group of friends working with me, uh they believe in me, and they are not afraid of pain and torture. So, we just started to uh to gain the results we achieved in these years. Let's take a look at what we did in 2014.

教师点评：译语内容和发布质量如前，总体还不错，但是仍有较多语言问题，其中不少应该和精力不足、记忆饱和、未能边译边自我监听有关，比如 a company 后隔了较远才用了谓语 become 导致语法错误，随后出现 although...but，a growth 等错误搭配，a few people originated 也许是想表达 originally? there's no limitation in its future glory，gain the results we achieved 等不地道。此外，I am nothing actually 体现了译员字对字横向加工模式，这里是中国人的自谦，意思在前面已经表达，这里可以不译。同传中，译员要有跨文化交际意识。

第一句可以顺句处理：a local company started in Tongzhou Beijing with 100-square-meter space and several employees not only survived but has grown to be a global brand。

"只要它一旦开始这个趋势就不可停止，这个未来的恢宏就不可限量"前面可以处理为 We are taking off with great momentum，之后听到后面可以追加信息 towards an unlimited future，或者 We are gaining momentum as we head towards a limitless future.

"我们才开始了我们过去的这几年所做出的种种结果"可以处理为：That is how we have become who we are today over the years.

14B 译语：And started from today, started from this year, a China local company which started in a Tongzhou house with just a few people, will become big in the world. We became very influential, although we started out with small dreams. I know we are just started on our journey, but this is a great change for all of us. It's a great leap. Once it started, the trend cannot be reversed. Our future prosperity is without limit. No matter what kind of difficulties we face, I will always remind myself that I was just started. No matter how many people told me that I've made great contributions, despite my young age. I would tell them that I was just started to see the world. I'm still young. I've just started to learn more about the world, especially the beauty of the world. I was nothing compared to the great world, and I'm honored to have such great partners and friends around me who believed in me and can weather through all the difficulties with me. That's how I started everything in the past. Let us look back in 2014, what we did in 2014.

教师点评：如前，译员对于需要快速横向加工的内容不太擅长，比如第一句，理解和表达都有问题，另外也有一些语言错误。也许因为该节主要表达发言人的自我感受，而非叙述，因此译员的纵向加工方式还比较适用，总体表现好于前面。

源语：现在我想用几个数字把刚才的那段视频再精简一下。8亿，我们在Q3的时候，全球移动用户总下载数超过了8亿，也就意味着全球曾经有8亿台手机使用过我们的软件。大家可以去对比那些所谓一线的厂商，我们曾经最大的对手，他们所披露的所有关于用户量的数据，在移动用户量上，我们其实已经开始超越那些曾经远远大于我们的公司。3.95。我们的移动月度活跃用户超过了3.95亿，这意味着在全世界每个月有3.95亿台手机在跑着我们的App。

14A 译语：Okay, now, I want to mention a few numbers to brief that video. 800 million. In Q3, our global mobile user download exceeded 800 million, meaning that 800 million phones once used our Apps. You can make a contrast, those so-called front-line manufacturers, the biggest rivalries we used to have, they disclosed some uh data about users. We actually uh started to uh surpass those much bigger company in mobile user net. Three uh our monthly active users passed 390 million, meaning that globally, 390 million phones run our Apps.

14B 译语：Now I'd like to show a few statistics to sum up the video that I showed. 800 million. In the third quarter, globally, our download have exceeded 800 million, which means 800 million phones have installed our apps, compared to those A-list companies, our greatest competitors, their disclosure of user information and mobile apps. We are started to exceed them, those who are much better than us in the past. 3.95. That's our monthly active users, which means around the world every month we had 3.95 phones running our apps.

教师点评：（1）商务话语中经常出现数字，可以根据源语情况使用简洁译语，如"超过"未必要译为 exceed, surpass 等，可以用 over, be/do better 等替代，如果源语较快，有时还可省略句子结构，直接用词组（表格法）。如"我们在 Q3 的时候，全球移动用户总下载数超过了 8 亿"处理为 in Q3, our global mobile user downloads, over 800 million。同样，install 可以用 run 代替。

（2）"用几个数字把刚才那段视频再精简一下"的意思应该是通过视频中的几个关键数字突出一下视频的主要信息，可以处理为 I will give you some numbers to highlight/emphasize what the video says. 或者 Let me share some figures to emphasize/underscore the video's message，或者更为简洁的 Let me highlight some numbers in that video. 此处两名译员的译语都不够地道、明晰。

（3）"大家可以去对比那些所谓一线的厂商，……曾经远远大于我们的公司"这一长句可以处理为：You can compare our data with those of the so-called top vendors, our once strong rivals. Their disclosed user data, in terms of mobile users, are no larger than ours'. 或者 You can compare our data with those of the so-called top vendors, our once strong rivals' disclosed user data. We are doing better than them.

（4）3.95 是中文，要注意英汉数字结构差异，即便前面说成 3.95，后面也要及时说出 395 million。两名译员的数字同传能力需要加强。

（5）译员 A 的商务语言资源有待加强。

译员 B 反思：我现在比较突出的问题是同传节奏把握得不是很好，有时候停顿较长，原因大概有两个：有些英语词我想不起来怎么说；我个人的加工方式比较脱壳，对译的能力比较弱，所以遇到不是特别了解，或者是听起来比较复杂的，我就会试图去解释，这样会导致我需要思考。但在和同学练习期间，我最近得到的反馈是我同传时节奏有点赶，想尽可能讲好一切，有的地方 EVS 会太短，所以译语听上去节奏不是特别均衡。未来除了加强对译训练，也想通过拉长前一句表达或者加强预测等，减少过长停顿。

我刚开始不是很理解老师为什么说我的翻译是偏深加工的，因为我一直感觉我也没怎么想，就是那样说出来了。但和对译的方式比较，会发现我的确是偏重于深加工的。我回想过去的学习经历，发现我的确是注重脱壳的，笔译、口译都是如此，我总觉得很多东西直译意思不太对劲。但也不是说我在这方面做得特别好，因为语言能力总有捉襟见肘的时候。我不太喜欢背诵，因为记忆力不太占优势，背了总是忘。加上没有经历过考研，没有背词条的经历，所以对译的能力没怎么训练过。由于以上种种，我在做视译的时候也会感觉有些别扭，但好在发现了这个问题，今后会加强这方面的能力。

教师点评：（1）两名译员的同传基本技能还可以，有忠实于源语内容的意识，译语发布总体较好（译员A音高可再低些，语气、语调再柔和些），但语言维度的问题较为凸显，除了提升英语资源丰富性、灵活性外，要进一步加强译语产出监管。

（2）两名译员的加工方式几乎相反：A自下而上，横向加工；B自上而下，纵向加工。比较明显看出两人在面对各自擅长的内容时，表现会更好，面对不适用自己擅长的加工方式时，问题凸显。但是会议源语类型丰富多样，纵向和横向加工都要熟悉，且能根据源语特征灵活切换。相比而言，纵向加工更适宜于生活表达，也是口译学习重点，一般先进行较长时间的横向加工训练，再转向纵向加工训练。

（3）两名译员的英语资源似乎有些差异，译员A生活口语资源更丰富，译员B中高阶语言资源更丰富。由于英语学习过程中输入资源的差异，学员英语资源的适用领域和语级常常存在差异。有的同学看美剧多，其英语生活口语资源丰富，但是中高阶的商务、行业、政治外交表达缺乏，有的同学大量使用中国政治话语英译材料，掌握较多正式用语，但是对生活用语或商务用语不熟悉。国际会议中商务、学术、技术话语较多，建议适当加强对此类语言资源的学习和积累，并根据个人情况及时补缺。

14C：

源语：我们从一个很小很小的小刷子开始了我们全球化之旅，我们用一把小刷子刷遍了全世界，刷出了每个月 3.95 亿用户。大家可以想象一下，不管是过去的任何一个媒体，任何一个产品能够在短短的 18 个月内，覆盖超过 3.95 亿用户，整个用户量增长超过七倍。这在过去的 20 年的历史里面，几乎很难看到有什么公司真的能做到这一点。当然了，也有人会说，即便用户量大，你们能不能做成商业化？工具产品和社交产品是否可比？但是我对这类回答一贯都是说，所有的创新都是从你看不起开始。第一辆汽车出现的时候，马车夫非常骄傲地和它赛跑，并且投来鄙视的目光。第一架飞机飞出去的时候，也没有人想到在 100 年后的全世界，我们可以到处坐着飞机，享受着极为便利的航空服务。3.95 亿对于这家公司来说是一个巨大的里程碑。因为它从用户量的规模上，使得猎豹移动已经超过了你们几乎说到的能够知道的几乎所有的公司，应该说仅次于类似于 Facebook、Google、微信，剩下的就不类似于了，剩下基本都被我们超过了，twitter、Line。还有什么？包括我认为 BAT 里的两家已经在用户量上都开始被我们超越了，除了微信大家用得太频繁之外。那么这么大的一个超越，就给我们开始了一个坚实的基础。在做清理大师 Clean Master 的时候，几乎所有人都会问你说，我们这么小的一个软件，怎么去不断改变全世界？

14C 译语：We started from a very little brush and then we started our globalization. We uh, make our brush go global. We accumulated 340 million users each month. Let's say, any media, any product that can uh uh in 18 month, cover over 395 million users with its user increase over 7 times, you know, it's quite unseen in the past two decades. Uh some may say: even with such a massive user volume, it's still a question whether you can go to commercialization. User products, utility products and social media are not comparable. But I answered: all innovations start from the place of disregard. When the first car appeared, the carrier driver proudly ran against it, and casting a contemptuous gaze. And when the first airplane appeared, no one anticipated that uh in every corner of the world, every one can enjoy the very convenient aviation service. 395 million, it's such a milestone. In terms of user scale, Cheetah Mobile outperformed all those companies that are known to you, only second to Facebook, Google, WeChat. And other companies, and twitter, Line and the two of BAT are lagging behind. And such a leap-forward lays a good foundation for us. When we were developing CM Master, all users asked us: how uh could you use such a small app to change the world?

译员反思：(1) 语言：灵活组句能力有待提高，"不管是过去的任何一个媒体……真的能做到这一点"一句的译语是名词短语+句子，不太符合组句规则，应丢掉语言形式框架，只译信息"within 18 months, we covered 395 million users with a 7-fold increase. In the past 20 years, few companies made it."

(2) 内容：表现还可以。

(3) 发布：较为薄弱，出现了很多 um, uh 等填充词，句首是由于启动过快，没听到信息就开口了，句中是由于转码不熟在进行思考，应多练习形成自动加工，还需努力提高发布监控能力；尽量避免不必要的语调上扬，如 "accumulated" "in 18 months" "7 times" 等都不需要用上扬的语调；减少句中停顿，如 "with ...its user increase"。

教师点评：质量总体较好，但仍有些问题需要注意：

(1) 内容上，有几处译语意思和源语有出入，第一个 3.95 亿错译，We uh make our brush go global 中的 make 应为 have made，And other companies, and twitter, Line and the two of BAT are lagging behind 没有表达出"用户量被我们超越"的意思，"几乎所有人都会问你说"应该不是 all users，而是业内人士或公司内部人士，既然此处没有明确指出，也可对译为 nearly all people。

(2) 语言上，时态有些问题，如刚刚提到的 make，还有 lays，可以改为 has laid；表达不正确，如 carrier driver 应是 coachman，and casting 应该去掉 and（同传时候由于记忆精力不足，译员可能会忘记前面语言的结构，导致后面的语言结构与前面不一致）；语言不够地道自然，如 all innovations start from the place of disregard 可以改成 all innovations start from a place of being overlooked/disregarded 或者更为简洁的 all innovations are not initially well-received，casting a contemptuous gaze 可以改为 giving a disdainful look 或 looking with contempt，how could you use such a small app to change the world? 可以改为 How could such a small app possibly change the world?；语言不够简洁，如第一句译语可以简洁处理为 with the little brush we have expanded our business globally，The little brush has become a global brand/presence，accumulated 可以简洁为 had。"不管是过去的任何一个媒体……几乎很难看到有什么公司真的能做到这一点"可以通过抓住关键信息（名词）做主语，弱化或后置谓语等其他结构形式，加上预测、顺句驱动处理：for any media, any product, within 18 months, a user base of 395 million/395 million users with an 7-fold increase, is/are rare over the past two decades/an achievement no other companies could match.

（3）发布上，非流利情形稍微有点多，确实要加强译语监管，另外有些词汇不需要用升调，comparable 重音错误。

源语：今天可以看到，我们从这么小的起步开始，猎豹移动在全球的下载量上，月度下载量一直排在前三名，仅次于 Facebook 和 Google。我们各项产品的指标其实都是在全球，原则上都是前50吧。Clean Master 一直高居我们的整个排行榜下载前四名，第四。CM Security 全球工具前三名，CM Browser 我们的海外版也迅速杀入了全球前40。还有我们的电池医生，作为我们当时移动破局的产品，也一直维持在非常高的位置，最重要的大家要看右边的评分。我们几乎所有的产品的评分都在 Google Play 上超过4.5分。这是什么概念呢？就是每一个用户给我们的评价，如果有人给我们投了一星评价，就有超过十二三个用户，必须给我们投五星评价，我们才能维持在4.5分以上。更重要的来自于 Clean Master 开始从一个工具变成一个平台。

14C 译语：Nowadays, we can see that we start from a small step and Cheetah

Mobile has achieved a lot. The global downloads,ranks the third in the world, only second to Facebook and Google. All the indexes of our products uh uh Top 50; Clean Master, Top 4; CM Security uh Top 3 in global utility market; CM browser overseas version also Top 40; and Battery Doctor, as a breakthrough product,also ranks high. Most importantly, you can see the rating.All the products are rated in Google Play over 4.5 points. What does that mean? Uh each user gives us a comment. If someone gives us one star, we need 12 or 13 users giving us five star. In such a way, we can retain 4.5 points. More importantly, CM Master used to be a utility tool. Now it's becoming a utility platform.

源语：我们有一套理论，尤其我自己说过，在工业时代是体系出单品；在移动互联网时代，是单品带体系，在一个非常扁平的世界里，我们只要把一个点做得足够高，就可以带起一整套巨大的体系，就像一个火车头带动了无数节车厢。不过我觉得背景音乐可以稍微关一下，打扰我的思虑，思考了。对，因为现在还不是小清新和文艺的时候，所以讲的比较具体的数据，请把背景关一下。背景音乐关一下。正是因为这样的一个认知，我们早在两年前开始进入了几乎全世界所有人都不看好的一个小的领域。就是我说的那把小刷子，这把小刷子今天已经开始变成了一棵庞然的大树。在 Clean Master 的带领下，我们的 CM Security, CM Browser, CM Launcher, 还有包括我们的电池医生，包括我们的 Photo Grid，包括我们等产品都开始繁茂生长，变成一个巨大的工具矩阵。这个工具矩阵下面再开始出现商业化，再出现和信息的连接，我们从工具这个侧翼市场开始切入全球的连接市场。

14C 译语：In the industrial age, it was about systems with individual products. While in the Internet era, uh we need individual products uh encouraging the development of a system. In such a flat world uh if we can uh have such a strong point, we can have a grand system that is very effective, like a locomotive pulling countless train carriers. I uh think you can turn off the background music. Yeah, now it's time talking about data and figures.

I'll continue now. Based on such understanding, two years ago, we entered an overestimated field—that little brush. That little brush has become a grown tree. Uh with Clean Master, CM Browser, CM Launcher, uh Battery Doctor, Photo Grid and other products are witnessing progress. They are becoming a tool matrix. And we start from the matrix to uh commercialize these products and then we connect them with the information system. Cheetah Mobile has transitioned from a tool market to a global connective market.

教师点评：这两节总体表现也还不错，问题与之前类似，主要是语言问题和流利性问题，也有少量内容问题（如 overestimated market 等）。

部分源语处理建议如下：

破局的产品：a disruptive product

"我们有一套理论，尤其我自己说过，在工业时代是体系出单品；在移动互联网时代，是单品带体系，在一个非常扁平的世界里，我们只要把一个点做得足够高，就可以带起一整套巨大的体系"：
We believe that in the industrial age, a product was created by an ecosystem, while in the mobile internet age, it's the opposite. In a flat world, a breakthrough in one product can lead to the creation of a huge ecosystem.

背景音乐这段，译员可以只说 please turn off the background music，可以提醒几遍。

"几乎全世界所有人都不看好的一个小的领域"：a neglected/overlooked market。

"这把小刷子今天已经开始变成了一棵庞然的大树"：the little brush has become a global brand/with the little brush we have created an ecosystem。

"这个工具矩阵下面再开始出现商业化，再出现和信息的连接，我们从工具这个侧翼市场开始切入全球的连接市场"：
Behind the tool matrix has emerged a business model/Around the tool matrix we have developed a business model. We have begun offering information connectivity solutions. Via the sideline tool market we have

accessed the global connectivity market.

猎豹全球年会 CEO 发言的剩余部分（源语较长，仅提供部分转写源语和译语供参考）：

源语：大家都知道，云存储在未来，未来就是一个连接的世界，就是一个云的世界，你可以想象，五年以后，当你掏出一部手机，如果还有手机的话，也许不是手机，也许是你大脑里的一个芯片，也许是你眼镜片上的一片视网膜的投影，也许是你一块手表！当你打开这些设备的时候，你会发现可能不是4G，可能是24G 的电信网络无处不在，包月不限时、不限流量也一定会存在，甚至如果没有牌照限制，我怀疑，即便是不用怀疑了，如果可以的话，猎豹移动也可以发射几颗卫星，搞几个热气球，然后免费地让大家上wifi，只要你打开，我就可以有源源不断的免费wifi。大家有没有想过五年以后如果是这样的话，你还需要一个巨大的本地存储吗？你的所有的数据都应该在云端，你不管拿出什么设备，你都是即时联网，实时在线，毫无障碍，那这样的话你的数据，你只是在用不同的设备去接触你的数据而已，而你所有的核心，不管是你的相片、你的生活，甚至包括你的身体数据，你每天的体温变化都应该存储在云端。这个时候在任何时候，即便你去体检或者什么样的时候，这些数据也不需要再拿一张破旧的病例，它随时可以看到，给你更精准的医疗呵护，给你更精准的食谱分析，给你所有所有数据，这让你变得更聪明。所以云存储一定是猎豹移动要做的战略性方向。

参考译语：Everyone knows cloud storage is the the future trend. We're headed towards a world that's connected through the cloud. Just imagine five years from now, when you reach for your phone, if we still even have phones by then, it may not even be a phone anymore. It could be a chip implanted in your brain, a projection on your glasses, or a watch. When you turn on these devices, you won't just be connected to 4G, but a 24G telecommunications network everywhere with a flat rate. If without requirement of a license, I think that Cheetah Mobile could launch a few satellites, set up some hot air balloons, and provide free wifi for everyone. As long as your device is turned on, you can have free access to wifi. Think about it, in five years, you won't need a large local storage anymore. All of your data will be stored in the cloud. No matter what device you use, you'll be instantly connected online in real time with seamless experience. Your data can be accessed from various devices. All your important data, from your photos to your daily body temperature changes, will all be stored in the cloud. When you go for a physical exam, you won't even need to bring old medical records. Medical data will be accessible at any time, providing you with more accurate medical care, more precise dietary analysis, and all the data you need to make smarter decisions. That's why cloud storage is a strategic direction for Cheetah Mobile.

源语：这个战略性方向，今天看起来，我们还只是在我们整个大战略里面的一个小的一环，但是从大方向上来说，没有一家公司不会是云公司。所以呢这个产品我们推出了仅仅两个月，我们现在的云存储用户已经超过了 2000 万。大家也可以想象一下，一天超过四五十万的用户注册，今天还有谁能真的认为我们只是一家工具软件厂商？我们每天的用户的注册数量已经开始超越了很多所谓社交软件产品，只不过是我们没有开始高调宣传。但是这个数据成长之快，其实也在超出我的预期。我终于知道我在两三年前做的预言是对的，就是看上去是个小工具，它最终会撬起一个移动互联网的生态系。云存储是我们走向这个生态系非常重要的一步。

参考译语：This strategic direction currently seems like just a small part of our overall strategy, but in the bigger picture, every company will eventually become a cloud company. Our cloud storage product was launched just two months ago, but we already have over 20 million users. Imagine, over 400–500 thousand users registering every day. Now who can still think of us as just a tool software manufacturer? Our daily user registration numbers are bigger than many social software products. We just haven't started promoting it loudly. But the rapid growth of the data is actually beyond my expectations. I realized that my projection made two or three years ago was correct. What seemed like a small tool would eventually leverage the entire mobile Internet ecosystem. Cloud storage is a crucial step for us to enter this ecosystem.

源语：不仅如此，我们不是靠简单的推广研发去完成我们对全球用户的构建，我们也非常重视用户体验。刚才说今天猎豹移动基本上所有产品的评分都远超同类竞争对手，不管是 Launcher，是 Backup，是 Battery，还是 Clean Master, CM Security，你可以把所有的同类的软件都搜出来，基本上，应该不是基本上，应该是没有谁的评分比我们高，因为在我们公司内部我们更看重的是用户对你的评价，只要这个评分低于对手的产品，你在公司内部拿不到任何资源，不会有任何兄弟部门去支持你，因为它在伤害我们的用户体验。用户的体验，是猎豹移动的成功之根本。所以即便在 Facebook 上，我们从今年 6 月份，2014 年 6 月份开始构建全球的粉丝网络，让更多的用户去关注我们，参与我们，并且变成粉丝文化的一部分。我们今天在 Facebook 上已经有了超过一千万的用户粉丝，这个数量也是所有中国公司在 Facebook 上最多的，包括小米等公司。所以有一次我跟雷总说，我说雷总，我从你那儿学到了粉丝文化，所以我们在全球不断地在努力在学习。雷总说，在国际化市场的粉丝文化构建上，你走在我们前面。所以最重要的是我们通过这样的一群忠实的用户，开始构建了我们面对全球的用户网络，知道全球用户需要什么，他们对我们产品有怎样的反馈，这样的能力才是我们的竞争对手所不能比拟的。

参考译语：Moreover, we don't rely solely on promotion and development to build our global user base. We value user experience. As I said earlier, almost all of Cheetah Mobile's products ratings are higher than those of our competitors, be it Launcher, Backup, Battery, Clean Master, and CM Security. You can search for all similar software, and there should be no one with a higher rating than us. Within our company, we value user feedback the most. As long as the rating is lower than our competitors' products, you won't get any resources or support from any other department in the company, because it would harm the user experience. User experience is the key to Cheetah Mobile's success. Even on Facebook, since June 2014, we have been building a global fan network. So that more users could know us, be part of us and part of our fan culture. On Facebook today we have over 10 million user fans, which is the most of any Chinese companies on Facebook, including Xiaomi and other ones. So one time I said to Mr. Lei Jun, "Mr. Lei, I learned fan culture from you and we are working hard on that globally". Mr. Lei replied, "You are ahead of us in building fan culture in the global market." Therefore, the most important thing is that through this group of loyal users, we have begun to build a global network of users, knowing what global users need, and what kind of feedback they have for our products. This is what our competitors fail to match.

源语：30%。这个数据看来不是特别高，对吧，但是这也是有着非常多的团队的努力。因为在2014年移动高歌猛进，但是PC全体整个的用户时长和用户量全行业下降，而我们珠海的同事们，珠海同事坐哪里？珠海的同事们在不断地输出给北京给广州人才的同时，也不断培养自己的新兴力量，并且在PC我们这个战略大本营上实现逆势增长。我们整个毒霸对整个导航流量的贡献在过去一年增加了20%~30%。我们双11给我们合作伙伴淘宝的贡献从毒霸那边增加了大概是6~7倍。所有这些都是在产品上不断改善，在用户体验上不断增强，在PC这个领域，其实我们还在不停地努力，才能做到这样的逆势增长。我们整个的这个产品界面，以前是移动向PC学习，现在PC开始学习移动，正是用这样的不停的体验的改进，使得用户发现金山毒霸不再是一个简单的杀毒类产品，它更是一个能够去帮助你管理你的电脑，更是能够去帮助你更快地获取信息的产品。所以这样的产品也被用户，即便在他们越来越少使用 PC 的情况下，整个的使用次数、使用时长反而在增加。除此之外，我们还有其他更多的产品，今天就不一一介绍了。

参考译语：30%. It seems not that high, but it's a result of our team's hard work. In 2014, mobile internet sector grew rapidly, while PC saw a decline in user engagement and traffic. Our colleagues in Zhuhai, where do they sit? They have been cultivating new talents not only for Beijing and Guangzhou base but also for itself. They helped achieve a growth against the trend of PC sector. Kingsoft Antivirus' contribution to navigation traffic rose by 20%~30% over the past year. During the Double 11 shopping spree, its contribution to our partner Taobao rose by 6~7 times. We achieved this by improving on our product and user experience. In PC sector, we have kept learning to make this happen. Mobile internet used to learn from PC but it is opposite now. Improving user experience impress users that Kingsoft Antivirus is not just an antivirus software anymore, but a tool that helps you manage your computer and access information faster. Despite the trend of declining PC usage, our users are spending more time on our products. We have other exciting products, but I'll leave those for another day.

源语：我们在硬件领域尝试了一款叫豹米的空气净化器，不能说我们是引导小米进入这个领域，应该说我们跟小米一起进入了一个暴利的领域，把整个的这个净化器的价格拉低到一千元以下，给用户提供了更好更优质的净化器产品。而对于我们整个战略来说，最重要的是我们通过一款小产品开始切入智能硬件这个领域，开始思考在未来 IOT 这个更大的范畴之内，猎豹移动怎样找到自己的立足点？你是通过边缘的硬件产品切入，还是通过生态系去知道这些硬件产品厂商怎样才能更好地去智能化，而我们帮他做些什么？我认为这款产品对我们最大的意义来自于此，来自于我们今又进入了一个新的领域，并且开始理解思考。那么像郑州的驱动之家，杭州的 Photo Grid，还有我们安兔兔这样的一些团队，其实都在他们的产品线上不停地成长。因为怎么说呢？应该说小伙伴们跑得太快了，所以今天我就没有把它们这些数字拿出来一一列举，虽然其实成长也很大，因为我们最近开这个年终总结会的时候，我们也感叹，所以以前我们总觉得自己是家小公司。今天突然发现你在这家公司做产品，如果你的用户量不上一个亿，你都不好意思跟人家打招呼。千万级的产品在公司说实话，这个重视程度想那么高不容易，这个百万级的产品基本上就会有很大的危机感。大家再去对比很多很多其他的公司，过千万过百万过亿已经是惊天动地的事情。

参考译语：In terms of hardware, we launched an air purifier called "Biaomi". It's not that we led Xiaomi into this field. Rather, we and Xiaomi entered a highly profitable market together and lowered purifier's price to below 1,000 yuan, providing users with a better product. It is our strategy that with such an offering we could enter smart hardware market and think about how in a bigger context of IOT, how Cheetah Mobile can find its place, whether it is through the edge hardware products or through the ecosystem to understand how these hardware product manufacturers can be smarter, and what we can do to help them. I think the key thing with this product is that we have entered a new field and started to think about and understand. Zhengzhou's MyDrivers, Hangzhou's Photo Grid, and Antutu among other teams are growing. Our teams have been growing very rapidly so that I cannot detail about their achievement. They have grown rapidly. When preparing for today's event, we were amazed because we used to think of ourselves as a small company. Today, if your user base is less than 100 million, you may not consider it a big success. Products with ten million users may not be highly valued in the company, and products with a million users may face great pressure. But for many other companies, one or ten million users are considered remarkable achievement.

源语：所以其实每个人的认知啊都来自于过去的经验，我们的确在过去的三年前是非常艰苦，也非常努力，有的时候也需要非常地谦和，当然现在还是需要很谦和。但是到今天我希望告诉大家一点，就是刚才那几个数据告诉我们，我们今天已经 totally different，我们已经开始成为全球移动互联网非常重要的一分子。我们在用户量的体系上已经开始和巨头媲美，我们在研发的能力上已经完全有机会有能力在短短的一两个月内进入一个新兴领域，并且快速地拔得头筹。我们在整个的创新体系上已经开始摆脱过去的那种只有单点、只有一项，而可以开始进入一个体系化的布局阶段。我们既可以在我们最擅长的工具领域开始持续地投入，我们也会开始对这种跨多个工具的 Launcher 领域开始投入，我们做的云存储，又开始项目的云端，开始展开我们的应该叫我们的触角。并且通过这样的云端化，又使得我们的产品更多地 ID 化，使得我们更多的用户的注册信息和我们发生关联。然后再通过这样的一些产品去实现了我们人和信息，人和机器，信息和信息的连接，开始构建，成了整个移动互联网非常重要的一环。

参考译语：Therefore, everyone's perception is based on their past experiences. In the past three years, we have faced many challenges and worked hard, and at times, we needed to be very humble. We still need to be humble today but the data we just saw tells us that we are totally different today. We have become an essential part of the global mobile internet. In terms of user base we are now comparable to giants. In terms of research and development, we are able to enter a new field within one or two months and become a leader there. In terms of innovation, we have begun to move away from the past single-point and single-item innovation system and have been able to make ecosystem-wide deployment. We will continue to invest in our tool field, and we will also start investing in the cross-tool Launcher field. Our cloud storage and our move to cloud will help us expand our reach. This cloud transformation will make our products more ID-oriented so that more user registration information is available to us and interact with our ecosystem. Through these products, we connect people and information, people and machines, information and information to build an essential part of the mobile internet.

源语：可惜啊，这个由于PPT做得有点仓促，我本来想把挂在珠海的那个横幅的照片放上去的。我们在珠海研发中心挂了一个非常巨大的对联。上联是祝猎豹移动12月收入超2亿，一骑绝尘，下联是，贺猎豹移动，下联是祝全球征战，横刀立马，舍我其谁。然后不负青春，横幅是舍我其谁，这么霸气的对联当然是我一个字一个字敲出来的。为什么要挂这么一个横幅呢？是因为我在一年半前，我在珠海有一次演讲，我跟所有的珠海同事说，我们要立一个志愿，三年收入超过西山居，然后大家反应平平，只有我在高喊。然后等我这个讲完以后，有人在QQ上问我说，傅总，我们能超得过西山居吗？西山居在我们心里就像一座大山，对吧，底下停的最好的车都是他们的。当然了，现在最好的车已经被姚辉的这个叫什么凯宴超越了，后来我被他刺激了，我只好也去买了个宝马的那个A8。但是这才过去了一年半。我不想，说实话，我不喜欢一个公司内部一片和谐，我觉得要有适当的竞争，我也更不喜欢大家是通过你好我好大家好来维持这个公司的凝聚力，我希望呢，通过你拼我赶谁做得更出色，我要跟出色的一起工作，我要变得比他更牛，这样不服输的志气，来让自己变得更牛。所以我当时在想，我说一定要超过，而且不需要三年。当我们12月超过收入是2亿的时候，西山居加WPS的收入，我忘了美金有多少？1.2亿有吗？听不见。我知道一年前超过了，我现在只是想说我们比他们加起来多得多得多。我只想说，其实有的时候在你心里的一个大的丰碑、一个大的石头都是这么一步一步走过去的，对吧。

参考译语：I was in a hurry in preparing the slides so I didn't have a chance to include a photo of the banner hanging in Zhuhai. In our Zhuhai R&D center we hung a huge couplet: one line reads wishing Cheetah Mobile to earn over 200 million yuan in December, while the other line reads wishing Cheetah Mobile to be a global leader. The banner reads "Who else but us?" and these lines are what I personally came up with. Why such a banner? A year and a half ago, I gave a speech in Zhuhai and told all my colleagues there that we need to set a goal: to earn more than Xishanju in three years. But there wasn't much of a response and only I was shouting. After my speech, someone asked me on QQ, "Mr. Fu, can we earn more than Xishanju? Xishanju is like a mountain to us. Even the best cars parked outside are theirs." But now the best car is Yao Hui's Cayenne. Then I was under pressure and had to buy the BMW A8. But that was only a year and a half ago. Frankly speaking, I don't like a company to be in quiet harmony inside. I think there should some competition. I hope that we can work with the best people and compete so that we could be much better. So I was thinking then that we must do better than Xishanju in no more than three years. When our revenue in December was over 200 million, Xishanju and WPS's revenue combined, 120 million US Dollars? Loud please. I know that we surpassed them a year ago and now we earn far more than them. So you see that we can make it though it did not seem possible at first.

源语：当然了大家别说我在年会上怎么看不起兄弟公司，我只是觉得我们值得骄傲一下，他们值得紧迫一下，然后大家再一起努力，互相帮助一下。因为我们自己找到了自己的发展之路，我们就一定可以能够更快，而且我有一个词叫一骑绝尘。一骑绝尘是什么意思？就是不可能被反超，只可能越拉越大，我们可以看看明年这个数字会不会变成4亿。我对此充满信心。更重要的是我们在过去的连续三年当中，收入增长持续保持在140。换句话来说，我们在两年前仅仅是在2012年的时候，我们的收入大概只有1.5亿还是1.6亿，小得我已经记不住了。2013年的时候我们是3.6亿。2014年的时候我们是7.6亿，今年我们应该会超过15亿以上，每年都会超过。说错了，17亿是吗？对，

17 亿以上，不好意思。每年都在 140% 增长。还有一点很重要。当然这个增长速度，大家可能对财报分析得不多。一个公司能连续三年保持季度对季度的增长超过百分之百，全球的公司放在一起应该不超过十家。连续三年，百度上市以后，曾经一度一直是超过百分之百。更重要的是什么？是在今年的第四季度，我们整个移动收入占比应该会超过 35%。而在去年的第四季度，我们整个移动收入占比大概只有 7%，也就是说在整个公司增长百分之一百多的情况下，我们移动收入占比迅速增长，超过 37% 的占比。我认为我们在今年一季度或者二季度，我们整个移动的收入占比超过整个公司收入一半以上。也就是说我们真正是猎豹移动了，别人不再说你们改了个名字叫猎豹移动，就变成移动公司了，你们收入大部分在 PC 上。我们从 5 月 8 号上市开始到现在只花了六个月的时间，我们海外的移动收入的增长是季度对季度超过十倍的增长，我们在海外收入的增长的规模上也是超出了所有投资人的预期。

参考译语：Of course, I don't mean to look down on our brother companies. I just think we should be proud of ourselves, and they should feel some urgency to catch up. Then we can all work together and help each other. As we have found our own path to growth, we can surely move faster and leave the others in the dust. As we continue to grow, we'll leave them further and further behind. Let's see if we can reach 400 million next year and I'm confident that we can. More importantly, in the past three years, our revenue has grown annually by 140%. Two years ago in 2012, our revenue was only around 150 or 160 million, so small that I cannot remember. In 2013, it was 360 million. In 2014, 760 million, and this year probably over 1.5 billion, 1.7 billion and every year it rose by 140%. One more thing. Most people don't often analyze financial reports. For a company to maintain quarter-over-quarter growth of over 100% for three consecutive years is very difficult, and globally there are probably no more than ten such companies. After Baidu went public, they were able to grow by 100%. More importantly in Q4 this year, our mobile revenue is expected to make up over 35% of total revenue, but in Q4 last year it was only 7%. That means when total revenue grew over 100% our mobile revenue also grew rapidly. I believe that in Q1 or Q2 this year, our mobile revenue will account for more than half of our total revenue. We are truly Cheetah Mobile now. We're not just a company that just changed its name to Cheetah Mobile and became a mobile company, and most of our revenue comes from PC. Since we went public on May 8th, it has only taken us six months to achieve over ten times quarter-over-quarter growth in overseas mobile revenue. The scale of our growth is greater than what any investor expected.

源语：所以最近整个股价的波动，大家可能也不知道是为什么，是因为很多投资人知道我们在海外移动收入上增长非常迅猛，我们今天还是Facebook全球移动合作伙伴里面给它贡献收入最高的伙伴之一，应该是它top级的合作伙伴。即便是今天像Facebook、Google这样的大公司，在面对猎豹，在移动互联网上跟它合作的时候，都非常地慎重，非常地重视。我们跟全球超过20个全球移动广告平台有合作关系，并且能够通过这20个移动广告平台给用户推送更好的信息，去满足用户信息的获取和商业化之间的关系。也就是说我们今年在第四季度，我们整个的收入增长，移动收入增长，整个收入结构发生了重大的改变。我们真正开始在移动互联网这艘大船上起航了。

参考译语：Recently there are fluctuations in our stock price because many investors are aware of our rapid growth in overseas mobile revenue. We are currently, among Facebook's global mobile partners, the biggest revenue contributor and we are Facebook's top partner. Big companies like Facebook and Google value their partnership with us in the mobile internet industry. We have partnerships with over 20 global mobile advertising platforms, which enable us to provide users with better information and promote user information acquisition and commercialization. In Q4 this year, our mobile revenue had rapid growth leading to significant revenue structure changes. We are truly embarking on a new journey in the era of mobile internet.

> 会议：中国国际技术转译大会亚欧科技创新合作论坛，亚欧重点前沿技术领域创新合作实践——亚欧科技创新合作中心领域中心搭建，太库科技创业发展有限公司代表

15A：

源语：感谢朱秘书长。同时我们今天也特别荣幸，就是太库被我们亚欧科技创新中心授牌产业孵化基地。因为刚才其他的这些嘉宾，大家都是围绕着专业化去讲的，然后我也结合我们太库现在在全球的一个资源平台的优势，然后跟大家分享一下我们现在在做的全球创业孵化平台这块，然后我们围绕亚欧科技创新中心可以提供哪些支持。

15A 译语：Thank you, secretary Zhou. It's a great honor that Techcode can be invited by ASEM CCSTI as an incubator. Many guests have talked about professional services. I'll brief you on Techcode's businesses on its global advantages, and I will talk about my...our global incubation platform services and what supports can we produce for start-ups.

译员反思：(1)"朱"（秘书长）听成了"周"，译前准备的时候应该把整个议程都熟悉一遍，先对整个会议背景有个了解，不能只看要练习的材料；同样，"专业化"并非 professional services，没有对 PPT 进行充分译前准备，应该深度理解 PPT 中的关键概念的内涵。

(2)"结合……全球的一个资源平台的优势"说完 businesses 后没法跟资源平台优势结合起来，又说了一个 on，语法出现问题。

(3) my 跟 our 出现改口，嘴太快了，脑子反应不过来。

(4)"围绕亚欧科技创新中心"因为说完句子主干后就没法插进去，导致信息遗漏。

(4) 语序错误，应该是 talk about ... what we can; produce 与 support 搭

配错误，以后练习时还要多监听自己的输出语言。

教师点评：译员译前准备不充分，缺乏基本的背景了解，这是一篇宣传、介绍太库科技的发言，译员应通过企业网站等途径充分了解太库科技的发展历程、理念、服务、成就等，并熟悉有关双语表达，还要了解其参加会议的背景，如太库科技为什么参会？以什么身份参会？和亚欧科技创新中心是何关系？通过参会发言希望起到什么交际效果，等等，这些内容译前准备材料中都有。了解上述内容有利于在同传中进行精准高效横向加工（专有名词、概念、术语等）。

除了秘书长的姓错译外，"秘书长"也错译，这是不该出现的。此外不了解背景导致"太库被我们亚欧科技创新中心授牌产业孵化基地"中的"授牌"误译为"邀请"，应该是 Techcode has been awarded an industrial incubator by ASEM CCSTI."专业化"的理解要看日程安排，本节的其他发言人都是代表具体分中心，侧重谈技术应用，因此此处"专业化"不是 professional service，可处理为 previous speakers discussed technological applications from the perspectives of the branch centers.

此外，由于本篇发言的口头语较多，语速较快，信息密度较高，充分译前准备能够促进译员运用预测、脱壳等策略进行高效纵向加工，及时去除有关语言框架，理解发言人要表达的信息，并以简洁、明晰语言传递信息。如果充分了解太库科技的情况，"我也结合我们太库现在在全球的一个资源平台的优势，然后跟大家分享一下我们现在在做的全球创业孵化平台这块，然后我们围绕亚欧科技创新中心可以做的哪些支持"中的"结合""在……这块""围绕""然后"等框架可以去除，直接译出命题，处理为 I will speak about Techcode's advantage of being a global resource platform and share with you how we serve as a global incubator for startups and how we support ASEM CCSTI，如果EVS较长，可以基于对太库的认识进行适当信息重组，处理为 I will share with you how as a global incubator we integrate our global resources to empower/serve startups and support ASEM CCSTI.

源语：我先介绍一下我们太库科技。太库，其实我们现在是主要致力于创新创业的全球化的资源的联动和发展。所以我们现在主要的核心的目标是三化，一个是全球化，一个是专业化，还有一个是品牌化。在全球化方面，太库现在在全球的 7 个国家、22 个城市一共建立了 30 个孵化器，然后也是包括我们现在在境外创新创业资源最聚集的美国硅谷、德国柏林、芬兰赫尔辛基，包括以色列特拉维夫，然后还有就是在莫斯科，都有我们自己的实体的办公空间。同时我们有专业的当地团队去运营我们当地的孵化空间，我们也是通过在全球去建立这样的一个平台，然后把全球最具创新创业的要素聚集在我们平台上。

15A 译语：First, something about Techcode. Currently, it's focused on start-ups' resources across the world. So our core target is that we can achieve three goals: profession...business-specific, globalization and become branded. Now we have seven businesses in seven countries, covering 22 incubators. And as for the most resources-concentrated areas like Silicon Valley in the US, and Israel, Moscow, Techcode has its physical offices. We have locally hired operating teams to operate the incubators. So we have a global platform to integrate innovation resources.

译员反思：(1)"致力于创新创业的全球化的资源的联动和发展"，提取出了部分关键词，但是英文表达还有很大提升空间，平时应该在视译的时候练练多样化表达。

(2) 被"三化"绊了一下，导致句子说得累赘，词不达意，且拖慢了后面的反应，需要控制这种一着急就多说的习惯。

(3) 讲者说了很长的状语才出来后面的核心词"孵化器"，导致说了 seven 之后没法接下去，没有当机立断进行预测，同时在 PPT 上找对应内容分了神，以后练习要找有 PPT 的真实会议，加强边看边听边说的能力。

(4) 罗列的时候跟不上，需要加强数字等练习。

(5) Locally hired operating teams，英语不够简洁，需要积累地道表达储备。

教师点评：(1)"致力于……联动和发展"处的问题主要是译员 EVS 过短，译得有点早，可以再稍稍等到"资源的联动"再译，处理为 integrate/provide global resources for start-ups，一般情况下，开口译的对象要么是比较独立、稳定的结构（如状语等），要么是关键命题信息已经清晰（即表达关键信息的主谓或者主谓宾等结构已经听到或者基本可以预知），这里的关键信息不是"太库致力于"而是"太库致力于×"，其中的"×"属于焦点信息，对于整个命题意义的影响比较关键，因此等到×说出后再译较为合适。

如果译员因为源语语速较快，需要缩短 EVS，减少记忆负担，那么谓语最好不用封闭结构 focus on，因为使用了介词，后面的语言灵活性空间十分受限，从而影响了对源语信息的传达，可以使用能够保持语言结构开放灵活的 serve/empower 等词汇，即处理为 serve/empower startups as a resource platform。

此外，如果译员做了充分译前准备，了解太库的业务范围等，此处也可通过预测进行翻译。

(2)"三化"的问题还是和译前准备有关，译员没有充分了解三化的内涵。如果译员之前没有拿到任何资料，此处应急的办法就是词汇对译：globalization, professionalization and branding，如果看了发言材料，就知道专业化是指专注于某些具体行业，因此可以处理为 industry specialization 或 industry expertise。全球化也可以是 global reach。

译员在译 core target 时，发言人已经讲到"三化"，因此没有必要说这么冗长的 So our core target is that we can achieve three goals，直接译"三化"就可以，或者先说 core target is three fold 再译"三化"。

(3)译员译完"三化"后，发言已经到了"7个国家、22个城市"，此种情形下，译员最应该做的是先不处理任何其他语言结构，先快速译出 in 7 countries and 22 cities，而不用先说 we have 等，这样会影响译员对后面转瞬即逝的信息成分的记忆保持和转换。在出现数字、专有名词、术语、大量罗列等情况下，一般都要先迅速对译这些成分，之后再根据语境搭配适当语言结构。后面的"美国硅谷……"处也是同样情形。另外，译员要明白，一般情况下，视译速度是低于听译速度，在有稿有 PPT 时，视译只能作为辅助和参考，不可因视译而影响加工效率，耽误了同传加工节奏。

（4）"境外创新创业资源最聚集的"这类长定语，如果源语语速过快，译员来不及全部译出，可以译出最关键/具体的信息，比如此处的 overseas startup-rich areas，长定语顺句处理的能力很大程度上取决于译员的形容词和名词表达资源。此外，发言人经常提到"创新创业"，根据发言 PPT 和语境，多数时候是指 startups，而非 innovation and entrepreneurship。

（5）locally hired operating teams to operate the incubators 表述的确有些烦琐，可以直接说 local（servicing）teams/professionals，后面的 to operate the incubators 也可以不说。译员可以多看多听地道的企业/行业英语表达。

源语：然后现在整个太库全球关注主要是三大产业，包括人工智能、大健康和新材料，所以现在我们也是围绕着三大产业的资源，然后做纵深的产业加速的孵化。所以我们也是在承接产业孵化基地的前提之下，可以为全球的这些要素，尤其是有产业化孵化产业化发展的这些要素，来提供垂直的产业化的纵深的平台。然后在品牌化方面，一方面我们是为全球的这些企业来打造一个高准入标准的全球共享的创新社区。同时我们也是围绕着产业化这块，然后为我们整个中国的区域的发展来植入强产业属性的创新产业集群的芯片。这个是我们现在整个太库全球的一个布局。我们可以看到我们现在在太库全球的这些空间，目前是有超过 4 万平米的一个孵化空间。然后我们会提供一个深度的孵化的服务。同时现在我们太库全球有超过 300 位的运营团队，然后 80% 以上都是当地的当地化的本地的雇员。

15A 译语：Currently, Techcode is mostly focused on three areas: AI, medicine...and we're helping with vertical acceleration. Hopefully, we can integrate factors for start-ups and providing vertical acceleration and platforms. As for building platforms, on the one hand, Techcode builds a high-threshold international sharing innovation community for startups. And also, we're focused on industry development to build industry-specific clusters. So that's our businesses across the world as you can see, we have lots of office spaces covering 40,000 square meters. We provide in-depth incubation services. Our operating teams have more than 300 locally hired employees, 80% of which are hired locally.

译员反思：（1）翻找PPT没跟上，因此把"新材料"给忘了。

（2）"承接产业孵化基地的前提之下"，没理解原文意思，所以遗漏过去，用自己的话糊弄了一下。译前应该看看类似的演讲，积累背景知识。

（3）停顿、语调、轻重音不分的问题很突出，目前在练shadowing，但是没有成效。可能还是太着急了，一句话说完，只想赶紧跟上，对自己的EVS没有把握。

教师点评：（1）第一句的情况如前，译员横向对译出现问题，耽误了后面。此处，根据发言"三大产业"，后面可以预知出现罗列，此时前面简洁处理，或者直接译具体的三个产业，即 Techcode specializes in AI...

（2）"在承接产业孵化基地的前提之下"，如果译前准备充分，这里脱去框架不难，即处理为 as an industrial incubator。

（3）发言的口语特征比较明显，语言较为啰唆，形式较多，可以基于译前准备，用简洁英语传达关键信息。"一个高准入标准的全球共享的创新社区"可以简洁处理为 top global innovation community，"为我们整个中国的区域的发展来植入强产业属性的创新产业集群的芯片"可以处理为 boost/empower China's regional growth with industrial clusters。

（4）"这个是我们现在整个太库全球的一个布局"不建议只说that's... 这是发言人对照PPT进行演讲，译员需要结合PPT为听众传达信息，处理为 this slide shows our global presence。有时如果发言人指具体某个图表、照片，译员需要明确其在幻灯片上的位置，如 the top-left/bottom-right table/picture shows...

（5）最后一句可以通过表格法＋简缩进行简洁处理，弱化或省略句子结构：we have over 40 thousand square meter space for (dedicated to) professional incubation with globally 300 professionals/by a global team of 300 professionals, 80% (of whom are) local.

（6）音韵有些问题，以恰当音韵凸显信息的能力有待提高，如部分句子间的停顿过短，部分非重点信息词汇不应重读。这里不建议译员练习 shadowing，因为一般认为 shadowing 的加工是语音，而非语义，这一练习可能会削弱语义和语用加工能力，也就是信息加工能力，而同传中以音韵凸显信息的能力离不开语义和语用的深层加工。可以通过多听多体会表达较好的一些发言，或者听知名电视节目主持人或记者的表达。

教师点评：译员总体表现还不错，语言资源和口齿伶俐性较好，信息加工能力稍弱。未来建议译员多思考感受语言与信息间关系，多训练脱壳、简缩、简洁表达能力；进一步加强快速横向加工能力、横向和纵向加工的灵活切换能力；加强地道的企业或行业英语语块学习和积累，让英语译语更简洁高效；强化以音韵包装和凸显信息能力；进行充分译前准备。

源语：然后我们太库现在整个的一个业务逻辑，尤其是针对海外项目，我们有12个字，叫全球技术、太库加速、中国创造，所以我们现在整个就是围绕海外这一块的项目，尤其是有进入中国市场需求的企业，然后我们会有一套我们自己的做法。我们会通过我们自己的课程的设计，然后帮助海外的这些项目去进行海外的前期的前置的孵化，也就是离岸孵化，就是这些项目如果有意向进入中国市场，我们会先就是培育它们在境外先去了解国内的市场，然后在我们国外的孵化器进行孵化。然后同时我们会给它开设各类的进入中国市场的这种课程的培训。然后当这个企业成熟了，可以在国内去拓展业务的时候，我们会依托国内的这些孵化的网络，把这些项目引进来，然后进行商业化的拓展、市场化的拓展以及产业化的落地的服务。通过我们一系列的课程的培训，和我们更深入的产业化的服务，来帮助项目在国内去进行市场化商业化和产业化的落地。

第三章 中英同声传译实战

15B：

15B 译语：In terms of our foreign business, we aim to provide China services and speed up global innovation. We serve companies, especially those with the intention to enter Chinese market. We have our standard, our classes for these companies to achieve offshore incubation. so they can understand Chinese market first, and we have a series of classes about Chinese financial market to brief them. When they are qualified to expand business in China, we'll uh introduce them with our network, and business expanding, industrial landing services. A series of classes, and our in-depth industrial services, we can help this project achieve market marketization, commercialization and industrialization.

源语：就我们整个在全球的发展当中，各级领导对我们太库的认可。左上角第一张图片是去年以色列开业的时候，延东副总理和万钢部长在我们太库以色列做了一个揭牌，当时延东副总理也是评价太库是中国孵化器出海的样本。然后包括我们今年在3月份的时候，然后我们做的中以的一个合作论坛，然后我们这边的李雪东副司长，也是一带一路建设工作领导小组办公室的一个领导，然后对太库的评价是：太库的国际化做得非常好，推动国际创新企业走进来，对于中外双方都非常有利，国际创新企业想来中国直接找太库就可以。

15B 译语：Leaders from different levels have acknowledged our work. You see that our vice minister and tech minister have acknowledged our works. And you see the you can see the bottom pictures, from the also from our national NDRC leaders. They acknowledged our work saying you can come directly for Technode for entering Chinese market.

教师点评：（1）译员采用了纵向加工模式和概译策略，基本以命题为单位，通过等待、深度理解、脱壳等提升了译语可用性，也基本传达了源语主要意思，但是总体准确性不佳，尤其是第一句，这可能与译员未进行充分译前准备有关。建议对于语速较快、信息成分较多的源语，将横向对译和纵向深加工相互结合。

（2）"然后我们太库现在整个的一个业务逻辑，尤其是针对海外项目"，要有交际意识，发言人是指着 PPT 向听众讲解，因此可以处理为 This slide shows Techcode's business logic/philosophy, particularly for overseas project.

（3）译语可以更加精简，those with the intention to enter Chinese market 可以精简为 those targeting Chinese market。

（4）"我们会给它开设各类的进入中国市场的这种课程的培训"可以处理为 we offer mentorship/coaching/courses to prepare them for the Chinese market。

（5）"当这个企业成熟了……商业化的拓展、市场化的拓展以及产业化的落地的服务"可以处理为：When they are mature/ready to expand their business in China, we rely on our domestic incubation network to bring the projects in and help with their commercialization, marketization and industrialization。"商业化的拓展、市场化的拓展"也可以根据具体语境处理为 market exploration and expansion。下一句又重复了这句的内容，英语需要避免完全重复，可以换种方式表达，如 bring the projects to fruition。

（6）第二段里有较多专有名词，而源语语速较快，需要快速对译，适当简缩，有些中国特色话语还需要一定认知补充。"左上角第一张图片是去年以色列开业的时候，延东副总理和万钢部长在我们太库以色列做了一个揭牌"可以处理为 the first top-left picture shows Liu Yandong, Chinese Vice Premier and Wan Gang, Minister of Science and Technology (present) at the launch ceremony. "国际创新企业想来中国直接找太库就可以"可以处理为 For international startups targeting Chinese market, Techcode is an ideal partner.

剩余部分：

源语：然后接下来汇报一下我们整个现在围绕国际化合作的工作基础。目前我们现在在全球的这个空间上，我们一共培育了1500个中小企业，然后这些企业都是集中在人工智能、大健康和新材料方面的，然后这些企业入驻之后也是获得了非常好的成长。我们可以看到整个我们太库在国内的一套商业逻辑，我们会每天每周每月包括每季度都会有各类的创新创业的辅导，通过全方位的课程的体系来帮助企业进行加速的深度的培育。当然我们肯定是依托于我们现在专注的产业，通过联动全球的资源，然后为企业实现促进它落地的目标，来达成最后的加速的进程。我们也可以看到我们一个孵化成果。企业在我们太库的平台上平均的上市周期缩短了五个月，并且企业入驻太库之后，它们的估值提高了平均2.5倍。然后目前在孵企业的估值也是5000万以上的已经达到了169家，估值一个亿的达到77家，3亿以上的25家。

参考译语：Let's move on to see what we did in international cooperation. We have currently incubated 1500 small and medium-sized enterprises specialized in artificial intelligence, health, and new materials. With our incubation, these enterprises have had significant growth. This shows our business logic. We have daily, weekly, monthly, and quarterly coaching for the startups to boost their development. With our industry expertise and global resources, we help bring these enterprises to fruition/success. Thanks to our efforts, the average time to market of these enterprises is shorter by five months, and their valuations up by an average of 2.5 times. Currently, we have 169 enterprises with a valuation of over 50 million, 77 over 100 million, and 25 over 300 million.

源语：这是我们现在一个培育得非常好的一个明星的案例。这个是在美国硅谷成长的企业。孵化美国硅谷之后，一年多的时间估值已经超过10亿美元。然后这个项目也是现在做得比较火的车联网的一个项目，然后目前我们也是结合现在我们在固安打造的智能网联汽车产业集群，然后已经把这个项目现在引入到我们北京，然后并且联动固安这边在进行区域的落地的发展。这是太库平台上的一些人工智能的明星企业，还有新能源方面的企业。这个也是我们太库在平台上做的一些活动，包括我们在国内的一些对接的考察团，同时我们也在联动境外的这些包括当地的政府，一些大型的机构一起做的境外的活动，包括去年我们在以色列做的DLD创新周，当时也是搭建了中以的合作的一个专场，然后也是帮助国内的这些投资机构、大型的企业和政府去深入以色列对接当地的企业的资源。

参考译语：This slide shows a success story. It's a company incubated in Silicon Valley and in just over a year it has achieved a valuation of over \$1 billion. It is a project related to internet of vehicles. As we are building in Gu'an, a city close to Beijing the intelligent and connected car industry cluster, we have brought the project to Beijing for an integrated development. These two slides show some successful AI and new energy companies on our platform. This slide shows various events we have organized. We have arranged some visits by domestic delegations, and we have worked with overseas local governments and large institutions in launching some events, for example, DLD Innovation Week in Israel last year, when we organized a special session to facilitate China-Israel cooperation and help matchmaking between China's institutional investors, big corporations and local governments and Israeli companies.

源语：然后因为现在太库承接的是我们整个产业孵化基地的一个工作的任务，所以我们也围绕着整个的产业基地做了接下来的一个目标和一个工作计划。因为我们是希望可以承接整个亚欧科技创新中心各国之间的这种资源联动，我们也愿意开放整个太库平台的这些孵化空间的载体和我们整个的深度孵化的一个服务，希望来支持我们整个亚欧两国之间的人才交流项目落地，以及产业化所有的相关的这这种服务。

参考译语：As Techcode is an industrial incubator for ASEM CCSTI, we have developed our goals and work plans to better serve ASEM CCSTI to facilitate the integration of resources across countries. We are committed to opening up our incubation space and offering in-depth incubation services to support the bilateral talent exchange projects and industrialization efforts.

源语：我们会通过我们现在太库平台上已经建立的这些合作的基础，通过我们现在有序的分工和我们自己的内部协同的分工，协同我们整个平台上的各类的资源，来进行垂直产业的一个系统的加速的服务，来最终依托我们的产业加速器和产业落地的资源，和整个资源的产业化的服务和产业化的基础。同时我们也会进一步来扩大我们全球的技术来源，因为现在太库在境外的六个国家分别有我们自己的孵化空间，我们下一步也会进一步去拓展我们在境外的合作的网点，所以我们也是开放的平台，希望跟各位在座的来宾一起来商讨，我们是不是可以一起来共同策划、共同谋划去建立我们的孵化器，建立我们的加速器，来更好地促进我们亚欧各国之间的科技资源的流动。

参考译语：Based on the partnerships on our platform, with well-organized division of labor and internal collaboration, we will coordinate all types of resources on our platform for an accelerated vertical industrial acceleration. We will rely on our industry accelerator and resources for launching industrial projects, as well as the industrialization services and progress. Meanwhile, we will further expand our global technology partnerships, as currently in six countries overseas we operate our own incubation spaces. Our next step is to expand our network of overseas collaborations. We are an open platform and hope to discuss with all the guests present if we can jointly plan and establish our incubator and accelerator to better promote the flow of technological resources between Asia and Europe.

源语：我们也希望来协同各位伙伴的资源，来依托太库平台的这些深度的服务，来提升我们在太库平台孵化器上的这些项目的加速的效率。所以我也希望能和在座的各位来进一步去商讨，来进一步来希望能吸引更多的这些平台的资源来加入我们亚欧科技创新中心，也进一步发挥我们太库平台的这些优势，来贡献更多的力量。所以最后我也想借用习近平主席的一句话，叫撸起袖子加油干，希望跟大家一起，我们 Just do it。谢谢各位。

参考译语：We hope to leverage our partners' resources and Techcode's professional services to make our incubation process more efficient. I look forward to discussing with everyone present on how we can attract more resources to join ASEM CCSTI and further fulfill our role. As President Xi Jinping said, let's roll up our sleeves and work hard together. So let's just do it! Thank you!

会议：IBM 中国论坛，圆桌会议：未来零售的关键能力，格风服饰有限公司副总裁

16A：

源语：感谢 IBM 的邀请。我们准备了一些 PPT 来跟我们各位阐述一下，作为零售业服装企业，在过去几年的一些艰难的一些变化。我在公司里面是负责除了销售和财务之外的，基本上所有的部门。我负责 IT、物流、商学院、人力资源，基本上除了销售所有的部门。所以我们知道在公司里面的转型的一些痛点在哪里。

译语：Thank you for inviting me to come here. I've prepared several slides of PowerPoint to help me introduce the changes we see in the clothing sector in the past few years. I am responsible to almost all the sectors excluded sales department. I'm responsible for HR and other, so I know the difficulties in the transition of the company.

教师点评：（1）译员要有现场交际感，"IBM 的邀请"不可遗漏，会议的主办承办机构、品牌名等非常重要。在处理类似"我们公司""公司"时，有时也需译出公司名"格风服饰"或品牌名"GLORIA/歌莉娅"。

（2）prepared，help me introduce 等表达反映了译员不熟悉会议用语或者英语基础不佳，可以处理为 I will walk you through several slides...

（3）"作为零售业服装企业，在过去几年的一些艰难的一些变化"应该是指格风服饰公司作出了一些调整，不是行业变化，可处理为 as a clothing retailer, in the past few years we have/Gloria has made/undergone some difficult changes/challenging transformations.

（4）"我在公司里面是负责除了销售和财务外的几乎所有部门"可简洁处理为 I am in charge of all, except for... 接下来列举部分漏译较多，对于列举，译员要迅速跟进，缩短 EVS，快速对译并适当记笔记。

（5）有些地方未能充分利用音韵凸显信息，如"痛点"（difficulties）一词应当重读，不可机械地将重读落在每句最后一个单词上。

（6）语法错误较多，语言基本功薄弱。

源语：其实我们跟所有的传统企业都是一样，我们在 2009 年的时候我们就开始触网，那么接着我们会开始开网店参加双 11。那么这时候我们也会经历过线上跟线下的品牌的文化相冲突的以及是消费者相不一致的地方。那么同时我们也经过整合，在这个时候我们开始跟 IBM 进行一个合作。那么 IBM 有些先进的理念或者在当时带进来，我们当时并没有非常地去了解或者清晰地去全面地思考说 IBM 的这些这些 concept、这些概念，而我们当时是用了 IBM 的 OMS 系统就是所谓的一个中台。那么在过去在我们这个中台系统搭建了以后一年多的时间，仍然会正如刚才那位主编讲的，这些零售业所遇到的困难我们都会遇到。这时候我们会发现企业需要的一个变化，不光是在系统上的变化，而且是在你的思维上和企业文化发生的一个变化。这是最最重要的。所以老板讲的是说，歌莉娅是一个地地道道的 local 品牌，本土品牌。我们是来自于当年的改革开放最前沿的广州西湖路的夜市，所以我们还是要回归到当时我们做这个批发的这样子的一个场景。所以我们要说回归初心，我们要以消费者为一盘货去经营整个公司，所以我们在过去的 18 个月到 24 个月里面公司进行了一些非常大的变革。

译语: Similar to other traditional enterprises, in 2009, we get in touch with Internet, and we started to open the online store. And we also experienced a period when the online and offline customers and brands are conflicted with each other. And then we integrated our business, and we cooperated with IBM at that time. IBM has many advanced philosophy and business models that we could learn from. We do not figure out that whether all these concepts could be applied to our system, and we apply the IBM system, that is the middleware, to our own enterprise. And in its construction, we still face many difficulties in retailing sales. So that's when we see that we need changes in both systems and mentality. So just like our chairman has said that Gloria is a local brand of China, we come from the market of Guangzhou that is at the frontline of reform and opening up. And we should back to the wholesale scenario. That is, we should find our aspiration and focused on consumer. So in the past 18 to 24 months, we've made many reforms in our company.

教师点评:（1）"传统企业" traditional companies。表示"公司""企业"的几个英语词汇有区别：enterprise 一般指大型或重要商业机构，用于比较正式场合，company 可以指任何类型商业实体，无论规模大小，使用场合更广，firm 一般指律师事务所、咨询公司等专业服务机构，business 表示企业的时候侧重指商业经营。

（2）"触网"可处为 started online business/e-commerce，get in touch with the Internet 有些不可思议，译员提前拿到的幻灯片中已给出该词，可见译前准备不充分。

（3）"我们也经历……不一致的地方"可以顺句处理为：we had online and offline brand culture conflicts and customer expectation inconsistencies/differences，当然这要靠译员的信息加工能力、英语基本功和商务英语能力。

（4）cooperate with IBM 可以简洁处理为 work with，"先进的理念"是同样问题，可以简译为 great ideas。

(5)"我们当时并没有非常地去了解……IBM 的这些 concept"属于非完整命题，没有表达出语境连贯的重要信息，可不翻。该源语选自会议的圆桌环节，发言形式比较自由，发言中存在较多不流利、不完整、不规范、不清晰的表达，译员需要基于平时的商业领域知识积累和充分译前准备，不受一些零碎、不当、不连贯表达干扰，不为一些语言形式羁绊，不以具体词汇为驱动进行逐词理解和对译，要透过语言形式提取命题信息、关键信息，去粗取精，去伪存真。

(6)对于包含术语、专有名词等成分的话语，如"IBM 的 OMS 系统就是所谓的一个中台"，译员要快速缩短 EVS，快速对译，"中台"是 middle-end，是幻灯片中有的词汇，和"后台"等都是本发言的关键概念，反映了译员译前准备不充分。

(7)"企业需要的一个变化……企业文化发生的一个变化"可处理为：A business needs to change not only its system, but also its mindset and corporate culture.

(8)对于"改革开放最前沿的广州西湖路的夜市"这类长修饰，译员可根据精力和时间状况选择不同处理方法，如果精力和时间不够，一般选择译出语境最相关、最具体、最关键信息，如"改革开放前沿的夜市"或者"夜市"，如果有足够时间，可以全译。另外，对于这类长修饰，一般应充分利用名词和介词资源顺句处理，如 reform and opening up-driven city - Guangzhou's nightmarket。

(9)"我们还是要回归到……回归初心"可以处理为：we should not forget our roots in night market wholesaling/how we did wholesale in night market and remain true to ourselves.

(10)"我们要以消费者为一盘货去经营整个公司"可以处理为：we should better serve our customers by integrating our channels/we should put our customers at the center and integrate online and offline channels.

源语：在我们公司里面有个口号，不能说口号，是一种说法，说与其让市场来革你的命，不如自己革自己的命。所以首先我们要想三个问题，第一个问题是我们的客户在哪里，我们当时在一直在澄清的问题是说，线上的客户和线下的客户能不能融合，我们全渠道能不能达成这一系列的东西，但是我们有没有真正地了解说我们的客户在哪里？以及是说我们未来的业务战略在哪里？客户和业务未来的业务战略有没有相交合的点，这是我们当时花了很长时间在讨论的问题。

译语：We've got a slogan in our enterprise that we don't want revolutionized by the market. We want revolutionized by ourselves. So we have to figure out three questions. The first one is, where are our clients? How can we integrate online clients with offline clients? How can we resolve all the problems in an all-channel way? And where are our clients, and where are our business strategies in the future? Is there anything that we could do to find our clients in our strategies? We paid a lot of time in discussing all these issues.

教师点评：（1）如前所述，对于口语特征比较明显的发言，译员要时刻警惕译语中的词不达意等情形，不能完全跟译发言形式（术语、专有名词、数字和列举较多的时候除外），需要适当等待或根据语境明晰信息，如"口号"不可译为 slogan，此处可以处理为 In our company/Gloria, we often say that...

（2）译员未充分做译前准备，对发言逻辑不清晰，加上发言不流利，导致这段译语较为混乱。

（3）"与其让市场来革你的命，不如自己革自己的命"可以处理为：Rather than waiting for the market to disrupt you, it's better to proactively disrupt yourselves.

（4）"我们要在想三个问题"可以处理为 we need answer three questions.

（5）"线上的客户……达成这一系列的东西"可以处理为 can we integrate/merge online and offline customers to achieve an omnichannel (approach).

（6）"未来的业务战略"，future business strategies 比 business strategies in the future 省时省力，译员需要加强简洁商务英语学习。

（7）"客户和业务未来的业务战略有没有相交合的点"可处理为 Can

we align customers with corporate strategies.

译员总反思：(1) 口语发布：较上一次上交反思的音频而言，在流利性方面有所进步，减少了重复和改口，避免了长时间的停顿；发音仍然存在较大问题，很多单词发音不够清晰或不够标准，如 store、business；容易受源语节奏影响，每个单词一顿，整体听感差、译语没有节奏感，忽快忽慢，这一点与加工单位有关；重音位置错配依然存在。未来要着力提高口语发布水平，通过较为简单的文本练习，为自我监控分配更多精力，逐步改善翻译节奏，注意重音凸显以提高译语可听性。

(2) 语言表达：语言质量依然不理想，单复数、介词搭配、冠词等出现错误，在口语水平较低的情况下未做好自我监控导致低级错误频出；译语臃肿，难以灵活简单地表达主旨，如"we experienced a period when..."，浪费时间和精力。这主要仍是受英语基本功所限，同时对精简压缩、去除框架等策略仍不够熟练。

(3) 内容传达：漏掉较多信息点，列举几乎完全没有译出，"IBM 的 OMS 系统""搭建以后一年多""广州西湖路"等信息也未传达，导致产出无信息语句，主要原因是反应速度不够快，无法迅速转码，在信息密度高的情况下容易认知负荷过载，无法边听、边记、边译。在未来的练习中，在紧跟原文的基础上，要注意保证信息完整度，多练习信息密集文本来提高反应速度和调整 EVS 的能力。

(4) 信息处理：加工单位小，没有做到"top-down"，担心大段遗漏信息而时刻紧跟原文，有时甚至以一个词语为单位，致使表达中出现较多停顿，大大降低了可听性，影响了对源语的理解。

(5) 交际思维：未意识到交际场景下翻译的重点，未着重强调品牌名，反而是将品牌名省略或泛化，应加强交际思维的训练，翻译时多加监控。

(6) 译前准备：译前准备不够充分；根据译前准备材料做了词汇表，但在翻译时听源语、看幻灯片和看词汇表三者不够协调，手忙脚乱，不知如何安置重点，词汇表几乎没有起到作用。

教师总点评：译员对同传问题的反思较为全面、细致，确实，在语言、内容、发布、同传策略等方面均存在不少问题。除了上述几个方面需加强努力外，译员要重点加强对商业领域知识和双语商务话语的了解与学习，理解发言逻辑与关键概念，加强对口语特征明显的发言源语的信息加工训练，强化源语听辨时的自上而下加工模式，提升商务语块翻译的准确性与效率。

剩余部分：

源语：那么首先我们要从思维上和组织上进行一个改变。组织上我们进行了调整，我们压缩了非常多的部门，让它更加符合互联网的这样子的一个企业的经营，同时呢我们也会说从门店的设置和门店的改变上做出一些调整。我们有关过店。在2015年底和2016年的时候，我们在很多城市都关店，包括我们的加盟商也关店。但是到了2016年的下半年，我们发现我们走出了这个谷底，我们的店铺数量在开始上升。那么同时呢就是我们发现是说你不光是在后端要改，在前端也要改，就是你的供应链也要改。你的消费者一定是喜欢爆款的。我不知道这里有多少是时尚行业的或者是服装行业的。那么当你的爆款的数量在你的这个销售的比例增加的时候，你的利润率是成倍地增加。所以你的供应链怎么样能支撑你的爆款，而让你的这个平销款的数量增加，这就是一个柔性供应链所要去达到的事情。最后我们要讲的是说我们后台的是不是原来的一些后台的部门，就像类似我以前管的这些部门，它是不是都可以整合在一起，而是原来我们有很多中心，比方说我们有品牌中心也好，我们有人事中心也好，现在我们都要所谓的这些部门是不是围绕着客户这个中心，我们有多少个部门的功能是不需要的。

参考译语：First, we need to change our mindset and organizational structure. We have streamlined our departments to align better with the needs of online business operations. Additionally, we've made adjustments to our store settings and closure. We closed some stores. At the end of 2015 and throughout 2016, we did that in many cities, so did our franchisees. However, in the latter half of 2016, we emerged from the slump and our store count rose. We've also realized that changes need to be made not only in the back-end but also in the front-end aspects, such as our supply chain. You know consumers are drawn to popular items. Particularly in fashion or clothing-making sector, as the proportion of popular products increases, so does your profit margin. Therefore, the supply chain has to support popular items and also boost the sales of regular items. This is what a flexible supply can do. Finally, as for our back-end departments, the ones I formerly managed, we must assess if they can be integrated. We used to have many centers such as brand center, HR center. We need check if they are customer-centric and necessary.

源语：所以在这一系列的指引下做了很多很多的事情，无论从人、事还有物流的产业链的角度上讲，我们发生了非常大的一些变化，特别是在过去的14个月里面。那么现在当然就是我们在基于OMS的这样子一个平台上，我们可以实现这样的一系列的功能。就是我们的，这个是第一点，就是大家所说的是全渠道。任何的订单，线上的订单可以线下发货，线下的订单也可以在线上发货。我现在有两个仓库，一个是线上仓，一个是线下的，那我们可以任意地发，只要是它系统找到它在哪里它就可以在哪里。北京的客户在网上下单，我们也可以从北京的店铺里面发货，这就是真正的全渠道，在今天我们已经做到了。

参考译语：With IBM's collaboration we've done a lot of work related to people, events and logistics industry chain. We've made a lot of changes especially in the last 14 months. Now with the OMS platform, we can do so much more. The first thing is omnichannel, where online order can be shipped offline and offline order shipped online. We have two warehouses, one online and one offline. We can ship from either one as long as the system knows customer needs. Customers in Beijing can place orders online, and we can ship from the physical store in Beijing. This is what true omnichannel means, and we've achieved it today.

源语: 同时我们在这里，我们要想象的就是说，作为我们服装企业过去的 20 年，我们的成功老板讲的说我们的成功是离不开加盟商的成功。在今天的变革过程中，我们要继续往前走，一定要维护加盟商的利益，如果我们把加盟商的利益抛在一边的话，我们企业做不大。所以在过去的 14 个月里面，我们另外的一个核心就是说一定是在企业的变革和发展中要维护加盟商的利益。所以我们在系统和人事的安排以及在流程的管理上，包括财务上面都非常地倾向于保证加盟商的健康的发展以及辅导加盟商的健康地发展。所以这是给大家讲的说我们在今年年底在回顾 2015、2016 年我们做的事情是说我们的库存下降了 25%，店铺里面的库存下降 25%，我们的单店利润上升了 15%。我们的前线的销售人员下降了 30%，这个是以前想都不敢想象到的。那么当我们做到这一点的时候，我们拿到这个编制的时候，老板都不敢相信在上面签字，但实实在在是我们甚至做到了这一点。

参考译语: At the same time, what we need to consider here is that as a clothing company, over the past 20 years we have succeeded, and our success, as our boss said, is closely tied to the success of our franchisees. As we change and continue to move forward, we must prioritize the interests of our franchisees. If we neglect their interests, we cannot grow. Therefore in the past 14 months, another key thing has been to ensure that as we make changes and develop we prioritize our franchisees' interests. In terms of system and personnel arrangements, process management and finance, we have been trying to ensure the healthy development of our franchisees and provide them with guidance. This slide shows that by the end of this year, when we look back at what we did in 2015 and 2016, we can see that our inventory has decreased by 25%, I mean the inventory in our stores. Our single-store profit has risen by 15%. Our frontline salespeople have decreased by 30%, which was unimaginable before. When we achieved this, our boss couldn't even believe it, but we actually did it.

源语：所以这个是一个最大的变化，就是说当你的思维发生了变化的时候，你坚持不懈地走下去的时候，你的结果就一定会做到。所以在公司里面通过这一轮的变化我们讲的对设计师来讲，我们是要做一种有故事的产品和有态度的设计。那么对于我们公司来讲，我们觉得我们是做衣服的，所以我们不是在以前，是说我们在做加加加很多东西做，我们是做诚衣的，我们讲的是诚心的诚，诚衣的。我们希望的是说我们真正能够打造客户喜欢、消费者喜欢的衣服。从设计的角度上来讲，我们从2015年开始我们就坚持地做减法。因为大家都知道服装的品类有非常的多的，有外套，有内衣，还有各种各样的。那么我们仅仅从我们公司角度上来讲过去的14个月，我们真正认识到是说我们就做两个品类的衣服，就是连衣裙跟外套。所以其他的会不会做，会做，但不是我们的核心，我们要真正知道说如何做减法，通过做减法来满足我们消费者的需求。

参考译语：So the biggest change is that when you change your mindset and persist, you will achieve your desired results. Through this round of changes, our clothing designers aim to create products with story-driven designs and with attitude. We are a clothing company. We should not just focus on creating more categories of products. Rather we have been making clothes with sincerity. We aim to produce clothes that customers will love. From a design perspective, since 2015 we have been trying to maintain our focus. As we all know, there are many different categories of clothing, such as coats, underwear, and so on. However, over the past 14 months, we have realized that we should only focus on two categories of clothing, namely dresses and coats. While we may still produce other categories, they are not our focus. We need to know how to be focused and meet consumers' needs.

源语：所以对于工匠精神我们认为是说很多人都会去讲，但是我们真正讲的是说我们是把柔性供应链和精益的销售能够带到前线带给消费者，这就是我们认为的工匠精神。对我们公司来讲是说，过去的一年的变化呢让大家每个人都会感觉到是说让之前的那种观念会发生变化。现在的观念就是说我们无论后台是要用心于产品，前线要交心于你的客户，这样子才能把你的销售做得很好。最后一个跟大家讲，就是说虽然现在在零售行业是，零售行业目前看来很多的企业已经走出了低谷，但是从我们第一季度来讲，我们第一季度同比去年的第一季度是有 20% 的增长，保守地估计。所以我们觉得我们在过去的 14 个月到 24 个月里面的一些变化还是比较成功，还是可以得到认可的。谢谢！

参考译语：Craftsmanship spirit is something that many people talk about. But for us it means we bring flexible supply chains and lean sales to the frontline and meet consumers' needs. This is what we mean by the craftsmanship spirit. Our company has changed a lot during the past year. Our mindset has changed. And now we focus on quality products in the back-end and keep customer-oriented in the frontline to drive sales. Finally, let me tell you that currently many retailers have emerged from the downturn. As for the first quarter, we went up by 20% over the same period last year. Therefore we believe that in the past 14 to 24 months we have made the right changes. Thank you!

四、学术、技术话语同传

会议：中国国际技术转译大会亚欧科技创新合作论坛，亚欧重点前沿技术领域创新合作实践——亚欧科技创新合作中心领域中心搭建，中国科学院光电研究院代表

17A：

源语：谢谢秘书长，谢谢各位专家和各位同仁，我代表中国科学院光电研究院呢感谢亚欧科技创新中心给中国科学院光电研究院这样一个机

会，我们去承接了现在的亚欧激光应用科技创新中心。那么在这里呢我向大家汇报一下我们的建设方案和我们未来的工作计划。我们激光应用领域的分中心呢，有几个合作单位，有几个合作方。一个呢是德国的夫琅和费激光研究所，还有白俄罗斯的激光信息技术公司，以及俄罗斯科学院应用物理研究所。同时呢我们还跟意大利的商务部、农业部，阿尔巴尼亚的科技部，泰国的科技部和澳大利亚的科技部都进行了相关的合作上的沟通。那么我主要从以下几个方面来展开介绍。

译语：Thank you, secretary. I would like to thank experts and partners here. On behalf of the AOE SAS, I would like to thank the cooperation center for giving us this chance to build a cooperation center on laser application. And I will give you a brief report on our plan for this center and our future work plan. This center has several partners, including Fraunhofer Institute of Laser Technology, Belarusian Laser Technology and Information System Company, Russia's IAT RAS. We are working with Italy's Ministry of Economic Development and their alternatives to Albania, Thailand and Australia. I will go over the following aspects.

教师点评：(1) 专有名词翻译问题多："秘书长"错译；AOE CAS 说成 AOE SAS，首次提到建议译全称；白俄罗斯及俄罗斯两个机构翻译不准确；their alternatives 应该是 their counterparts，但这里不太合适，因为这里谈不同的几个部。这些内容都在发言 PPT 中，译前准备不充分。

(2) "承接"可以用 host 或 assume；"汇报"很多时候是谦虚说法，不建议译作 report，除非实指下级对上级的汇报关系，此处可直接处理为 I will brief you about/present you；"建设方案"可以译作 development plan。

源语：那么我们中心建立起来的第一步的工作计划呢，就是首先呢计划建成这个我们领域分中心的运营机制。那么亚欧激光应用合作创新中心呢是以中国科学院光电研究院为核心平台。首先我们设置一个日常的执行机构。那么这个执行机构呢会跟上述的合作伙伴共同建立一起运营的工作机制。那么这个办公室呢设在我们中国科学院光电研究院，具体的事务部门呢根据合作的这个需要，联合其他亚欧中心的国家建立一个开放的互动的对话机制。并且呢我们在中心里面呢还希望吸纳一些具有实力的央企和上市公司作为我们的董事单位，这样的话呢推动我们科技成果的转化和落地。第二个呢我们计划在 2017 年和未来的 2018 年，搭建激光应用信息的共享平台。那么整合亚欧激光应用科技创新中心各单位的科研资源，以及项目资源、人才资源，设立中心的项目库、专家库，以及质量检测设备的分享库，形成标准化的共享机制，以此呢来促进亚欧激光产业的合作交流和共享。

译语：Our first step is to build a central management mechanism. This cooperation center has AOE CAS as its core platform. We will build an office for daily execution. It will be working with the partners above to build a smoothly operating mechanism. It is located in the AOE CAS. We would satisfy the realistic requirements and work with Asian-European countries to build an open communication mechanism. We will also work with central SOEs and publicly-traded companies to roll out our outcomes. We will plan that in 2017 and 2018, we will build an information sharing platform, which would integrate the R&D resources and programs and professionals from different centers and build database of programs, professionals and equipments to form a standardized shared mechanism, to promote communication and sharing.

教师点评：（1）"分中心的运营机制"误译为"中心管理机制"，此处可处理为 we will first of all work out the operational mechanism 或者 how the center operates/runs；译语的 mechanism 重音错误。

（2）"我们设置一个日常的执行机构"可以处理为 we will set up an executive body/a secretariat/an office for day-to-day operations；to build a smoothly operating mechanism 可以改为 to develop joint working mechanisms。

（3）对于第三句和第四句的 it，建议至少将其中一个明确为指代对象，同传中代词不可过度使用，否则会影响译语的清晰度和可理解性。

（4）would satisfy the realistic requirements 有些匪夷所思，译员要加强对命题信息的听辨，而非词汇层面拼凑、堆砌、编造。

（5）"吸纳……董事单位"可以处理为 invite them to serve on /become members of our board of directors.

（6）"推动我们科技成果的转化和落地"可以处理为 implement/ materialize our scientific and technological findings。

（7）"激光应用信息的共享平台"不可漏译最关键的词——激光应用，平时可加强这类多词汇长短语的快速对译。"整合……资源"一般用 pool 或者 bring together；equipments to form a standardized shared mechanism 加强译语监控，避免语法错误。

源语：第三个呢就是我们计划在全国范围内，尤其是在京津冀鲁豫这五个地方呢设立亚欧激光应用中心的分支机构。那么我们先后呢和天津的武清区、东丽区，北京的亦庄开发区，还有杭州，另外郑州和济南都进行了多方的会谈和交流。那么在今天的我们的分会上，然后这些省市的领导也都到会，然后第一对我们表示成立的祝贺。第二呢他们也表示就是在下一步要支持咱们亚欧科技创新中心的建设。那么我们计划呢在济南分中心建设以激光显示和激光医疗以及激光通信的技术和平台。那么在郑州呢主要进行激光纳米材料的相关的技术和应用的主题。那么在承德呢就是以光通信和激光芯片为主，主要与德国开展合作。那么在重庆呢我们现在也在探讨，就是把激光和汽车产业里边的应用相结合。那么现在呢主要的合作方有美国的 ITU，还有这个德国的莱布尼兹轻量化研究中心。

译语：Next, we also plan to build sub-centers in Tianjin, Beijing and other regions. We've been working with Tianjin District, Dongli District in Tianjin, and Hangzhou, Zhengzhou as well as Jinan Province in the form of communication and exchanges. The directors from these regions are here, and they've delivered their congratulations for the building of this center. And they also make it clear that they will support our work in building this cooperation center. We plan that we will build a laser display, laser medical, laser communication platform in Jinan, and a center for nano new materials in Zhengzhou. And in Chengde, a light communication and laser chip centers working with German partners. In Chongqing, we will build a center integrating laser and cars with ITO from the US and the research center from Germany.

教师点评：(1) 该段专有名词与术语的错译、漏译、概译等问题比较集中。需要优先处理专有名词、术语和列举，以免短期记忆容量不足造成错漏，例如第一句可以顺句先译出"京津冀鲁豫"，第二句可先译"天津的武清区"等列举。

(2) "省市的领导"可以处理为 heads of the provincial and municipal governments；delivered their congratulations for the building of this center 可改为 congratulated us on/offered their congratulations on the launch of this center。And they also make it clear that they will support 可以简洁处理为 vowed their support，接前一句。

(3) 译员多次使用 we plan that，可以改成 we plan to...

(4) "激光和汽车产业里边的应用相结合"可处理为 application of laser technology to automotive industry。

译员总反思：(1) 听说协调还需继续提升，偶尔还是会出现嘴瓢、词不达意的情况，而且发布节奏不够均匀，句子内停顿过多过长。

(2) 脱壳不够，很多表达还是在机械对应原文，要在平时的练习中有意识地纠正，以便下一次同传时能瞬间反应出脱壳程度更高的说法。

(3) 信息列举的部分翻得不好，没跟上、没翻全、翻得不准确，在 EVS 的调整上不够灵活。针对这一部分，策略是先翻信息密集列举的部分，再讲句子的其他内容，这点要在接下来的练习中巩固。

(4) 代词过度使用，应该点明代词的指代对象。

教师总点评：(1) 译员有自己优势，如反应快，表达较为伶俐，语言资源较为丰富，但纵向的信息加工稍弱，因此转换与表达总体要好于听辨理解，建议在同传中加强听辨，尤其是命题信息的深度理解与脱壳，同时加强命题信息成分（专有名词、术语与列举等）的横向加工训练，熟练掌握横向加工策略，提升加工速度，做好纵向加工和横向加工的自由切换。

（2）多处开口点选择不恰当，导致译语不流利、节奏不匀称，需要加强顺句驱动、EVS动态调节与策略运用训练。

（3）同传要更严谨，更严格要求自己的同传加工颗粒度与同传内容、语言和发布质量，加强译语监管。

（4）加强行业领域与政策性话语的双语语块学习，提升译语准确性、地道性。

（5）态度上要更端正，做足译前准备，尤其是专有名词部分。

剩余部分：

源语：那么第四个呢，就是开展高层的互访，那么我们通过这个亚欧激光应用中心以及各地的分中心呢，将对德国、意大利、阿尔巴尼亚、泰国和澳大利亚等国家，针对激光显示、激光医疗、纳米金刚石、光通信以及智能汽车的领域进行广泛的技术交流和考察，同时呢邀请各国参加亚欧激光应用中心的国际会议。目标呢就是通过了解和沟通，深入地推动激光技术的发展，探讨呢多种的可能的合作形式和模式，为引进和输出激光技术做好基础和准备。

参考译语：Fourth, we will conduct high-level exchanges. We will leverage the Laser Technology Sub-center and its various branches. Germany, Italy, Albania, Thailand, and Australia, among other countries, will be visited. Laser display, laser medicine, nanodiamonds, optical communication, and intelligent vehicles are fields for extensive technical exchanges and investigations. Besides, these countries will be invited to participate in the international conference of the Laser Technology Sub-center. By deepening our understanding and communication, we aim to drive the growth of laser technology, and explore diverse possibilities for cooperation. Through these efforts we can be prepared for importing and exporting laser technology.

源语：那么首先呢我对激光应用领域做一个简短的介绍。那么激光应用领域呢大家可以看到，就是它在军用和民用上都有非常广泛的用途。那么在我国呢共有五个国家级的激光技术研究中心，有十多个研究机构。那么在这个里面呢光电研究院作为五个光机所的总体院，是具有非常突出的优势的。并且呢光电院呢它形成了产品定型和一定的生产规模。那么每年呢激光应用领域，它的产品和相关的服务，整个的市场产值高达上万亿。那么在这个领域内呢国际需求和合作也是非常旺盛的。那么南美、中东、亚洲和亚太的国家对激光技术的需求非常旺盛，那么在光通信、材料、检测、医疗美容等领域也有非常大的市场潜力。

参考译语：First, let me give you a brief overview of the fields in which lasers are applied. As you can see, in both military and civilian fields lasers have a wide range of applications. China has five national-level laser technology research centers and over ten research institutions. Among them, the Academy of Optoelectronics is the leading one among the five Institutes of Optics and Precision Mechanics with outstanding advantages. The Academy of Optoelectronics has developed product specifications and achieved a certain production scale. Ever year laser applications generate a market worth trillions of RMB. This is a field in which international demand and cooperation are very strong. Countries in South America, the Middle East, Asia, and the Asia-Pacific region have very strong demand for laser technology. Optical communication, materials, detection, and aesthetic medicine are fields with great market potential.

源语：但是呢这个领域具有以下几个特点，那么第一呢就是整体的研发水平参差不齐，那么亟待呢就是通过开展多方的合作来达成技术的升级。第二呢在"一带一路"的战略的引导下呢我们也希望通过激光应用中心，能够实现中国的激光技术的走出去的战略，并且呢搭建国际合作的桥梁，促进激光产业的交流合作与发展。那么现在呢在国际上慕尼黑光电展是全球最大的光电展，那么我们光电研究院呢在每年的9月份到11月份之间，都会在深圳呢主办一个深圳光电展。那么我们这次呢借由承接亚欧科技创新中心激光应用分中心的机会呢，我们也希望在原来的展会的基础上，进一步扩大我们展会的规模，做成一个全球的光电博览会。今天我们院长到会的时候呢也对相关的工作做了具体的部署。

参考译语：This field has some distinctive features. First, the overall research and development performance varies greatly, and cooperation is necessary for the technological upgrading. Second, under the guidance of the Belt and Road Initiative, through the the Laser Technology Sub-center, we aim to expand China's laser technology globally, and build a platform for international cooperation to advance the development of the laser industry. Currently, Laser World of Photonics Munich is the world's largest of this kind. Every year from September to November, our Academy hosts in Shenzhen the International Optoelectronics Exhibition. We would take the opportunity of hosting the Laser Technology Sub-center of CCSTI to expand our exhibition and turn it into a global optoelectronics expo. During today's meeting, our Academy's director has outlined specific plans for that.

源语：那么简短地介绍一下光电研究院的基础，那么光电研究院呢在航空航天应用科技以及光电工程领域呢都开展了非常多的工作。那么咱们的海南卫星发射场里面的指控系统，还有海军司令部的指控系统，是光电院的激光投影保证了咱们军队以及航天工程的圆满执行和完成。那么我们光电院呢还是定量遥感信息的重点实验室，以及并且呢我们在青岛还建立了光电研究院的分支机构。那么这是我们跟立陶宛和德国的夫琅和费激光研究所，以及德国的亥姆霍兹卡尔斯鲁厄研究中心,即将展开在激光制造和皮秒激光以及飞秒激光半导体芯片方面的这个研究工作。那么我们现在呢在与泰国的合作当中,把中国的北斗卫星技术和多光谱相机用于泰国的农业。那么我们和白俄和俄罗斯都进行了相关的激光器件和产品的共同开发。俄罗斯的科学院呢,我们在等离子物理以及光学声呐等方面也开展了合作和技术交流。并且呢我们和白俄罗斯的激光信息技术公司呢开展了多项,比如说OPO激光器的联合开发。

参考译语:Now let me briefly introduce you about our Academy. In aerospace technology and optoelectronic engineering we have carried out a lot of work. The control system in Hainan Satellite Launch Center and that in the Navy Command use the laser projection technology developed by our Academy, which has ensured the success of military and aerospace missions. The Academy also boasts a key laboratory for quantitative remote sensing information. And we have set up a branch in Qingdao. With Lithuania's counterpart, and Germany's Fraunhofer Institute for Laser Technology and Helmholtz Association Karlsruhe Institute of Technology, we will work on picosecond lasers, femtosecond lasers, and semiconductor chips. Currently, we are working with Thailand to apply China's Beidou satellite technology and multispectral cameras to Thailand's agriculture. With Belarus and Russia we have jointly developed laser devices and products. With the Russian Academy of Sciences we have collaborated and exchanged technology in plasma physics and optical sonar. Furthermore, with Belarusian laser information technology company we have jointly developed projects, such as OPO laser development.

源语:那么总体目标呢就是我们在科技部和北京市科委的指导下,坚持平台开放、资源共享的原则,汇集一流人才,创造一流的科研条件,达到一流的管理水平。那么努力呢形成核心的产业技术集群。那么近期的工作刚才已经向各位专家进行了汇报,那么这个呢是我们激光应用中心的一个初步的组织架构。那么是在理事会领导下的秘书处负责制。那么我们下设呢四个机构，一个是标准化委员会，这个是我们是SSTC487标委会。那么我们光电院呢还有一个质量监督检验中心，那么也在今年通过了认监委的认证。那么第三个呢就是我们会成立一个专门的科技交流的工作委员会，来推动和上述合作单位和国家的合作。那么在这里呢我也是特别感谢北京市科委，然后咱们亚欧科技创新中心，其实已经搭建了一个非常好的国际交流的平台，那么我们下一步呢也要继续，然后依托咱们这个亚欧科技创新中心呢去开展国际合作。

参考译语：With guidance from the Ministry of Science and Technology and the Beijing Municipal Science and Technology Commission, we aim to maintain an open platform and shared resources, attract top talent, create world-class research environment, and achieve exceptional management standards. By doing this, we aim to form a core industrial technology cluster. These work plans have been presented before. This shows the organizational structure of the Laser Technology Sub-center, which operates under the leadership of the Council and the Secretariat. We have four subordinate organizations: first the Standardization Committee, which is the SSTC487 Standard Committee; second, the Quality Supervision and Inspection Center, which has been certified by the Certification and Accreditation Administration of China this year; third, a specialized Technology Exchange Working Committee, which will promote cooperation with our partners and relevant countries. We are particularly grateful to the Beijing Municipal Science and Technology Commission and the ASEM Cooperation Centre for Science Technology and Innovation for providing an exceptional international exchange platform. Going forward, we will continue to utilize the cooperation center to further international cooperation.

会议：车路协同自动驾驶论坛，主旨演讲：新一代车路协同技术及展望，北京航空航天大学教授

18A：

源语：尊敬的各位同仁，各位专家，大家下午好！在学校里面这个时段讲课是需要勇气的，因为都困了，或者到下午这个时段疲了，我试着把它讲下去。今天是应冉教授的邀请，讲一下车路协同这个概念，就刚才赵校长介绍的时候，实际上中国的车路协同在2009年我们在写"'十二五'交通科技发展规划战略"的时候，当时我们在专家组里是第一次提出来的。所以大家看到在2011年2月份的话，中国启动了一个国家的863计划，叫智能车路协同关键技术研究。当时也是清华、北航很多单位联合起来来做这个项目。所以那个时候我们就开始从国家的层面来推车路协同工作，实际上这项工作在国际上也是非常瞩目的。我们从美国的V2I到Connected Vehicle一些项目，也都是力主推动车路协同的。所以从整个的发展维度上看，实际上就是无外乎在整个交通系统当中，人和车之间是高度耦合的，车跟车之间也是高度耦合的。那么车跟路之间又是高度耦合的，所以这是一个复杂的信息物理系统，特别复杂。

译语：Dear colleagues, uh, distinguished experts, Good afternoon. It takes courage for one to teach at such a time in university, because everybody is getting drowsy. I will try my best to get you interested. At the invitation of professor Ran, I will speak about CVIS. As you have heard, CVIS has already been brought up uh at our expert panel at the 12th 5 year plan for scientific development. The nation launched a 863 project for key technologies which also involved uh Tsinghua University. We started our work back then. This project caught worldwide attention from artificial intelligence to connected vehicle. A lot of projects all feature CVIS. From the external environment of vehicles, both uh there is there are high integrations between uh CT, uh V2V, V2P and V2T.

教师点评：（1）"在学校里面……"属于会议常用语，可以把信息表达得更加明晰，如 It can be quite challenging to speak after lunch, as it's often difficult to keep you alert and engaged during this time. 类似的会议用语还有"我是午饭前最后一个发言人，所以我尽量讲简短点" I am standing between you and lunch so I will be brief.

（2）"中国的车路协同在 2009 年……"这句的困扰点主要有两个，一个是谓语"提出"前存在比较长的状语，另外一个是较长的专有名词"'十二五'交通科技发展规划战略"。译员采用了预测策略，将"提出"提前译出，这是可取的，问题是随后未能及时顺句快速对译出专有名词，不仅导致记忆饱和，翻译不准确，还导致精力和时间消耗过多，EVS 过长，影响接下来几句的处理。这句有两种处理方式：一是预测＋顺句，即 China's CVIS was first proposed in 2009 when we were drafting the 12th 5-year plan for Transportation science and technology development；二是断句＋顺句，即 as for China's CVIS, in 2009 when....we proposed the concept. 需要反复强调的是，对于学术、技术话语，术语、专有名词或列举的部分，需要采用横向加工，及时快速对译，不建议采用纵向深加工，进行等待、脱壳和句子重组等。

（3）"中国启动了一个国家的 863 计划，叫智能车路协同关键技术研究"可以处理为 China launched a 863 program project to research key technologies for CVIS。口译中，在译前未能精确准备的情况下，专有名词和固定语块建议模糊处理，传达基本意思即可，比如某书名、论文名、项目名等，不建议处理为 titled 之类，某人说过的话，也不宜处理为 quote someone as saying... 或 someone said... 可以表达为 talked about...said something to the effect that...

（4）"我们就开始从国家的层面来推车路协同工作"可以处理为 Then the nationwide efforts on CVIS began.

（5）接下来有两处"陷阱"，"这项工作"不是指这项具体研究项目，是指 CVIS 这一领域，随后的"我们"只是汉语口语的习惯性表达，不是实指，不应处理为 we，直接从"美国的 V2I"开始译。译员将 V2I 理解为 AI，可能是译前准备不充分，也可能是因为 EVS 有些长，记忆出现问题所致。

（6）本段最后一句的处理，问题还是在加工策略上，译员应该采用横向加工，及时快速顺句对译，而非纵向加工，试图进行深度理解、脱壳、概括、重组等。似乎也与译员译前准备不充分有关。这句可以处理为：Pedestrians and vehicles are highly coupled/interconnected, so are vehicles and vehicles, vehicles and roads, creating/resulting in a very complex cyber-physical system.

源语：那么在这个情况下，就是说我们想到在这样的系统里让它高效地安全地运行，能不能通过车路之间的信息交互这样的手段来实现协同管理，这是最初的初衷。所以从2011年开始，我们国家推动这事以后，到目前为止，实际上是大概在前年吧，工信部又推动了叫"基于宽带移动互联网的智能汽车和智能交通应用示范"，也选择了五个应用示范的城市，还有两个示范区，还有一个试点示范的一个国际合作的一个项目。那么这些都是国家在推这方面的事情。

译语：To effective, efficiently and safely operate in such a network we started on our work. Since we started our project in January we have done a lot already. Uh the year before the last the Ministry of Industry and Internet Information Technology uh also launched a project of CVIS and ICV-based on platform in it.

教师点评：这段的问题同前面，译员纵向加工模式导致整体同传节奏有些滞后，造成数字、专有名词、列举等错译、漏译等。一方面译前准备非常重要，包括"工信部"等在内的专有名词，在PPT中都有，即便没有，发言中常提到的部委的英文名称的全称和简称，应该做到脱口而出。

源语：实际上从亦庄，离我们最近这个，就是北京的亦庄，搞开放环境下的车路协同的这种示范，现在是总面积是，总长度是十公里的道路，有七个路口，这里面有一些公交专用道，也有一些潮汐车道。同时在信号灯，在一些路侧设施上做了很多这样的改造，包括我们的LTE-V

的基站、Wi-Fi，包括路侧的设备，DSRC 也包括一些视频，还有信号灯的联网，以及一些网联车，这些都做了一些很好的基础性改造，目的是通过这样的一个示范来推动在车路协同的维度下驾驶的诱导、盲区的预警，包括信号的协调、公交的优先，这些车路协同的典型的示范和测试。

译语：There are there were also a number of other national pilot zones. Yizhuang in Beijing is also a pilot zone in terms of open roads. It was the first time in our country. There are a total of seven crossroads featuring uh bus lanes and also reversible lanes. We did a lot of transformations including LTE uh basis traffic lights uh sign boards and the connected uh sign boards and traffic lights. There were a lot of good practices to help give more guidance to driving to blind spot alert traffic coordination and bus priorities.

教师点评：译员的问题同前。术语、专有名词等，要进行充分译前准备；开始翻译前，进行双语快速对译热身，提高产出准确性、流利性和效率。"北京的亦庄，搞开放环境……也有一些潮汐车道"要快速顺句对译，Yizhuang in Beijing is piloting a CVIS project in open environment, on a 10-kilometer road with 7 crossroads, bus lanes and tidal lanes。后面部分术语更多，是非常典型的技术性话语，缩短 EVS，快速对译（包括音译、重复等），保证术语和专有名词准确性，简化语言表达是基本策略。

剩余部分：（囿于篇幅，加之同传策略主要为横向加工，仅提供部分转写源语和译语供参考）

源语：实际上在这个过程当中，刚才克强教授也讲到，很多单位都参与了这些示范，也有相关的一些装置和设备在示范运行当中来做。所以我们北航那边，我们也是在 2011 年在北京率先拿到了一个车路协同的重点实验室。我们也在亦庄那边做了很多的自己研发设备的测试和示范。同时刚才也讲了，发达国家其实做得也挺早的，我们在欧盟来看的话，它 2013—2017 年的 ITS 行动方案当中，也把车路协同作为一个重点。日本和美国都有相应的一些推进计划，其实昨天王笑京教授也讲了，日本做得是比较好的，也比较高效的。那么综合起来看，实际上我们这些面向应用场景的车路协同的示范推动，应该说在跟国际上在很大维度上都是同步在推进相关的工作。

参考译语：As Professor Li Keqiang mentioned earlier, many organizations joined these demo projects, and some equipment and devices were involved in the process. In 2011, Beihang University became the first in Beijing to establish a key laboratory for CVIS. In Yizhuang there are also numerous tests and demos of independently developed equipment. As mentioned earlier, developed countries have been working on this for some time. European Union's ITS Action Plan 2013 to 2017 identified CVIS as a key focus. Japan and the United States also have some plans on this, and as Professor Wang Xiaojing mentioned yesterday, Japan has been quite effective and efficient in this area. Overall, the practical scenario-oriented demos we have been doing are basically keeping pace with international efforts.

源语：为什么叫新一代车路协同，或者是叫车路协同的另外一个阶段，我就总结一下，我们过去做车路协同，可能大家更加关注于车车、车路信息的交互，更加关注于车车、车路协同安全或者它的一些预警，或者一些辅助的预警，更加关注车跟信号灯之间的这些协调控制，也就是车、车队跟信号灯之间的协调管理。所以在这个层面上来讲，实际上它更加依靠的是 DSRC、蜂窝这样为代表的一些 V2V、V2I 的一些信息交互技术。一会儿陈总还要讲 5G 和信息交互的事儿。实际上更加令大家关注的是人车路的系统安全的模式，更加关注从被动的一些危险辨识，向辅助安全的预警这方面的转变。我们觉得这样的一个车路协同体系，它是基于现状的，是基于目前已有的车辆的水平，道路状态的水平的。那么这样的体系走到现在，走到了基于场景的一些示范推动,也就是说来把车路协同这个事情通过关键技术的研发突破到落地,那么走到了现在这个阶段,我们觉得它已经完成了这个段的历史使命。

参考译语:Why is it called the new generation CVIS, or CVIS at a new stage? Let me summarize. The past CVIS prioritized the V2V and V2I interaction. It focused more on V2V and V2I safety and the warning system involved. And it looked more at the coordination and control between vehicles, vehicle fleet and traffic signals. This coordination relied more on DSRC, cellular technology, among other V2V and V2I information exchange technologies. Later, Mr. Chen will talk about 5G and information exchange. In fact, people are more concerned about human-vehicle-road system security, and going from passive danger identification to auxiliary safety warnings. We believe that CVIS at this stage is based on the current vehicle performance and road conditions. This system is currently on the stage of scenario-oriented demos. So CVIS, with some key technological breakthroughs, has become a reality. We can say that it has fulfilled its historical mission.

源语:那么从下一步看,实际上我们目前车路协同阶段,它还有它的局限性。刚才讲到了,一个是从车的角度来说,是基于信息化辅助的一些人工决策操控的,由人工来决策操控的,信息化是一种辅助的手段。从设施的角度,基础设施和交通工程的角度来说,现在很多的测试都局限在单一的交叉路口,做一些协同的测试和管理。那么从通信的角度来说,大家尝试着用 DSRC 在交叉口上做布局,多模通信做主导的这么一个模式来推进。那么从局限性上来看,为了满足未来的这种交通出行的智能化、运行管控的全局化和信息服务的泛在化,那它肯定是有差距的。那么从这个角度来说,我们觉得 1.0 的版本需要更新了。

译语:Looking forward, we can see that the current stage of CVIS has its limitations. As mentioned earlier, from the vehicle perspective, it is based on information technology-assisted manual decision-making and control, with humans in charge and technology playing a supportive role. From the perspective of infrastructure and traffic engineering, many current tests are still limited to single intersections for cooperative testing and management. From the perspective of communication, we are using DSRC for the intersections with a multi-mode communication-led model. So the current system has its limitations. Looking forward, we need intelligent transportation with global operation control and ubiquitous information service. Therefore, we believe that the current version 1.0 needs to be updated.

源语：所以我们从学界上感觉到这是一个变革。那么从变革的维度来说，从局部的感知到单车的预警，将来我们一定要走向大范围的区域感知到系统的决策和管控。刚才讲到云控，云管云控，这都是系统级的一些控制和管理。所以现在很多车企在开发单车智能的时候，它也注意到了，包括昨天百度也在给很多专家发了聘书，搞了顾问，它也注意到要朝智能交通上走了，因为光有单车智能是不够的。所以我们讲局部的协同到区域的协同是一个明显的一个转段。那么从过去的信息化的辅助，人工决策到未来的半自动决策，甚至到将来的有条件的自动决策，再到完全的自动决策，这个肯定需要转段。所以我们感觉未来的这种交通信号的联控，路网的整个道路交通状态的云管云控以及自动驾驶汽车的协同、编队的管理，都是我们新一代车路协同的一个特点。

参考译语：So the academia recognizes this as a transformation. In this transformation, local perception and vehicle early warning will give way to a broader regional perception along with system decision-making and control. Earlier, we talked about cloud-based control and management, both of which operate at a system-level. Therefore, many automakers, while developing intelligent bicycles, have also noticed this shift. Yesterday Baidu brought on board a number of experts as consultants so as to move towards intelligent transportation recognizing that having intelligent bicycles alone is not enough. So we can see that the transition from local collaboration to regional collaboration is evident. The past information-assisted, human decision-making will transit to a future of semi-automatic decision-making, and conditional automatic decision-making, and ultimately fully automatic decision-making. Therefore we believe that the coordination of traffic signals, cloud-based management and control of the entire road network's traffic conditions, as well as the coordination and management of autonomous driving vehicles and fleets, are all features of our new generation CVIS.

源语：那么基于这特点，我们在这里就把车路协同的第二代的特征做了一下描述。我们认为第二代的车路协同，从载运工具的角度来说，它一定要具有广域的感知能力和人机共驾的这样系统，至少要是L3级的这样的智能汽车，是吧，然后具备人和系统协同决策这样的一些功能。从基础设施的角度来说，这个不是讲要有三块云嘛，是吧？除了传统的基础设施之外，还要有中心云、边缘云、车云这几块云来协同进行管控。然后从管控的范围来讲，基础设施肯定是在单一路口的维度下更大范围的一个全局的优化和控制，这是它的一个特点。那么从通信角度来说，未来以LTE和5G为代表的一个主流通讯，加上在一些特定场合特定背景下的一些多模通信的结合，也是下一步通讯的一个特征。

参考译语：Having said that, let's move to the features of the second generation CVIS. In terms of vehicles, it will have broad-area perception capabilities and a human-machine co-driving system, and at least be equipped with L3 intelligent vehicle technology to enable collaborative decision-making between systems and humans. In regards to infrastructure, there will be three cloud components: the traditional infrastructure, along with the central cloud, edge cloud, and vehicle cloud, working together to enable coordination and control. In terms of infrastructure, there will be three clouds. Besides the traditional infrastructure, there will also be the central cloud, edge cloud, and vehicle cloud to enable the coordination and control. The infrastructure will go beyond individual intersections to optimize and control a broad area. In terms of communication, the future will be featuring LTE and 5G among other mainstream communication technologies, along with the scenario- and context-specific multi-mode communication.

会议：城市雨洪管理与景观水文国际研讨会，主旨演讲：智慧与现代科技结合治理城市内涝，华南理工大学教授

19A：

源语：非常荣幸能够参加清华和两个单位一块办的雨洪管理的国际会议，我觉得他们那个理念非常好，多个学科交叉，这是将来我们整个科研还有治理雨洪重要的方向。中国古代有许多防止城市内涝的经验，主要是规划建设和管理好城市水系。古城水系的排洪，河道的密度和行洪断面是两个重要的技术指标。古城水系调蓄能力是防止雨涝灾害的重要因素。明清紫禁城和赣州古城是两个防内涝的典范。那么我们现在城市内涝的主要原因是什么？可将古代的智慧与现代的科学技术结合起来，治理城市的内涝。我的一种想法是建立大、中、小三个排水系统的设想。

译语：It's an honor to be here at this event hosted by Tsinghua University. I think the cross-, uh, discipline research is a very good idea. That's what we should focus on in the future. In ancient China we have many experience to prevent urban waterlogging. It's mainly about planing, building and administering the water system well. Density of escape canal and flood cross section are two important technical indicators. The flow management and storage capacity of the canal are very important for preventing waterlogging in a city with. The Forbidden City in Ming and Qing

Dynasties and Ganzhou Ancient Cities are the two great examples. What causes flood in the cities? With ancient wisdom and modern technology we can build a large and middle and small drainage systems.

教师点评：(1) 第一句开场白的翻译存在语言问题，内容也不够准确，信息不够明晰、连贯，译员要熟知会议背景信息，具有会议情境和交际意识，当然，会议知识是需要逐步积累的。此处，发言人是想说这次会议体现了学科交叉，这也是未来各个领域科研以及雨洪管理领域科研的方向，可以处理为：This event demonstrates an inter-disciplinary approach, which is the direction for future research and the research in stormwater management.

(2) "中国古代有许多……"一般不建议处理为译员的状语+主谓的方式，直接处理为主谓 Ancient China had... 以节约时间和精力。

(3) 这一段的中后面，译员的 EVS 有些过长。学术、技术话语同传中，术语可能随时出现，译员需要保持警惕，保持较短 EVS，在预知术语或专有名词即将出现时，要进一步缩短 EVS，以便快速准确对译这些转瞬即忘的信息成分。因为译员在译"中国古代……"一句稍稍滞后，加上接下来有几个术语，导致译员未能理解或记忆"古城水系的排洪"（flood discharge/drainage），这一漏译影响了该句翻译的准确性、完整性。

(4) 译员将该段源语最后两句译为一句，可能是直接视译了 PPT 上的句子，这在一定程度上影响了源语意思的传达，没有传达出发言人提出设想这一意思。问题的根本原因应该是译员滞后。同传中，译员可能由于视译 PPT 而滞后，也可能因为滞后而视译 PPT，一般建议译员以听源语为主，PPT 内容供译前准备和译中参考。这两句可以处理为：we can combine ancient wisdom with modern technology to address waterlogging. To achieve this I propose building large, medium-sized and small drainage systems.

(5) 一小段译语中存在时态、主谓一致、单复数等多种语言问题。

源语：下面我们简单地介绍一下近年来频繁的城市内涝，这个大家已经比较熟悉就过一下。这是北京的特大的暴雨，就是 2012 年 7 月 21—22 号的，造成了比较重大的损失。这个 07 年西安内涝，11 年 6 月 19 号，武汉的雨洪内涝。这是上海的，13 年的。这是广州的，这是南京、深圳、汕头、浙江的宁波余姚。那么解决城市雨洪引起的内涝灾害，已成为城市建设和管理的当务之急。为什么我们的现代城市这么脆弱，一场暴雨就引发一系列灾害，造成严重的损失。为什么明清紫禁城建成至今已经近 600 年，从来没有暴雨后的洪涝灾害出现，为什么在近年许多城市暴雨后出现洪涝灾害的时候，保有宋代排水系统福寿沟的赣州城却平安无事。那么中国古城在排水和防涝上有什么好的经验？能否将古代的智慧和现代的科学技术结合起来，治理好城市内涝，这是我一个想法。

译语：Next we will briefly introduce the frequent urban waterlogging in recent years. I will be brief in this part. This is the heavy rainstorm in Beijing which happened in July the 21st to 22nd 2012. This is the waterlogging in Xi'an in 2007. And this is the 2011 waterlogging in Wuhan. This is what happened in Shanghai in 2013. And this is the rainstorm in Guangzhou in 2012. And Nanjing, Shenzhen, Shantou, Yubo Yuyao also suffered from heavy rain. And to solve the waterlogging problem has become a priority for city management and construction. Why does our urban city become so fragile? A heavy rain can cause so many disasters and loss. And Forbidden Cities in the Ming and Qing Dynasty have been built for 600 years but haven't seen any rainstorm or waterlogging disasters. Why there are so many cities suffering from the waterlogging disasters? But the Ganzhou city are is safe from all the disasters. What are the experience of the ancient cities? How can we combine ancient wisdoms and modern technology to treat urban waterlogging?

教师点评：（1）"我们简单介绍"显然是表达不当，可能是"我们简单看一下"和"我简单介绍"的杂糅，译员要加强源语信息听辨和译语表达监控。

（2）发言人对着图片、照片、表格等做介绍时，译员可根据同传 EVS 情况，有意识地添加 this picture shows 等，如果一页上有多个图、表，译员需要在译语中具体定位某个图、表在 PPT 中的位置。

（3）介绍几个地方内涝部分，时间、地名出现一定的错译、漏译，也有语言错误，原因应该还是 EVS 过长，译语有些冗余，消耗了时间。译员不用每次都说 this is... 而直接用"表格法"，提及时间、地点等即可。

（4）Why does our urban city become so fragile? urban city 应为 modern cities，表达可以更简洁，why are modern cities so fragile?

（5）"宋代排水系统福寿沟的"漏译，此处可以顺句处理为 Song Dynasty's Fushou canal/drainage system in ancient Ganzhou made the city safe；同样由于滞后（滞后的原因之一是译员语言冗余，safe 足够，不需要再说 from all the disasters），随后的"排水和防涝"漏译。

（6）同前面，单复数问题较为凸显，如 Forbidden Cities, Ganzhou city are, what are the experience，wisdoms 等。

源语：第二个，中国古城避免内涝的智慧，营建和管理好古城的水系。这是我们国内发现的最早的一个古城，就是湖南澧县城头山古城，距今有 6000 年的历史，这个古城是个圆形，它城墙的外面有一圈护城河，这是很重要的古城水系的组成部分。中国古城的水系有环城的壕池和城内外河渠湖池组成，具有多种功能，被誉为城市之血脉，有十大功用，包括供水、交通运输、溉田、水产养殖、军事防御、排水排洪、调蓄洪水、防火、躲避风浪、造园绿化和水上娱乐、改善城市环境十大功用。其中排水排洪和调蓄洪水两大功用，对防止城市灾害、涝灾至关重要。

译语：Second, Chinese ancient cities' wisdom for avoiding waterlogging, managing and building uh water systems in the ancient city. This is an ancient city in Hunan Li county which has a history of 6000 years. There is a canal around the city which is a very important component of ancient Chinese cities. A Chinese ancient water system is composed of canals around this city which are deemed the blood stream of the city. They are used for supplying water, transportation, irrigation, military defense, entertainment, and other factors, among which draining water and preserving flood is very important for cities to prevent waterlogging and flooding.

教师点评：(1) 第一句，发言人在读PPT的标题，不建议译员直接对译，而是理清逻辑，明晰信息，处为 Ancient Chinese cities had the wisdom to avoid waterlogging by building and managing water systems，如果已经译出前半句才发现逻辑关系，可在后面加上 is reflected in，以便提高译语可用性。
(2) 这一段不少细节内容漏译，如"城头山""圆形""内外河渠湖池""水产养殖"等，原因同前，应该还是滞后较多引起，另外，发言内容基本都在PPT中，可见译员译前准备不够充分。

源语：中国古城水系营建和管理的历史经验，那么通过对汉长安城到明清北京城历代京都城市防洪的研究，有如下的重要发现：一个城市排洪河道密度和行洪断面是两个重要的技术指标，对防止内涝十分重要。第二个，城市水系的调蓄能力是城内防止雨涝之灾的重要因素。第三个，城市水系的管理十分重要。我们介绍一下明清紫禁城，紫禁城呢，这是它们那个图，它是从明永乐四年开始兴筑工程，十八年基本竣工，到现在已经快600年。它利用了元大都原来的排水系统，并做到多方面的改进。一个是开凿了绕城一圈、又宽又深的护城河筒子河，第二个是开挖了城内最大的供排水干渠内金水河。第三个是设置了多条排水干道和支沟，构成了排水的沟网。第四个是采用了巧妙的地面排水方法。第五个方面是排水系统的设计施工都很科学精确，管理非常妥善，因而坚固耐用。

译语：Now I have talked about the historical experience for building a city water systems in ancient times. I have researched the ancient cities and we have the following findings. The density of escape canal and flood cross sections are two important technical indicators for preventing a waterlogging in a city. And the preserving capability of the water systems are is important. And the management of city waters is also very important. Now let's look at the Forbidden City in the Ming and Qing Dynasty. The city was built in the Ming Dynasty and completed in 1420 with 600 years of history. It pre-, let's say the original drainage system in the Yuan Dynas- and Dynasty but had a wide and deep uh canals around the city and also built the biggest drainage channel. It has a very uh sophisticated drainage measures for the ground. And the design, the implemen-, the constructions are scientific and accurate so they will last for a long time.

教师点评：（1）第一句误译了，发言人再次阅读标题，译员要补充交际信息，处理为 Let's move to.../I will now talk about...

（2）后半部分由于术语和专有名词密集，译员准备不充分，加上双语对译慢，内容、语言和发音问题都较多。后半部分"它利用了元大都原来的排水系统……"可处理为：It utilized the original drainage system of the Yuan Dynasty's capital, and made various improvements. First, around the city, a wide and deep moat, Tongzi River, was dug. Second, within the city the largest water supply and drainage canal, Inner Jinshui River, was built. Third, multiple drainage canals and branches were built, forming a drainage network. Fourth, ingenious surface drainage methods were employed. Fifth, the design and construction of the drainage system were scientific and precise, and the management was good making the system durable.

教师总点评：译员纵向加工痕迹更明显，且译前准备不够充分，导致术语、专有名词等的对译速度稍慢、准确性不够高，听译与视译尚不够协调，译语表达不够简洁，上述因素又导致 EVS 过长，影响理解和记忆；同时译语存在较为明显单复数、主谓数的一致、搭配等语言问题，也存在一定的音韵问题。建议译员强化学术、技术话语的同传训练，细化译前准备，加强术语等的横向快速对译训练，简化译语表达，加强译语监听,努力减少基本语言问题。

剩余源语:(囿于篇幅,加之同传策略主要为横向加工、发言内容基本在 PPT 上,仅提供部分转写源语和译语供参考)

源语:这是筒子河。它宽 52 米,深 6 米。它是直来直上直下的一个石砌的河帮,河长约 3.8 公里,不仅有利于军事防御。我们看很多电影跟武打小说,就是说要过筒子河是非常困难不容易,很宽,52 米嘛是吧。而且它作为排水干渠和调蓄水库有两重作用,它的蓄水容量是 118 万立方米,即使紫禁城出现极端的大暴雨,就历史上最高的,日雨量达到 225 毫米,它的径流系数取 0.8、0.9。外面有洪水困城,它没法排到城外,但是把紫禁城内的径流全部泄入筒子河,也只是使筒子河的水位升高不到 1 米。那么这是内金水河,它是弯弯曲曲地流过了故宫。

参考译语: This is the Tongzi River. It is 52 meters wide and 6 meters deep. It has a straight stone embankment. The river is about 3.8 kilometers long, which is good for military defense. We often see in movies and martial arts novels that crossing the Tongzi River is extremely difficult because it is 52 meters wide. The river serves as both a drainage channel and water storage reservoir, with a storage capacity of 1.18 million cubic meters. Even during extreme downpours, such as the historically highest recorded daily rainfall of 225 millimeters, with a runoff coefficient of 0.8 to 0.9, the Tongzi River can play its role. As there is flooding outside the city walls, the water cannot be drained out of the city. Even if all the runoff within the Forbidden City is discharged into the Tongzi River, the water level only rises by less than one meter. This is the Inner Jinshui River, which meanders through the Forbidden City.

源语:明清紫禁城外绕筒子河,内贯内金水河,两河长度约 6 公里,那么河道密度达到什么程度呢?每平方公里 8.3 公里这么的一个指标,和宋代的水城苏州相媲美。明清紫禁城的排水系统以规划设计的科学完善，排水方法的巧妙有致，水系调蓄能力大，而成为我国古城排水系统最完美的典范。紫禁城内共有90多座院落，建筑密集，如果排水系统不好，一定会有雨潦致灾的记录。然而自1420年竣工，到现在已经600年，没有一次雨潦致灾的记录，排水系统一直沿用而有效。这不仅是中国城市建设史，也是世界城市建设史上的奇迹。

参考译语：The Forbidden City in the Ming and Qing dynasties was surrounded by the Tongzi River and connected to the Inner Jinshui River, with a total length of about 6 kilometers. The river density was as high as 8.3 kilometers per square kilometer, comparable to the water city of Suzhou in the Song dynasty. The drainage system of the Forbidden City was well designed and planned, with effective drainage approaches and a large water storage capacity. It has become the perfect example of ancient city drainage systems in China. Within the Forbidden City were over 90 courtyard houses, a poor drainage system would have caused rainfall disasters. However, since its completion in 1420, in the past 600 years, there has not been a single record of such a disaster and the drainage system has remained effective. In the history of either Chinese or international urban construction, it is a miracle.

源语：下面我们介绍一下赣州古城的福寿沟，这是清代的图。福寿沟我们一直还沿用着，尽管其中有一部分已经是废掉了，但大部分还在起作用。赣州城，这是赣州城的城墙和它的炮楼。赣州地处亚热带，降水强度大，那么如果我们不注意排水，它肯定会有雨潦之灾。那么宋代开始就是水利专家刘彝知赣州做了福、寿二沟，福、寿二沟到现在还在起作用，这是福寿沟的现在部分的情况。

译语：Now, let's move to the Fushou Canal in the ancient city of Ganzhou. This is a map from the Qing Dynasty. This canal is still in use. Though some parts of it have been abandoned, most of it is still functioning. This picture shows the city wall and cannon tower of ancient Ganzhou City. Ganzhou is located in the subtropical zone with heavy rainfall, and if the drainage doesn't work well, there will certainly be rainfall disasters. In the Song Dynasty, the hydraulic expert Liu Yi became the mayor of Ganzhou and built the Fushou Canal. The Fushou Canal is still functioning today, and this is how part of the Fushou Canal looks like today.

源语：当代城市暴雨后内涝的原因有多种，包括城市建设挤占河道、行洪河道，使江河洪水位升高，等等。填占河湖的水体、洼地，使城市水系缺少调蓄能力。还有都市化洪水效应加重了内涝，海平面上升使排水困难，等等。还有土地开发忽视排洪防洪排涝工程的建设，增加了洪涝风险。超量开采地下水使地面沉降。还有现代化城市在水患面前变得更脆弱，灾害更加严重。还有北京城市内涝与排水管道断面沉积物多影响排水有关，这些都反映出城市排水设计和管理的弊病。

参考译语：As for the reasons for urban waterlogging, they include urban development encroaching upon flood discharge channels by urban development, raising the flood level of rivers and lakes. Filling water bodies and low-lying areas reduces the storage capacity of urban water systems. Additionally, urbanization has worsened flooding and waterlogging, and rising sea levels have made drainage more difficult. Also during land development, absence of flood control and drainage projects has increased flooding risk. Over-extraction of groundwater has caused land subsidence. Furthermore, modern cities have become more vulnerable to water disasters. And Beijing's waterlogging is linked to the accumulation of sediment in drainage pipes. All these problems point to the inadequacies of urban drainage design and management.

源语：那么下面我们把对于古代智慧和现代科技结合治理城市内涝的对策介绍一下。现在我们城市排水有什么困境呢？包括城市现有的水系消失，原有的水系消失或者残缺不全，市政排水管网取代了城市水系，排水管网的标准普遍偏低，更不具有调蓄能力，因此暴雨后常常出现内涝。还有一个都市化洪水效应，增加了排水负担，使内涝更为严重。

参考译语：Now, let's see how we can combine ancient wisdom with modern technology to address urban waterlogging. Currently, urban drainage system faces a number of challenges, including the loss of existing water systems, total or partial loss of original water systems. Also municipal drainage networks have replaced urban water systems and the drainage networks are generally of low standard and often lack storage capacity. As a result, heavy rainfall often leads to waterlogging. Second, the urbanization exacerbates flooding, adding pressure to drainage systems and worsening waterlogging.

源语：第三个方面，假如我们想借鉴国外的巴黎、伦敦、东京等城市的地下排水隧道、大型地下蓄水池的做法，需要城市一次投入相当规模的财力和物力，对已经形成规模的建成区、老城区，那么地下的管线非常多，你要做这样的一个隧道，即使你有钱，难度也是非常大的。那么这是巴黎的地下水道的管网，这是巴黎的下水道，这是巴黎的下水道溢流的堰室。东京的下水道也是很巨大的规模，把上面的雨洪统统地排到地下的大的管道，花费的钱财是非常巨大的。

译语：Third, if we borrow the practices of cities like Paris, London, and Tokyo in building underground drainage tunnels and large underground water storage facilities, that would mean a significant investment of financial and material resources. For the established urban areas, underground pipelines are numerous, and building such tunnels if very challenging even with enough funding. This picture shows Paris' drainage pipeline network. This shows paris' sewers. This shows its overflow chambers. Tokyo's sewage system is similarly extensive, with all rainwater collected and drained into large underground pipes, requiring a great deal of financial investment.

源语：那么我们应该怎么办？我们就提出建立大、中、小三个层次的排水、城市防洪排蓄一体化的系统，一个是大排水系统，一个是中排水系统，一个是小排水系统。大排水系统，就是立足排蓄并举、排蓄互补的设计理念，构建以河、湖、渠、池等城市水系为主体，地下调蓄的隧道，调蓄池的设施为辅的城市排水大系统。

译语：So what is our solution? We propose establishing large, medium and small drainage systems, integrating flood prevention, drainage and storage. So we have large drainage system, medium and small ones. As for the large drainage system, it is based upon a design concept of drainage and storage combined and complementing each other. Urban water systems such as rivers, lakes, canals, and ponds will play the major role supplemented by underground storage tunnels and storage facilities, to create a large urban drainage system.

五、互动话语同传

互动话语的出现场合包括访谈、圆桌会、咨询会、头脑风暴、小组讨论及发言问答环节等。与致辞、演讲相比，互动话语的同传存在一定挑战，需要采取相应应对策略。

第一，话语内容与形式可预测性低，发言人、发言主题、发言内容、发言思路变换多，变换快，语言表达风格丰富多样，译员的听辨理解压力大，译员要加强源语信息听辨，确保理解优先。第二，由于即席交互性强，互动话语的语速常常较快，不同发言人的轮换快，译员需要保持较快的加工速度，且常常需要保持较短 EVS（问答环节的提问部分可以适当拉长），快速跟进发言，快速译出，多采用横向加工的方式进行翻译，多用简单清晰的词语和句子结构。译员 EVS、语速或风格等可据源语情形随时调节，要关注译语的可用性。第三，即兴发言往往口语特征强，用语不规范、形式不清晰、意思不明晰、思维混乱、语言啰唆反复等情形多，译员需要去伪存真（及时识别口头语、不当表达、未完成表达等），去粗取精（合并、压缩、概括啰唆冗余表达的意思），显化源语信息，确保源语简洁、清晰、高效。平时可以多训练找到在非常口语化的话语中快速搜寻、翻译命题的方法，并确保所译的命题语言衔接，信息连贯。第四，有时发言人切换太快，而译语滞后，听众在译语中听不出话轮，分不清译语在翻译哪个发言人的话。此时，译员可以在转向译另一个发言人时，稍稍改变语气语调，以提醒听众所译的发言来自不同的人。第五，在中外嘉宾互动时，中文与英文发言的切换可能特别频繁，译员需要及时切换译员机的中英文频道。第六，交际方对译员常常较为依赖，口译的质量与交际效果立竿见影，译员听不懂、译不出、表达不规范、不地道、信息不凸显等情形都可能导致听众听不懂，影响现场交流效果。译员在同传中，要注意观察听众表情、动作（如译语已经结束，但听众双手捂着同传接收机不愿放下），了解听众理解情况，以便变换表达，重复表达，加以解释，直到其理解。第七，在出现发言人未打开麦克风，未对着麦克风说话，多人同时说话，一人说完未关麦克风导致发言听不清等情形时，译员可在译语中及时提醒（可视现场情况用双语提醒），要突出自己的"翻译""interpreter"身份，避免用"我……"进行提醒。

建议同学多进行互动话语口译训练，对比英汉互动话语的平行语料或文本，体会英汉发言人表达思想观点的方式差异，训练"去粗取精，去伪存真"的信息加工能力，积累英汉互动话语的程式语和简洁用语的语块，培养用精简、清晰语言表达连贯信息的能力。

会议：以下源语节选自《航空大都市——我们未来的生活方式》新书首发暨《一起读书吧》系列节目启动仪式的对话环节。主持人为时任央视节目主持人崔先生，嘉宾包括《航空大都市》作者卡萨达先生、时任河南省人大常委会副主任张先生、北京航空航天大学经济管理学院教授张先生、《航空大都市》译者曹先生。同传是汉英双向，但此处仅点评汉英同传。

20A:

源语：崔：马上要请上的这位朋友是我的一位河南的朋友，铁杆朋友，他也是一位著名的节目主持人，但是大家都不知道。他的公开身份是河南省人大常委会副主任，今天他来跟我一起主持这个节目，我们欢迎他，张大卫先生，欢迎他。

译语：Cui: Now, I will invite a friend of mine from Henan province. He's also a famous anchor, but maybe you don't know that he has another identity. He is the vice chairman of Henan People's Congress. And today he will co-host with me in today's show. Welcome, Mr. Zhang Dawei.

教师点评：（1）"马上要请上"是指请上台，可用 we will invite... onto stage 或 we'll have... on stage。

（2）"节目主持人"建议用 TV host 而不是 anchor（新闻节目主持人）。

（3）"大家都不知道"指的应该是"节目主持人"这一点。

（4）"他的公开身份"不宜处理为 public identity，可直接处理为 He is the Vice Chairman of the Standing Committee in the Henan Provincial People's Congress. 此处源语语速不快，也可处理为 He holds the official position of/His official position is... 职务名在译前准备材料中有，嘉宾的名字、来自机构、职务等是译前准备最基本的内容，译员不该译错。

（5）welcome Mr. Zhang 是对张先生表示欢迎，此处主持人请观众一起欢迎，应该是 Let's welcome... 或者 please join me in welcoming ...

（6）该段中（中间和后面），译员 EVS 有些过长，译语滞后发言较多，以至于欢迎掌声响起后，译员还没译 welcome。互动话语中，尽量缩短 EVS，以保证互动交际效果，这一点在主持人逐一介绍嘉宾，嘉宾起立致谢等环节尤为重要。

（7）"铁杆朋友""著名节目主持人""公开身份"等都与主持人的幽默风格有关，后面还有很多此类表达。幽默是同传的难点，一方面因为同传时间压力大，幽默话语的双语转换困难，另一方面，由于文化和审美等差异，幽默话语即便译出，往往在译语文化中也很难收获源语中使用的效果。译员在译前准备阶段可以多向客户索要有关材料，现场译前多和主持人沟通，译中积极听辨、根据语境谨慎处理。互动话语同传中，一般以交际主题信息为主，话语风格信息的传达，要视具体语境、情境和译员状况而定。

源语：崔：大家好像不知道你以前主持过节目。

张：我小时候说过相声，就这么大历史，其他没主持过，真没主持过。

崔：拜过师吗？

张：无师自通啊，那时候也没电视，也没什么的。

崔：要说这个可能也能说一个小时，但是今天我们的主题是航空大都市，对这本书您看过吗？

张：这本书我属于那种先睹为快的人之一。

崔：就是还没出版，您就看了？

张：偷看的。

崔：看的盗版？

张：不是，我们翻译了，它这个翻译的手稿，需要有些人帮着看一看翻译怎么样，我属于这批。

译语：Cui: The audience didn't know you have been an anchor.

Zhang: I studied xiangsheng.

Cui: Do you have a teacher to learn this?

Zhang: No, I didn't have a teacher or materials like television shows.

Cui: But today our theme is aerotropolis. Do you read this book?

Zhang: I have read this before it's published.

Cui: The piracy?

Zhang: No, I have read the manuscript because they need someone to help them to examine the translation.

教师点评：(1) 这一节源语语速快，话轮转换频繁，译语内容忠实性较弱，语言问题较多，语法问题（如时态、搭配等）多，表达不地道。

源语并不难，时间压力下，译员的薄弱的英语基本功充分暴露。对于此类源语，译员应提高加工速度，抓关键信息译，以最简洁语言表达。如，第二句可简单处理为 I did crosstalk but have never hosted a program. 第四句可简单处理为 self-taught. 当然，这要靠译员的信息加工能力与英语资源丰富性、灵活性和可用性。有些同学平时接触较多的政治话语或行业话语，对于简洁生活用语不熟悉，资源不够。反之，也有些同学经常看美剧，较为正式的话语接触少。平时应多接触、多训练不同语级、语域的话语。

（2）同前面一节，译员的加工节奏不太合适，开口译的时间有些晚，EVS 有些过长。对话一快，译语就跟不上，影响交际效果。好在此处是两个中国人交流，交际双方不依赖口译，如果是中外交流，影响会很大。

（3）译员需要时刻听辨理解主题信息，同时加强自我监控，警惕一些中式玩笑话，因为这些话语可能不仅难以跨文化传递，难以起到效果，还可能引起负面效果。在此语境中，"偷看的""盗版"等明显是主持人在开玩笑，建议过滤不译或弱化或语义上行，以免引起外方误解。"偷看的"可以处理为 Yes（对问题的回答），"盗版"一句可以过滤不译或者译为 how。

（4）部分译语语调不合理，如 But today our theme is aerotropolis, I have read this before it's published 两句用了升调，而相邻处有问句，也是升调，前者升调的误用不利于听众的理解。

（5）话轮转换处缺少音韵提示，听众可能难以将话语与说话人对上。

（6）部分源语处理建议：

"要说这个可能也能说一个小时，但是今天我们的主题是航空大都市"
Without further ado, let's move to aerotropolis.

"这本书我属于那种先睹为快的人之一"
I was one of the first to read it/I was among the first readers.

"它这个翻译的手稿，需要有些人帮着看一看翻译怎么样，我属于这批。"
Its translation needs to be reviewed. I was among the reviewers.

源语：崔：今天的观众都是大学生，我给您出难题，三句话，把这本书说清楚，我来说，航空大都市……

张：我现在就开始说三句话，实际上让我说三条心得，这个我们从小学中学大学过来都是呢，这个什么主题思想啊、段落大意啊，这我们都经过训练是吧？这本书呢我觉着呢给我们开启了一扇窗户。第二呢向我们提供了一种强大的智慧的支撑。第三呢它是我们的一个美好的愿景，我再说第四，航空大都市的愿景最终可能最先在河南人手中把它变成现实。

崔：告诉您一个喜讯，也许是不太好的消息。这本书的翻译者和作者我们今天都请到了现场，他们会验证您说得对不对，来先看看他们是谁。

译语：Cui: Maybe you can use 3 sentences to describe this book, Aerotropolis.

Zhang: Three sentences to describe my ideas. We all studied in primary schools, secondary schools and we are good at describing the main ideas, sort of things. This book provides us a window. And second, it provides us a support in wisdom. And third, it is also our vision. But fourth, aerotropolis, this vision can be realized first in Henan province.

Cui: I want to tell you a good news, maybe not so good. The translator and author of this book are invited in today's show and they will know.

教师点评：（1）这一节的内容问题较前一节少（可能因为话轮少，语速慢），主要在"说三条心得""他们会验证您说得对不对"未译出，"But fourth"错译，但本节的语言问题仍然较多，语法问题包括 provides us 后面没有 with, a support, a good news 中不用冠词 a, the main ideas 不需要 the, invited in 应是 invited to，另外还有不地道表达，如 support in wisdom, I want to tell you a good news 等。这些问题凸显译员的英语基本功较弱。此外，同前，译语升调误用，因为语速快，有些译语听不清。整体产出速度仍然稍慢。

（2）"今天的观众都是大学生，我给您出难题"不太好处理，因为前后的逻辑和连贯性不清晰、不确定，说话人的意思有可能是：今天的听众是大学生，所以出个难点的问题，也有可能是：今天的听众都是学生，我们就像在学校一样，所以我要来考考你。在即兴讲话，尤其互动话语中，经常有此类表达，说话人觉得有内在关联，但是对于译员来说关联不明显，逻辑不清晰。译员常用的策略包括：不译，照字面译，脱壳或信息显化，但每种策略都有风险，不译可能遗漏发言人认为重要的内容，照着字面译，听众可能听不懂，译员如果自己进行脱壳或信息显化处理，也可能译错源语意思。这个问题主要是源语内容逐步展开、译员渐进式理解这一同传工作方式特征造成的。如果是重要信息，译员在听到后面突然明白源语逻辑后，也可以在后面译语中通过重复或植入，将源语信息表达出来。

（3）互动话语同传中，译语可以视语境尽量精简，用短句替代长句，用短语替代短句，如 The translator and author of this book are invited in today's show 可以简洁处理为 We have both the translator and author here, you can use 3 sentences to... 直接可以简略为 3 sentences to... 译员可以复听译语，或者将之转写为文本，看看能否删除一些语言形式，而不影响源语信息表达。

（4）部分源语处理建议：

"我给您出难题，三句话，把这本书说清楚"
I'll challenge you to summarize the book/tell us about the book in just three sentences. 或者 Just three sentences to tell us about the book.

"我现在就开始说三句话，实际上让我说三条心得"，OK, three sentences, or three key takeaways.

"给我们开启了一扇窗户" It opens up a window for us.

"向我们提供了一种强大的智慧的支撑" it is a powerful source of wisdom.

"告诉您一个喜讯" I have some good news.

"他们会验证您说得对不对" They will check if you are right.

20B：

源语：崔：曹先生是这本书的翻译者，您是怎么发现的这本书，现在书太多了？

曹：很早的时候应该说在八年前就跟卡萨达教授认识，因为那个时候我们需要做临空经济航空大都市，卡萨达教授呢是这方面的杰出代表，所以我们在网上发现了他。到 2007 年卡教授准备做这本书的时候，派了第二作者林赛，然后呢卡教授给我了一封 e-mail 说希望林赛到了中国，我能够接待他，介绍一下中国临空经济的发展。所以在 2007 年我就知道这本书是要出。

译语：Cui: Mr. Cao is the translator of this book. The microphone is not working. Mr. Cao is the au, the translator for this book. How did you discover this book, because there are so many book. And why did you decide to translate this book?

Cao: About 8 years ago, I met Professor Kasarda. And we're focusing on the topic of the civil aviation, aero-metropolis. And Professor Kasarda was the lead in this sector. And in 2017, when he decided to wrote this book, he sent me the e-mail that he wanted that when he arrive in China, I can be the receptor and also introduce him the China's civil aviation bases. So in 2017, I knew that I am can be the translator of this book.

教师点评：（1）内容和语法的问题都较多。内容方面，以下部分的译语不忠实，"跟卡萨达教授认识""需要做临空经济航空大都市""所以我们在网上发现了他""派了第二作者林赛，然后呢卡教授给我了一封 e-mail 说希望林赛到了中国""中国临空经济的发展""这本书是要出"。语言方面，语法错误比较多，如 so many book 应是 so many books, we're focusing 应是 we were focusing, lead 应是 leader, decided to wrote 应是 decided to write, when he arrive 应是 when he arrives, introduce him 应是 introduce him to, I can be 应是 I could be。表达方面，有一些修正、犹豫，有的地方重音不恰当，如 this book, arrive in China, (translator of) this book。此外，译员译前准备不足，航空大都市说成 aero-metropolis, 此后虽然发现这一问题，但是 aerotropolis 的读音存在问题。另外，"林赛"也没有准备到。但是也有值得肯定的地方，如"您是怎么发现的这本书，现在书太多了"，译员在译完该句字面意思后，又追加了 why did you decide to translate this book，较好地传递了源语信息。此外，译员的表达伶俐性较好。

（2）"我们需要做临空经济航空大都市"中的"做"内涵不清晰，可能是指郑州要发展临空经济，也可能是发言人要研究临空经济，此时可以语义上行模糊处理为 we need to work on aviation-based economy and aerotropolis。"卡教授给我了一封 e-mail 说希望林赛到了中国，我能够接待他，介绍一下中国临空经济的发展"：Professor Kasarda emailed me hoping that when Lindsay arrives in China, I can receive him and tell him about China's aviation-based economy.

源语：崔：现在您的问题和张先生的问题一样：三句话说说航空大都市说的是什么意思。
曹：航空大都市说明的是一种未来的新兴的城市形态。
崔：这是第一条？
曹：第一条。
崔：您不是说的是窗户的事吗？
张：我们每个人感受的不一样。对我们这些从事具体工作的人来讲呢，它给我们打开了一扇看世界的窗户。
曹：第二条它代表了这个时代城市的发展方向。第三条，这是中国未来城市发展的方向。

译语：Cui: And please, give us three sentences to brief on the aero-metropolis.
Cao: It is about the future city model.
Cui: And you're talking about the windows.
Zhang: Perhaps we have different feelings. For us in the government work, I think it opens a window for us.
Cao: And the second sentence from Mr. Cao is that this represents city development of this time. The third sentence is that this is the future urbanization for China.

教师点评：(1) 本节比较明显的问题是译员翻译不同发言人时，未以音韵提示做区分。不过，在翻译曹先生发言时，由于曹先生讲完第一句后，张先生插入了一句，译员加上了 from Mr. Cao，反映出不错的交际意识。互动话语同传中，为了听众理解便利，要谨慎使用代词，有时还会将一些代词处理为名词，明晰为所指的具体人或物名词，或者增加具体名词，如第一句的"您"可以明晰为 Mr. Cao，It is about 中的 it 明晰为 aerotropolis，you're talking 中的 you 可以明晰为 Mr. Zhang。另外，如果讨论嘉宾的姓或者头衔，译员需要在译语中通过称呼全名等方式加以区分。

(2) to brief on 应为 to give a brief on，这句也可以处理为 please describe aerotropolis in three sentences；"您不是说的是窗户的事吗"可以明晰为 But Mr. Zhang, you mentioned that aerotropolis opens a window；"对我们这些从事具体工作的人来讲呢"可以不译，张先生的两句话可以处理为 People have different feelings/perspectives and I believe it opens up a window；of this time 应为 of our time；最后一句译语不够准确，可译为 It is about/describes/points to the future of Chinese cities.

源语：崔：告诉你们二位一个不太好的消息——作者在这呢！现在我们要跟卡萨达先生对一下，您是这本书的作者，您这本书是介绍郑州的窗户吗？

Ka: yeah, includes Zhengzhou city as an emerging aerotropolis. Yes it does.

崔：我没听懂，我这没有声音。

张：他说这是窗户，是很多城市的窗户。

崔：我得听懂，要不然我不知道您说得对不对。

调试设备

崔：对不起，卡萨达先生，刚才张先生说您这本书《航空大都市》讲的是郑州的窗户，对吗？

Ka: It is about the window for cities around the world of which Zhengzhou is one that is quickly emerging as an important window on the world.

崔：您在这本书里提到"郑州"这两个字了吗？

Ka: yes.

崔：您是什么时候发现郑州有这个潜力？

Ka: About 4 years ago, I was doing research on the movement of business and industry around Asia and became clear that one of the magnets was Zhengzhou city. And then when Foxconn located here, it reinforced that idea that this was an emerging global center that was tying together supply chains. That's parts and components around the world, assembling products and then shipping them around the world. Today Zhengzhou accounts for almost 70% of the iPhone 5 production with the parts and components coming from 7 different countries, shipped to an 8th and then distributed through an ninth around the world. It is an exemplary globalization.

译语：Cui: And let me talk to you some bad news. The author is here. And Professor Kasarda, you're the author of Aero-metropolis. Is this book about the Henan window?

Ka：郑州确实是现在航空港发展的一个领先者。确实是如此。

Zhang: He said this is the window. And it is the window for many cities.

Cui: I need to understand what Professor Kasarda said.

Cui: Sorry, Professor Kasarda, Mr. Zhang said that your book Aerometrop, aerotropolis is about the window of zhengzhou.

Ka：是关于世界上所有城市的窗口，而郑州也是其中一个非常重要并且不断发展的窗口。

Cui: You mention zhengzhou in this book?

Ka：是的。

Cui: When did you discover that zhengzhou has such potential to be the aerotropolis?

Ka：译语略。

教师点评：(1) talk to you some bad news 应该是 tell you 或者 share with you some bad news；

"我们要跟卡萨达先生对一下"可译为 Let's check with Mr. Kasarda；后一句译语可改为 Is this book about the window of Henan？

(2)"这是窗户"中的"这"可以明晰为 aerotropolis，在互动话语中，this, it 等有时候不易理解。

(3) 主持人说自己听不到同传的声音，此类话语也需要翻译，以便其他交际参与者，或者让现场工作人员了解情况，协助解决相应问题。尤其是在中方组织的会议上，外方在发言中提及需要解决有关问题时，更需要翻译，有时候需要翻译几遍，直到现场有关人员响应。此处可以译为 I can not hear the translation（据笔者观察，很多会议口译用户更喜欢用 translation 而不是 interpretation）。

(4)"刚才张先生说您这本书《航空大都市》讲的是郑州的窗户，对吗？"这是个问句，需要加上 is that right？

(5) mention 应为 mentioned；When did you discover that zhengzhou has such potential to be the aerotropolis? 可以简洁处理为 When did you find zhengzhou's potential to be the aerotropolis? 或者 When did you discover zhengzhou as a potential aerotropolis?

(6) 在英汉发言人互动环节，双方高度依赖同传，对比源语和译语会发现，同学的同传速度明显低于译员现场的同传速度，因为一方提问后，译员还没翻译完，另一方已经开始回答，学员与职业译员往往在反应速度、加工效率和交际效率上有显著差异，这与子技能和策略不娴熟、子任务协调不娴熟、技能一体化不熟练、语言能力薄弱、领域知识与会议知识不足等都有关。

源语：崔：现在说专业的问题了。你们也听不到是吧？

张：这会儿听到了。说到 iPhone，郑州生产智能手机的70%。

崔：我们还是先说一点通俗的吧，要不然一开始我就没话说了。您是研究航空大都市的，卡萨达先生，有一个问题，您坐过飞机吗？

Ka: I flied quite a bit. Yes, You have to experience the aerotropolis to write about the aerotropolis, so I was in Zhengzhou city 3 times in the month of May.

崔：您坐过多少次飞机呢？

Ka: I have probably traveled thousands of times by plane.

崔：没有一个准确的数字吗？

Ka: I don't know the exact number but I can give you an idea of how many miles, 8 million miles.

崔：800万英里，这个太好算了，张先生，您给算算这是什么意思？

张：这个说明他的生活方式是在云端，on the cloud，他是属于在云端。

译语: Zhang: When we are talking about iPhone, it produced more than 70% of the iPhone across the world.

Cui: Let's be general. Professor Kasarda, you did research on the aerotropolis, and I have a question, have you ever traveled in airplane?

Ka：我已经坐过很多次飞机，并且我在5月份的时候来到过郑州3次。

Cui: How many times have you been travel in airplanes?

Ka：可能有数千次了吧。

Cui: Let's be specific, and also be exact.

Ka：我并不知道确切的数字，但是我可以告诉你大约我飞行了多少里程，大约有800万公里。

Cui：8 million miles, Mr. Zhang, please let's do the math.

Zhang: And this can show that Professor Kasarda is living on the cloud.

教师点评：（1）第一句未译，可能是因为该句与前面的英语源语叠加，这种情形在互动话语交流中比较多见，译员一般通过适当提高加工速度，权衡不同源语的信息价值，选择相对重要的信息译出。此处的第一句对交流的信息价值不高，可以不译。如果在互动中出现多人较长时间同时发言，译员可以适当提醒。

（2）互动话语同传中，译语的精简对于听众的理解和译员的精力节省都非常重要，第一句译语 When we are talking about iPhone, it produced

248

more than 70% of the iPhone across the world 有些烦琐，可能也是导致译员下一句译语 let's be general 不够忠实的原因。该句可以简洁处理为 When it comes to iPhones, it produces over 70% of them worldwide.

（3）"我们还是先说一点通俗的吧，要不然一开始我就没话说了。"的意思是先说点简单点的，不是宽泛的，可以处理为 let's start with something simpler/more straightforward.

（4）"您是研究航空大都市的，卡萨达先生，有一个问题，您坐过飞机吗？"处理这句译语时，译员语言不够简洁高效，导致滞后源语较多。此外，travelled in airplane 应为 travelled by airplane。此句可以简洁处理为 Mr. Kasarda, you research the aerotropolis/you are aerotropolis expert, then have you ever flown?

（5）译语 How many times have you been travel in airplanes? 再次出现语法错误，该句可处理为 how many times have you flown?

（6）"没有一个准确的数字吗？"可以处理为 (is there) an exact number? 这比译语 Let's be specific, and also be exact 简洁清晰高效。

（7）"800 万英里，这个太好算了，张先生，您给算算这是什么意思？"中，"这个太好算了"是主持人的幽默，"算"指的应该是 800 万英里相当于坐了多少次飞机，该句可以译为 How many trips/journeys would it take/are needed to reach 8 million miles, Mr. Zhang, can you do the simple math?

（8）Professor Kasarda is living on the cloud 可以改为 Professor Kasarda lives on the cloud.

教师总点评：两位译员虽然基本能够跟上源语，但是内容准确性和完整性、语言的正确性、地道性和可用性问题较多。互动话语同传对译员的语言能力和同传技能、策略的要求极高。互动话语语速快、内容和形式可预测性低、话轮转换频繁、口语特征强，交际方对口译高度依赖，给译员带来较大压力和挑战，要求译员反应速度快，信息听辨和加工效率高，外语资源足够丰富、可用，双语转换灵活高效，译语简洁清晰，交际性强。因此，互动话语同传的教学一般安排在同传教学的中后期，在学员基本掌握、能较为娴熟运用各种同传技能和策略之后进行。学员要进一步提升外语作为口译工作语言的能力，深度训练各种同传技能与策略，加强互动话语同传的刻意练习，了解英汉发言人在互动环节的思维差异与表达方式差异，积累相关简洁高效双语语块。

剩余源语较长，仅提供一小部分转写源语和汉英译语供参考。

崔：咱们要围着郑州走一圈是多少公里？

Cui: How many kilometers is it to go around Zhengzhou?

张：郑州啊，小学生的算数。我们现在城市建设规划区面积400平方公里，那就是400平方公里呢，那就是20×20公里，一个边就是20公里，400平方公里，20走一圈乘以4，是80公里。

Zhang: Simple math. Zhengzhou's planned development zone covers 400 square kilometers, that is, 20 by 20, 20 kilometers each side. If you go along all four sides, it would be 80 kilometers.

崔：卡萨达先生，您算算您飞行了8万公里，等于绕郑州多少圈？我就不信我谈不过理论家！

Cui: Mr. Kasarda, You've flown 800 miles（此处主持人说错数字了）, which is equivalent to how many circles around Zhengzhou? I will challenge Mr. Kasarda to do the math.

Ka: Maybe about 200 thousand.

崔：曹先生，您觉得写这样一本专著，这是不是一个基础条件？

Cui: Mr. Cao, do you think you need to frequently travel by air to write "Aerotropolis"?/do you think frequent air travel is a prerequisite for writing "Aerotropolis"?

曹：我觉得这是最基本的，只有真正去了解全球的航空大都市的发展的基本状况，因为在翻译这本书当中，卡萨达教授和林赛考查了20多个国家，这样才能掌握全球的航空大都市的发展的趋势。

Cao: Yes. True understand of the global development of aerotropolis is necessary so Professor Kasarda and Lindsay visited over 20 countries to grasp the trends of global aerotropolis.

崔：那在空中旅行实际上就成了卡萨达先生的生活方式,是不是这本书的很多内容,很多章节都是在空中完成的?

Cui: So air travel has become Mr. Kasarda's way of life. Is it true that many chapters of this book were completed in the air?

Ka: That's absolutely true. The plane is a great place to get some writing done.

崔：对,因为水平很高嘛,一出手就会水平很高。您怎么看您这种生活方式,就是经常在天上飞?

Cui: I agree. When you flied high your writing level would be high. How do you view your lifestyle, one involving frequent air travel?

Ka: Well sometimes I don't know exactly where I'm going but I know I'm going to get there fast.

崔：其实航空确实给我们带来了生活方式的变化,让我们一起看一看有什么样的变化。

Cui: Aviation has indeed changed our way of life. Let's see what changes it has brought about.

播放短片

崔：大家一定非常羡慕这种生活,而且很多朋友可能已经感受到了这种生活。这里面只有一处,我觉得描述得不对,就是说白天可以在世界上的一个地方,晚上回家就可以看"一起读书吧"。哪有人看这么严肃的节目,都是看选秀节目现在。但是这是我们对未来的幻想。我们可以不吃世界各地的新鲜水果,但是一定要看世界各地新出的书,丰富我们的头脑。刚才张先生和曹先生都用三句话来描述了这个航空大都市,卡萨达先生可能三句话不够,可能还不能空口说,那我们有一个模型图,您对照着这个模型图再给我们介绍一下您的这本专著吧。

Cui: Many people must envy this kind of lifestyle, and many friends may have already experienced it. There is only one thing that the video is not right about, that is during the day, you can be in any part of the world, and in the evening, you can go home and watch "Let's Read Together". Nobody watches such serious programs anymore and people watch talent shows nowadays. However, we still hope that people can read more. We can skip having fresh fruits from around the world, but we must read new books from around the world to broaden our minds. Earlier, Mr. Zhang and Mr. Cao described the aerotropolis in three sentences, but perhaps three sentences are not enough for Mr. Kasarda. Here we have a model chart. Mr. Kasarda, I would like you to introduce your book based on this model chart.

播放短片

崔：模型图在这儿，那个是虚晃一枪，您看看这张图，给我们做个讲解。

Cui: This is the model chart. Please tell us about the aerotoplis with this model chart.

Ka: Yes, as you can see on the model here in front of you, an aerotropolis is a city built around an airport. It is basically a city with runways and the businesses locate around the airport because it connects them quickly and efficiently to long distance, that is faraway customers, faraway suppliers, faraway enterprise partners, and these customers, these suppliers, these business partners, halfway around the world are as important to these businesses in or around the airport as they are in their own city, in their own region. So it is about global connectivity and it is about speed, and it is about the ability to compete. So I wouldn't take the three sentences and put them into three words to start our conversation. The aerotropolis is about speed. It's not the survival of the fittest, it's survival of the fastest. It's about agility, the ability to change, to adapt quickly to market changes, environmental changes, whatever that might be. And it's about connectivity both locally in the city where there could be connected but more importantly globally. So the aerodropolis is how speed, agility and connectivity lead to businesses forming around airports that makes them more competitive. It creates jobs, it attracts investment as we're seeing here in Zhengzhou creating a very powerful magnet to move the economy to the next higher level.

崔：我听了很多，我觉得他最关键词就是郑州，一直在说郑州，他对郑州情有独钟。您也觉得郑州有这样的优势？

Cui: I heard that Mr. Kasarda kept mentioning Zhengzhou and he has a special fondness for Zhengzhou. Mr. Zhang, do you also believe that Zhengzhou has such advantages?

张：我觉得卡萨达对郑州的爱，首先是郑州先爱上了卡萨达先生和他的理论，他这本书，否则的话呢，我们过去一句常话，没有无缘无故的爱，世界上有那么多大都市那么多地方发展航空，为什么他在很短的时间内来到郑州三次呢？我们郑州人啊通过看卡萨达的书爱上了这位非常睿智博学的教授对不对？

Zhang: I believe that Kasarda's love for Zhengzhou comes from the fact that Zhengzhou first embraced him and his theories. As the saying goes, there is no love without reason. With so many metropolises and places worldwide developing aviation, why did he visit Zhengzhou three times in such a short period? The people of Zhengzhou, by reading his book, have developed an admiration for the knowledgeable professor, haven't they?

崔：您也喜欢郑州是吗？

Cui: Mr. Kasarda, you also love Zhengzhou?

Ka: Absolutely!

崔：那您知道胡辣汤和铁棍山药吗？

Cui: Then do you know the local spicy and sour soup, and the Chinese yam?

Ka: I had the soup last night. It is a delicious soup.

……

张：我现在有一个基本判断，卡萨达先生正在坐飞机的时候思考来写第二本书——《航空大都市》，他第一本书的副标题呢叫我们未来的生活方式，他现在正在筹备的写第二本书，也就是航空大都市的第二册，叫郑州航空经济区的实践与趋势，我觉得我能猜得差不多，不信你试试，你问他。

Zhang: I feel that while Mr. Kasarda is on the plane, he is thinking of writing his second book on aerotropolis. The subtitle of his first book is *The Way We'll Live Next*. He is now planning to write the second book on aerotropolis with a title *Zhengzhou Aviation-based Economic Zone: Practices and Trends*. I believe I am quite close in my guess. You may check with him.

Ka: It sounds like a good title, Mr. Zhang.

张：我们还希望那个卡萨达先生多来几次，包括也多吃点我们的山药和胡辣汤，然后喝点我们的酒，然后和我们郑州人一起把这本航空大都市第二分册写好。

Zhang: We also hope that Mr. Kasarda can make more visits, enjoy more of our Chinese yam and spicy and sour soup, try some of our Chinese liquor, and work together with the people of Zhengzhou, to complete his second book.

崔：我其实我也赞成，我觉得如果他在这儿多喝点酒，他说不定就会说这本书是我写的呢。

Cui: I agree. I feel that if he drinks a bit more here, he might even say that this book was written by me.

张：你肯定有贡献。这里边呢一定会给您留个位置。所谓留个位置呢就是里边一定有一张图片，也就是今天咱们四个人这个图片，不是你一个人独享，四个人分享。

Zhang: Surely you will be recognized. He will make sure to include you in the book, perhaps by putting in the book a photo of the four of us from today.

崔：航空大都市。既然我们说到航空大都市，我觉得我们就没有必要从头到尾坐在演播室里，我提议咱们做个洲际旅行怎么样？都坐头等舱，咱仨不花钱，用他那张金卡。您累计的公里数是不是足够换我们机票了？

Cui: Since we are talking about aerotropolis, I don't think we need to sit in the studio the whole time. I suggest we go on an intercontinental trip. We could all fly first class, using his gold card? Do you have enough accumulated miles to cover our airfare?

Ka: we will take everybody with us.

崔：那我们现在就到了机场，我们听听广播，它往哪儿飞，我们就买哪儿的票。

Cui: We are now at the airport. Let's listen to the announcement and buy our ticket for the flight.

播放短片

崔：这里是阿姆斯特丹，我一下飞机就买了一束郁金香，这个郁金香需要一荷兰盾，相当于人民币3块7，为什么只有我买了呢？因为他们三个没带钱。您看到这个会不会非常亲切？

Cui: Here is Amsterdam. As soon as I got off the plane, I bought a bouquet of tulips, which cost one Dutch guilder, equivalent to 3.7 Chinese yuan. I bought it as the other three didn't bring any money. Mr. Kasarda, do you find the flower very familiar?

Ka: It is a beautiful flower.

崔：荷兰的郁金香，但是在全世界现在都可以轻易地看到它，这就是一个航空都市的一个魅力。曹先生可以跟我们分享一下。

Cui: Dutch tulip can now be seen all around the world. This is the beauty of an aerotropolis. Mr. Cao could share some thoughts with us.

曹：我觉得这一次能拿到这样的一朵鲜花，确实是卡萨达教授的这种理论的真正的实现，因为在两年前我也去过荷兰阿姆斯特丹机场去调研，它的郁金香应该是遍布了全球。实际上不仅是这样，我们更多地包括海鲜，包括电子产品、生物医药，正是因为有了这样一个全球化的生日，速度经济空间的到来，那么航空大都市的建设才使得我们生活会越来越好，才能使得我们在这个舞台上能够能见到这样一朵美丽的花朵。

Cao: I believe that having such a flower is truly the realization of Professor Kasarda's theory. Two years ago, I also visited Amsterdam Airport for research, and found their tulips were widely available worldwide. But it's not just tulips, but also seafood, electronics, and biopharmaceuticals. With globalization and economies of speed, building an aerotropolis leads to a better life for us and allows us to see on this stage such a beautiful flower.

六、政务话语同传

政务话语的出现场合包括由各级政府、事业单位、人民团体举办的，以政治、外交、经济、社会、文化、环境等治理为主题的会议，由上述机构举办的各种庆典、仪式，包括会议开幕式与闭幕式、签约仪式等，以及其他类型会议，如行业会议、学术会议的致辞环节与主旨报告环节。相对于商务话语、学术话语和互动话语，政务话语同传的主要挑战与应对策略如下：

第一，政务话语一般有演讲稿，讲稿字斟句酌，语言或华丽或凝练，内容程式化，书面结构多，信息密度高，译员应尽量提前拿到讲稿，在发言开始前不断获取更新讲稿，提前备好、更新译语，多阅读、视译译语，确保发音精准、表达流利。政务话语中的中国特色政治话语常常较多，涉及国家的价值观念、政治理论、政治制度、发展道路、内外政策等内容。这类话语既包括治理概念（名词词组）、治理举措（动词词组）和领导人讲话引语等，也包括各类专有名词，如人名、职务，机构名、会议（报告）、规划、倡议名，政策、法律、法规名、区域、地区名，项目、活动名等。对于这些特色政治话语的译语，译员要积累、使用由权威部门公布的译语版本。对于没有公布译语版本的表达，要注重以地道英语表达特色话语的意义和内涵。

第二，政务话语的发布一般以读稿为主，也可能读稿与脱稿交替，译员需要娴熟运用带稿同传能力，采用顺句驱动、断句顺接等策略，并且注意以下几点：（1）不可完全依赖稿件视译，需要积极听辨，以防发言人稿件与译员稿件存在差异，或者发言人脱稿即兴发挥；（2）加工节奏不可过快，避免过快阅读译语，超过源语发布节奏；（3）也不可过慢，视译加工往往比听译加工速度慢，译员要警惕译语过于滞后，遗漏源语信息，影响交际效果，如介绍嘉宾、嘉宾起立、观众鼓掌欢迎环节，译语滞后过多会严重影响交际效果。（4）充分忠实于源语，双语转换一般以横向对译为主，谨慎使用脱壳、压缩、概译等策略。

第三,政务话语同传一般在比较重大、庄重场合使用,对译语的语言与发布质量要求更高,译员应加强译语监管,避免语法错误,确保语级、语域契合场合要求,发布流利,语气、语调庄重,节奏平稳,音韵恰当。

> 会议:第二届"一带一路"国际合作高峰论坛"数字丝绸之路"分论坛,主持词、致辞

21A:

源语:尊敬的各位来宾,女士们、先生们,第二届"一带一路"国际合作高峰论坛"数字丝绸之路"分论坛正式开始,有请论坛主持人国家发展和改革委员会任志武副秘书长上台,掌声有请。

译语: Distinguished guests, ladies and gentlemen, the Second Belt and Road Forum for International Cooperation—Thematic Forum on Digital Silk Road is starting now. Let's welcome the host, National Development Reform Commission for the PRC, the Deputy Director Ren Zhiwu.

教师点评:(1)这节是会场播放的提前录制好的音频。会议现场有时候会播放一些中文或双语音视频:如会议开始前对会议及主办机构的介绍视频,提醒会议即将开始,请参会人员回到会场,或者会场人员就座,宣布会议正式开幕,介绍会场安全、餐饮、同传设备使用等会务信息等。一般情况下,对于第一类的会场的暖场音视频,译员无须翻译,对于提醒会议开始、宣布会议开幕、介绍会务信息,如果是中文单语,则需要提供同传,如果译员翻译了一句后发现是中英对照,则一般不需要提供同传。

(2)"分论谈正式开始"可以处理为...is commencing/beginning 或者 begins/commences;大会主持人一般用 chairperson。

(3)"国家发展和改革委员会"应是 National Development and Reform Commission of China/People's Republic of China,也可以将 China 放在前面,但是一般不用缩写 PRC,尤其首次提及时。此处的基本的机

构名出现错译，着实不应该。

源语：尊敬的利亚伊奇阁下，尊敬的拉法兰阁下，尊敬的松薇女士，尊敬的林念修副主任、杨小伟副主任，女士们、先生们、朋友们，大家下午好。万物复苏，春意盎然的北京，热情欢迎远道而来的高朋宾客共议数字繁荣。第二届"一带一路"国际合作高峰论坛将"数字丝绸之路"作为新设分论坛之一，由中国国家发展和改革委员会与国家网络信息化办公室联合主办，由国家发改委"一带一路"建设促进中心、创新驱动发展中心和国际合作中心承办。由城市和小城镇中心、新华社中国经济信息社协办。

译语：Distinguished His excellency Ljajić...（耳机里突然没有源语声音，所以没译）
The Second Belt and Road International Cooperation Forum take the belt and road as the thematic forum hosted by the NDRC and CAC, and co-hosted by the International Cooperation Center and China Center for Urban Development of NDRC and China Economic Information Service of Xinhua news agency.

教师点评：(1)"尊敬的＋姓名＋阁下"可处理为 Your Excellency Mr./Ms.＋姓名，无须使用 distinguished 或 respected，"尊敬的松薇女士"可处理为 Ms. Songwei，"尊敬的林念修副主任，杨小伟副主任"可处理为 Vice Chairman Lin Nianxiu, Vice Minister（据主办方资料）Yang Xiaowei，如果源语语速慢，时间允许，也可处理为"Mr./Ms＋人名＋职务＋机构名"，如 Mr. Lin Nianxiu, Vice Chairman of China's National Development and Reform Commission。
(2)"万物复苏……"这句可处理为 In the vibrant/blossoming spring in Beijing, where everything is rejuvenating, we warmly welcome distinguished guests from afar to gather and discuss the prosperity of the digital era.
(3)译语的语法错误较多，"作为新设分论坛之一"可处理为 has

included...as one of the newly-established/new sub-forums，主办一般用host，联合主办用co-host，承办用organize，协办用co-organize，支持用support，赞助用sponsor，但有些会议的主办和承办会混用，比如本次会议的主办方译为organizer，承办方译为co-organizers，具体以本次会议英文会议手册中的版本为准。此外，CAC首次提及要用全称Cyberspace Administration of China，机构名和一些其他专名第一次出现时要用全称，后面可以视情况再将全称和简称一起使用1~2次，之后可以使用简称，但是在多个简称相同或相似时，还是建议用全称。

源语：出席今天论坛的主要嘉宾有：塞尔维亚副总理兼贸易、旅游和电信部部长利亚伊奇阁下，法国前总理拉法兰阁下，联合国非洲经济委员会执行秘书松薇女士，古巴信息和通信部部长佩尔多姆先生，埃及通讯和信息技术部部长特拉阿特先生，格林纳达基础设施发展、公用事业、能源、交通和执行部部长鲍恩先生，老挝邮政电信部部长古玛西先生，缅甸交通和通讯部部长丹心貌先生，沙特阿拉伯通信和信息技术部大臣施瓦赫先生，泰国数字经济和社会部部长杜龙卡韦罗先生，土耳其交通和基础设施部部长图尔罕先生，津巴布韦新闻宣传和广播服务部部长穆茨万格瓦女士，以及来自爱沙尼亚、匈牙利、印度尼西亚、韩国、新加坡、英国等30多个国家和国际组织的官员和贵宾，让我们以热烈的掌声欢迎各位嘉宾的到来。

今天的会议议程主要包括开幕致辞、部长论述、签约文本交换仪式、对话交流等环节。首先有请主办方中国国家发改委副主任林念修先生致辞，大家欢迎。

译语: Today, we have guests H. E. Mr. Rasim Ljajić, H. E. Jean-Pierre Raffarin, Mr. Vera Songwe, H. E. Perdomo, H. E. Talaat, H. E. Gregory Bowen, H. E. Thansamay, Minister of Post and Telecommunications of Laos, H. E. Thant Sin Maung, Minister of Transportation and Communications of Myanmar, H. E. Abdullah AlSwaha, Minister of Communication and Information Technology of KSA, H. E. Pichet Durongkaveroj from

Thailand, H. E. Mehmet Cahit Turhan, H. E. Ms. Monica Mutsvangwa, and Estonia, Korean, England and other 20 countries. Our guests and representatives. Let's welcome their presentation.

Today, the schedule includes the opening remarks, the speech by the ministers, document exchange ceremony and panel discussion. First, let's welcome the deputy director of NDRC, Mr. Lin Nianxiu.

教师点评：（1）本节的嘉宾信息在会议手册中都有。嘉宾介绍部分，译员需要注意以下几点：第一，无论如何一定要在会议开始前拿到主持词，并且备好译语，在开始前的最后时刻确认更新版本（有时候会议开始后还会收到最新版本），标注去除或新增的嘉宾，介绍顺序改变的嘉宾等，建议译员打印出来，更便于各种调整和标注，也能避免因电子产品出故障无法视阅；第二，节奏要和源语精准匹配，不能超前，也不能滞后到差距一个嘉宾，诸如出现主持人介绍 B 后，B 起立，但译语还在介绍 A 的情形，影响交际效果；第三，一般是听完"机构＋职务＋姓名"后，至少在听到"职务"后，开始按照英文相反语序译出，既可是"姓名＋职务＋机构"，也可"职务＋机构＋Mr./Ms.＋姓名"（机构名太长或有几个机构职务时），不建议在听到机构时就超前译出人名与职务，因为可能会出现同一机构的出席嘉宾调整；第四，译员需要提前通过和主办方、嘉宾等确认所有姓名的正确发音，并且多次阅读，形成肌肉记忆，以免在高压力下出错；第五，要标记清楚嘉宾性别。本节中，译员遗漏了多个机构和职务名称，对部分姓名的读音不正确，而且将松薇女士性别说错。这些信息会议资料中已经提供，可见译员没有充分准备。

（2）除了专有名词外的英语表达几乎都不正确，如 we have guests 应是 Distinguished guests attending today's forum include，"以及来自……官员和贵宾"可处理为 We also have guests from 或 Guests present also include, Let's welcome their presentation. 应是 Please joining me in warmly welcoming them with a round of applause, Today, the schedule includes 应是 Today's agenda/Our agenda today includes，随后的两环

节名称错译,根据会议手册,分别应是 keynote speech from ministers, Cooperation Documents Exchange Ceremony,此外国家发改委副主任应是 Vice Chairman。

(3)除了内容和语言问题,译语不够流利,语气、语调不够庄重。

综上,本段译语在内容、语言和发布上都存在许多问题,质量不可接受。译员除了没有充分准备外,对此类话语,尤其是会议程式语的英译不熟悉。

21B:

源语:尊敬的利亚伊奇副总理,尊敬的委拉松薇女士,尊敬的拉法兰先生,各位来宾,女士们、先生们、朋友们:

大家下午好!欢迎各位嘉宾来到北京,出席"一带一路"国际合作高峰论坛"数字丝绸之路"分论坛,共商21世纪数字丝绸之路建设,共谋数字经济发展。作为本次论坛的主办方,我谨代表中国国家发展改革委,对远道而来的贵宾、各位嘉宾朋友们表示热烈的欢迎和衷心的感谢!

译语: His Excellency Mr. Rasim Ljajić, Her Excellency Ms. Vera Songwe, his Excellency Mr. Jean-Pierre, distinguished guests, ladies and gentlemen, good afternoon! Welcome all of you come to Chin- uh Beijing and this thematic forum on digital silk road to talk about the 21st -Century Digital Silk Road and the digital economy. As the organizers of this forum, on behalf of the NDRC, I would like to extend my heartfelt gratitude and welcome to all of the friends coming from afar.

教师点评:这一小节有不少问题,如 His Excellency 应为 Your Excellency, Ljajić 读音错误, Welcome all of you 后面需要加 to, Beijing 前出现口误 Chin- 和有声停顿 uh, to talk about 建议改为 discuss, all of 应去掉 of。

源语:当前,新一轮科技革命和产业变革孕育兴起,以大数据、人工智能为代表的新一代信息技术蓬勃发展,开启了信息化发展的新阶段,数字经济成为全球经济增长的新引擎。全球信息化、网络化的大趋势使得各国网络平台和数字经济的联系越来越重要。中国国家主席习近平多次指出,中国希望通过自己的努力,推动世界各国共同搭乘互联网和数字经济发展的快车。要将"一带一路"连接成21世纪的数字丝绸之路。

译语: Currently, the new round technological and industrial reform is are emerging. The big data, AI and the new generation of information technology has ushered in a new phase. The digital economy has become the new driver for global growth. Global information and network-based trend has made the network platforms and digital economy all the more relevant. As the Chinese President Xi Jinping has mentioned, with our own efforts, we would like to put the world into the fast lane of network and digital economy. We would like to build the Belt and Road Initiative into the 21st-century Digital Silk Road.

教师点评:(1)发布上,本节除 is are emerging 一处需修正外,发布质量较好。

(2)语言问题不少,如 new round 应是 new round of,has ushered in 应为 have ushered in, Global information and network-based trend 可改为 the global trend of digitalization and networking,国家领导人"多次指出"建议用 noted on numerous occasions,would like to 建议改为 wish to/aim to, we would like to put the world into 一句的意思显得有些过于张扬。

(3)内容上,两句译语不够忠实。"以大数据、人工智能为代表的新一代信息技术蓬勃发展,开启了信息化发展的新阶段"可以处理为 Big data, AI, among other new-generation information technologies, have ushered in a new phase of/has opened up an new era of digitalization/digital transformation;"全球信息化、网络化的大趋势使得各国网络平台和数字经济的联系越来越重要"可处理为 The global trend of digitalization and networking has made the connection between national network platforms and digital economies increasingly important. 另外，"中国希望通过自己的努力……"还可处理为China wishes/aims to help enable all the countries to get onboard/ride the express train of internet and digital economy。

源语：近年来，中国政府积极部署电子商务、智慧城市、大数据、"互联网+"、人工智能等一系列重大举措，取得了显著成效。据有关统计，2018年，中国网民规模达8.29亿人，98%的农村实现了光纤通达，互联网平台带动就业超过5000万人，全国网上零售交易额达9万亿元。同时，中国政府秉承"开放创新、包容普惠"的宗旨，大力推进数字丝绸之路建设合作，分享数字化转型的变革红利，为古老的丝绸之路注入了新元素。

译语：Currently, the Chinese government has deployed e-commerce, s- smart city, big data and AI, which has come a long way. According to the statistics, the in 2018 the netizens in China exce- exceeded 829 million. 50 million jobs was created by the online platforms, and the online retail reached 9 trillion yuan. At the same time, the Chinese government will uh stick to the principle of innovation and inclusion to talk about the cooperations and bring dividend of digital economy transformation, which brought new impetus to the to the traditional Silk Road.

教师点评：（1）本节的非流利情形较多，重复、修正、有声停顿等共计7处（其中the in处可能是因为源语声道问题导致），在高规格政务活动同传中，应尽量避免非流利情形出现。
（2）还是有基本语言问题，如jobs was created应为were created，cooperations应为cooperation，Chinese government will stick to应为sticks to/has been sticking to。
（3）内容方面，"近年来"不是currently，"互联网+""一系列重大举措""全国网上零售"等漏译，最后一句不够忠实，该句可处理为 The Chinese government, guided by/adhering to/upholding the principles of "openness, innovation, inclusiveness, and shared benefits", actively promotes/advances cooperation in the construction of the Digital Silk Road, shares the dividends of digital transformation and injects new elements into the ancient Silk Road.

剩余部分：

源语：我们致力于加强政策沟通协商，凝聚发展共识。与超过16个国家签署了"数字丝绸之路"建设合作协议，联合7个国家共同发起了"一带一路"数字经济合作倡议。我们致力于建设数字基础设施，架起互通桥梁。与"一带一路"沿线国家建成超过30条跨境陆缆、十余条国际海缆，国际通信出入口总容量达到了87.6Tbps。我们致力于扩大数字经贸合作，培育增长动力。2018年，中国跨境电子商务零售进出口额达到了1347亿元，同比增长50%。中国ICT企业到海外投资日益增加。我们致力于大力发展信息惠民，增进民生福祉。在50多个国家探索远程医疗合作，与40多个国家的相关企业合作开发移动支付等新应用。

译语：We are committed to enhancing policy communication and consultation to foster consensus for development. With over 16 countries we have signed cooperation agreements on the construction of the Digital Silk Road. With seven countries we have jointly initiated the Belt and Road Digital Economy Cooperation Initiative. We are dedicated to building digital infrastructure for better connectivity. With countries along the Belt and Road we have established over 30 cross-border land cables and over 10 international submarine cables, with international communication capacity hitting 87.6 Tbps. We are devoted to expanding digital trade cooperation and cultivating growth drivers. In 2018, China's cross-border e-commerce retail imports and exports reached 134.7 billion yuan, a 50% year-on-year increase. Chinese ICT companies are increasingly investing overseas. We are committed to promoting information accessibility and improving people's well-being. With over 50 countires we are exploring telemedicine cooperation and collaborating with relevant enterprises from over 40 countries to develop new applications such as mobile payments.

源语：女士们、先生们、朋友们！中国有句俗话"朋友多了路好走"。"一带一路"沿线各国虽然国情不同，但是目前都在致力于繁荣数字经济。这些年的实践证明，只要我们携起手来，加强合作，一定能够更好地把握时代脉搏，共创数字经济美好的未来。我们愿本着共商、共建、共享的原则，以加强政策沟通、设施联通、贸易畅通、资金融通、民心相通为目标，与各方共同推进数字丝绸之路建设，共同开展以下工作。

译语：Ladies and gentlemen, friends! The Chinese saying goes, "With more friends, the road becomes easier to travel." Countries along the Belt and Road , despite having varying national conditions, are currently committed to digital economic prosperity. The practice over these years has proven that with concerted efforts and enhanced cooperation, we can better grasp the pulse of/keep up with/stay in tune with the times and create a bright future for the digital economy. Guided by the principles of extensive consultation, joint construction, and shared benefits, we are committed to promoting policy communication, infrastructure connectivity, unimpeded trade, financial integration and people-to-people ties. Together with all parties involved, we will advance the construction of the Digital Silk Road and carry out the following tasks.

源语：一是深化需求对接，找准共同发展的合作方向。围绕各合作国经济社会发展的实际需求，共商合作计划，明确时间表和路线图，拓展面向信息基础设施、信息通信技术、数字化转型、数字技能培训等领域的合作空间，让各国人民共享数字经济的发展福祉。二是深化项目对接，形成优势互补的合作成果。充分发挥数字丝绸之路建设合作、东盟智慧城市网络等机制的作用，共商共建跨境光缆、卫星导航等重要信息基础设施，推动城市间、企业间围绕大数据、电子商务、智慧城市等落地一批务实合作项目，共同推进数字经济创新发展。

译语：First, we will further align our demands and identify areas of cooperation. Considering the practical needs of economic and social development in each country involved, we will engage in discussions on cooperation plans, establish clear timetables and roadmaps. And in areas such as information infrastructure, information and communication technology, digital transformation, and digital skills training, we will expand our cooperation. These efforts will enable people from all countries to share the benefits of digital economy. Second, we will synergize our projects and leverage complementarity to deliver better outcomes. The cooperation in the construction of the Digital Silk Road and the ASEAN Smart City Network, among other mechanisms, will be utilized to jointly build cross-border optical cables, satellite navigation systems among other important information infrastructure. We will enable cities and enterprises to cooperate in areas such as big data, e-commerce, and smart cities, and jointly implement projects, aiming at innovative growth of the digital economy.

源语：三是深化人才对接，筑牢坚实稳固的合作基础。鼓励科研机构、企业等加强人才交流合作，通过联合设立研发中心、创新平台等多种形式，共同培养高层次创新和技术人才。支持各类机构、企业开展多层次的交流培训活动，促进数字技能的普及提升，让民众更加便利地利用数字化工具获取信息，促进文化交流、民心相融。四是深化治理对接，构建公平正义的合作环境。完善网络空间对话协商机制，共同研究制定全球互联网治理规则，进一步加强在知识产权保护、个人隐私保护、跨境数据流动等方面的合作，共同构建网络空间命运共同体。

译语：Third, we will promote talent exchange and build a solid foundation for cooperation. We encourage research institutions and enterprises to enhance talent exchange and cooperation. Through joint establishment of research and development centers, innovation platforms, and other forms of collaboration, we will jointly cultivate high-level innovative and technical talents. We support various institutions and enterprises to carry out multi-level exchange and training activities, promote the popularization and enhancement of digital skills, enable people to conveniently access information through digital tools, and promote cultural exchange and mutual understanding. Fourth, we will further collaborate on governance and build a fair and just environment for cooperation. We will improve dialogue and consultation mechanisms in cyberspace, jointly research and formulate global internet governance rules, further strengthen cooperation in areas such as intellectual property protection, personal privacy protection, and cross-border data flow, and jointly build a community of shared future in cyberspace.

源语：女士们、先生们、朋友们！数字经济发展前景广阔、潜力巨大，定将绽放异彩。我们衷心地期待与各国一道努力，共谋合作，共享机遇，共赢发展，希望与会嘉宾深入交流、集思广益、畅所欲言，为推动"21世纪数字丝绸之路"建设献计献策，共同谱写数字经济新篇章。最后，预祝本次论坛取得圆满成功，谢谢大家！

译语：Ladies and gentlemen, friends! The digital economy has great potential and promising prospects. We sincerely look forward to joining countries worldwide to seek cooperation, share opportunities, and achieve win-win development. We encourage all participants will to actively engage, exchange ideas and contribute suggestions and strategies to shape the "21st-Century Digital Silk Road" and usher in a new era of the digital economy. Lastly, we wish this forum great success. Thank you all!

会议：世界交通大会，主旨报告：构建现代交通运输体系，交通部副部长

22A：

源语：主持人：各位嘉宾、女士们、先生们、朋友们，上午好。非常荣幸有机会主持主旨报告环节的演讲。本届大会期间的学术交流有主旨报告、专题论坛、学术论坛和学术报告栏等多种形式组成，将有来自世界各国的1500多位专家学者，在会议期间发表自己的学术观点。今天上午的主旨报告环节，我们邀请了国内外知名学者、专家，就现代交通运输体系的建设和未来交通发展的有关问题做演讲。今天主旨报告环节第一位演讲的嘉宾是中华人民共和国交通运输部副部长刘小明先生，刘小明先生曾任北京工业大学副校长，北京市教委主任，长期从事交通运输的教学和行政领导工作。作为知名学者，拥有学界、业界双重丰富经验的刘小明教授，主要的学术研究方向，包括城市交通的控制系统，交通的信息处理和分析技术，等等，并取得了一大批有较大影响力的学术成果。下面有请刘小明副部长做演讲。有请。

译语：Distinguished guests, ladies and gentlemen, dear friends, good morning! It's my great honor to have this opportunity to host the keynote speech section. During this conference, we have reports, symposium, and academic reports sessions. We have over 1,500 experts, both at home and abroad to express their views. This morning, we have the experts on the public transportation system and future issues. And our first speaker is Liu Xiaoming, Vice Minister of Transport China. He was once Vice President of Beijing University of Technology, Director of Beijing Municipal Education Commission. And he has worked in this field for a long time. As famous experts, he has rich experience both in the industry and in the academy. It mainly focus on the control system, public transport analysis technology with a great number of academic results. Now let's warmly welcome Mr. Liu Xiaoming for his keynote speech.

教师点评：（1）演讲前主持人对演讲人的介绍是会议同传的一大挑战，因为一般是读稿，而译员常常拿不到讲稿，且该部分的信息比较密集，表达比较凝练。译员应缩短 EVS，采用顺句横向对译为主的策略，提高加工速度，传译相对重要信息，这更加注重译语信息的准确性（而非完整性）。

（2）keynote speech session 比 keynote speech section 更常用。

（3）"专题论坛""学术报告栏"分别为 thematic forums, academic presentation posters, symposium 应用复数。

（4）to express their views 可改为 to share their insights。

（5）This morning, we have the experts on the public transportation system and future issues. 不够忠实，该句可处理为 During the keynote speech session this morning, we will have well-known scholars and experts from around the world to present on modern transportation system construction and future developments in transportation.

（6）"长期从事交通运输的教学和行政领导工作"可处理为 He has long been engaged in teaching and administrative leadership roles in the field of transportation.

（7）As famous experts 应为 As a famous expert 或 As one of the famous experts。

（8）对于"主要的学术研究方向……学术成果"一句，如果译员时间宽裕，习惯较长的 EVS，可处理为 His main research areas include urban transport control systems, transport information processing and analysis techniques. And he has published extensively and influentially in this field，否则一般优先处理术语部分，句子其他内容后置，即 urban transport control systems, transport information processing and analysis techniques are among his main research areas. 具体见下一条。

（9）译员对"现代交通运输体系的建设和未来交通发展""城市交通的控制系统，交通的信息处理和分析技术"等术语、罗列的加工策略有待改善。面对这些密集的信息成分，译员应尽快完成之前的译语，迅速顺句对译该部分（如有必要，也可记笔记），或者先行处理这部分内容，将之作为主语，句子的其他内容后置，以免记忆负担过重造成漏译。此外，译员也可通过部分源语提前预测，及时调整策略。在处理"现代交通运输体系的建设和未来交通发展"时，译员在说 experts, on, the 三个词的时候，每个词后的等待都有些久，实际在译员听到"现代交通运输体系的建设"时，便可顺着语序将之对译为 modern transport system construction。对于后例，译员在听到"主要的学术研究方向"时便可预知随后的术语罗列，此时可将非术语部分后置，尽快准备好优先加工术语部分。

（10）译员发布质量总体较好。

源语：刘：谢谢主席先生的介绍。尊敬的各国交通运输部部长，尊敬的各位来宾，女士们、先生们、朋友们，大家上午好。这一次大会的主题是交通让世界更美好。众所周知，交通运输关乎人类最基本的生产生活需要，是经济社会发展的先决条件和国家强盛的重要支撑。正如亚当·斯密在国富论中所讲，一切改变以交通改良最有实效。特别是在现代社会，交通运输是联系国内和国际，城市和乡村，生产和消费的重要纽带，在支撑国家开发开放，新型城镇化建设，扶贫脱贫，区域协调发展和经济转型等各个方面，发挥着十分重要的基础性、先导性和战略性作用，是重要的现代服务业。这里我想和大家分享和交流三个方面的情况和思考。

译语：Thank you for your kind introduction. Distinguished Ministers of Transport, distinguished guests, ladies and gentlemen, dear friends, good morning. Our theme today is "Better Transport, Better World". As is known to all, transportation has a lot to do with our basic demands and also the precondition for our national prosperity and socioeconomic development. Just as Adam Smith, in his book, he wrote that the public transport conditions improving is very important. Especially in nowadays society, public transportation is the links between the urban and rural, the domestic and international community. And it plays a basic leading and strategic role in supporting national development and opening up, new type urbanization, poverty alleviation, regional and coordinated development and economic transformation and upgrading, and it's a very important modern service industry. Here, I'd like to walk you through the following three aspects.

教师点评：（1）"这一次大会的主题"建议处理为 The theme of this convention。（2）has a lot to do with 不够正式，不适合该会议场景使用，可改为 plays a crucial role/is vital for/is closely related to 等。Just as Adam Smith, in his book, he wrote 应是 Just as Adam Smith stated/emphasized/expressed in his book，在翻译名人名言或引语时，如果译前没有查证到准确译语，译员一般不直接译作 said, wrote 可将"说过""写过"模糊处理为 according to... 或其他表达。此处是外国人的话被译成了中文，再回译到原外文，挑战极大，翻译主要意思即可：The most effective way to bring about/drive social change is through improvements in transportation.

（3）nowadays society 可改为 today's society。

（4）译员将"交通运输"误译为 public transport, is the links 语法错误。同前，译员处理接下来三个罗列时的策略不太妥当，在听到"国内和国际，城市和乡村"时，应尽快简化之前的译语，腾出精力尽快处理罗列，如 public transportation is the links between 改为 transportation links... 也可先快速顺句对译罗列部分，其他部分后置：Between domestic and international realms, urban and rural areas, production and consumption, transportation is the very bridge. 同样，在处理"在支撑国家开发开放……"一句的5个短语的罗列时，也可采用这一策略，尤其是这些罗列部分没有出现在译员手边材料中时。此处，需要指出的是，译员在译该句时，在阅读PPT上的译语，而译语是笔译版本，和源语语序存在较大差异，译员在发言人还没有提及"发挥着十分重要的基础性、先导性和战略性作用"时就提前读出译语，有一定风险，建议译员参考译语顺句驱动：in supporting national development and opening up...transportation plays... 此外，译语中 regional and coordinated development 应去除 and。

源语：第一，改革开放40年来，中国交通运输取得了重大的成就。改革开放40年来,中国交通运输实现了跨越式发展,取得了历史性成就,有力地支撑了经济繁荣和社会和谐进步。人民群众的幸福感、获得感显著提升。

译语: First, over the past four decades after the reform and opening up, China's great achievement in public transport. Over the past four decades after the reform and opening up, we have made great progress and remarkable achievements, which is beneficial to improving people's sense of gaining and people's well-being.

教师点评:(1)第一句译语表达有问题,短语要改成句子 China has made great achievement in transportation。两句中的 after 都应改成 since。
(2)译员多次将"交通运输"误译为 public transport。同传中,译员对于主题词要确保精准,翻译中要加强译语监管。
(3)"幸福感""获得感"分别是 sense of happiness, sense of fulfillment。此外,"经济繁荣""社会和谐进步""显著提升"等未译出。政务话语同传中,忠实性非常重要。

源语: 一是基础设施建设突飞猛进,五纵五横综合运输大通道基本贯通,综合交通运输网络不断完善。截至2017年底,综合交通网总里程突破500万公里,全国铁路营业里程达到12.7万公里,其中高速铁路2.5万公里,居世界第一,占世界高铁里程的66.3%,拥有万吨级及以上的泊位2366个,居世界第一,是改革开放之初的18倍。全国(发言人口误,应为全球)港口货物吞吐量和集装箱吞吐量排名前10位港口中,中国占据全球的七席,高速公路通车里程13.6万公里,居世界第一,农村公路里程达到400万公里,建制村通畅率达到98.35%。"十三五"末将兑现小康路上不让一个地方因交通而掉队的庄严承诺。

译语: First, rapid progress in infrastructure construction. Comprehensive transport channels has been set. Comprehensive transport network is improving. By the end of 2017, the comprehensive transport network mileage reach 5 million kilometers, railway operating mileage 127,000 kilometers, among which high speed railway 25,000 kilometers, ranking the first in the world, accounting for 60 66.3%. Berths of 10,000 tons and above is 2,366, No.1 in the world. Top ten ports in the world in terms of global port cargo and container throughput, seven, we have seven Chinese ports. The rural the highway mileage is ranked the first in the world, among which rural highway mileage 4 million kilometers. Accessibility rate of administrative villages reach 98.35%. At the end of the 13th Five-year Plan, we will fulfill our commitments.

教师点评：(1)"五纵五横综合运输大通道基本贯通"可处理为 Five vertical and five horizontal trunk lines/corridors are largely in place。

(2) reach 应该是 reaches。为了避免语法错误，减少语言加工精力，提高翻译效率，数字较多的部分可以尽量精简语言，如减少流水句的使用，多使用"一个句子加挂若干短语"的做法，但是也要避免短语和句子错搭，此外也可将短语与音韵相结合（即前文所谈的"表格法"）。本节中，短语与句子错搭、误用问题较多，如 railway operating 前需要加 with, among which 后面需要句子，或者不用 among which, high speed railway 后加 accounting for, 66.3% 后需要加上 of world's total, Berths of 10,000 tons and above is 2,366 可以去掉 is，在 2366 前适当停顿，倒数第二句译语的 reach 应该用单数。

(3) "是改革开放之初的 18 倍""高速公路通车里程 13.6 万公里"漏译，数字较多的部分，需要提高语速，简化语言，结合笔记，突出关键信息点的传译。

(4) "小康路上不让一个地方因交通而掉队的庄严承诺"可处理为 we will fulfill the solemn commitment that in building a moderately prosperous society, we should let no place fall behind in transportation/we will take every area on board in terms of transportation。

教师总点评：译员的发布质量总体较为平稳，流利，音韵运用也较好，但内容忠实性问题不少，语言问题更多，建议译员加强此类话语的同传训练，提高部分同传策略（如术语的横向顺句对译、数字部分简洁处理等）运用的娴熟度，提升源语内容翻译的准确性、完整性，加强对译语的自我监管，尤其是基本语法的监管，减少语法错误和口误。

22B：

源语：四是行业治理体系逐步完善，交通运输行业持续改善改革创新，不断增加交通运输发展的动能和激发交通运输发展的活力。综合交通管理体制、法规标准体系初步形成，市场体系逐步完善，基本形成统一开放、竞争有序的交通运输市场，国际合作水平和国际影响力明显提升。40年来，中国的交通运输发展经历了从瓶颈制约到总体缓解，再到基本适应经济社会发展需求的历史性的转变，已经成为名副其实的交通大国。

译语：Fourth, system of industrial governance gradually improved. We have made great innovations and stimulate the vitality of transport development, and our rules and regulation have has formed and our market system, which is unified, open, competitive and orderly transport market is formed. Over the past 40 years, China's transport development has experienced many stages, and it has made a historic leap to become a major player.

教师点评：（1）译员语调过平，可能会影响听众理解。

（2）本节的不少内容在PPT中有，但译员基本没有使用PPT中已有译语，似乎也没有在译前准备适合译语，而是选择即兴听译。政策性话语即兴口译的挑战较大，因此本节中内容和语言问题较多。

（3）语言问题包括：gradually improved 前要加 has，stimulate 应为 stimulated，rules and regulations have formed，which is 后面应该加上 a，is formed 改为 has formed。此外，transport 一般指运输行为和过程，如果指运输行业、体系等，一般用 transportation。

（4）内容上不够准确的地方也不少。"交通运输行业持续改善改革创新"可处理为 The transportation sector proceeds with reform and innovation;"不断增加交通运输发展的动能"可处理为 increases momentum/cultivates new growth drivers for the transportation sector;最后一句可以处理为:China's transportation has moved from being constrained by bottlenecks to overall alleviation, and further to essentially meeting the demands of economic and social development, making China a major transportation player.

源语:回顾 40 年中国交通运输发展的历程,我们有 5 个方面的深切体会,一是必须充分发挥中国特色社会主义体制优势和制度的优越性,凝聚中央地方和人民群众的各方力量,形成共同推进交通运输事业发展的强大合力。二是必须毫不动摇地坚持和加强党对交通运输工作的领导,确保交通运输发展始终坚持以人民为中心,始终符合国家经济社会发展大局。三是必须不断解放思想,改革创新,与时俱进,坚决地破除阻碍交通运输高质量发展的体制机制障碍,不断地增强交通运输发展的内生动力。四是必须加强交通运输发展的顶层设计,充分发挥规划的先行引领作用,确保交通运输发展一张蓝图干到底。

译语:Over the past 40 years, I have five thoughts. First, we must give full play to the socialist system with Chinese characteristics, which can pool strength of all parties to jointly promote transport growth. Second, we must uphold and strengthen the party's leadership in transport and ensure that develop of transport conforms to the overall situation of the country's economic and social development. Third, we must unleashing, emancipate our mind, reform and innovate, and also break down the institutional barriers that hinder the high quality development of transport. Fourth, we must strengthen the top-level design of transport development and give full play to the leading role of planning to ensure that the development and transport can go all the way through.

教师点评:(1) develop of 与 must unleashing 充分反映译员缺乏译语监管。

（2）第一句译语过于简单、不正式，可改为 Looking back at the 40-year journey of China's transportation development, we have gained experience in five aspects.

（3）译员漏译"始终坚持以人民为中心"（Transportation development should always be people-centered），是因为译员直接阅读了 PPT 上的译语，而 PPT 上并没有这句话，可见译员在带稿（PPT）同传时，需要以听辨源语为主，手边材料作为参考，警惕发言人更新了稿件或脱稿发挥。此外，在译前准备阶段，应充分检查客户所提供的译语是否准确可用。

（4）"不断地增强交通运输发展的内生动力"可处理为 keep enhancing the endogenous driving force of transportation development/promoting the endogenous development of the transportation sector；"确保交通运输发展一张蓝图干到底"可处理为 turn the blueprint for transportation development into reality/fully implement the blueprint for transportation development。

源语：五是必须坚持立足国情，准确把握交通运输发展的阶段特征，把国外交通运输发展的先进经验与中国交通发展的实践相结合，不断地探索具有中国特色的交通运输发展的道路。甘而不忘苦，安而不忘忧。中国交通运输在快速发展的同时，仍然存在着一些需要特别关注的突出问题。一是交通引导发展理念尚需加强，交通追随发展模式仍占主导，综合交通运输体系顶层设计和实施路径亟待强化，引导国土资源开发和产业布局、城市土地利用的能力和水平急需提升。

译语：Five, we must adhere to the national conditions and combined advanced overseas experience with the practice of China's transport development, and explored the path of transport with Chinese characteristics. Be willing not to forget pain and anxiety. Now we still have many problems which are prominent. First, we need to have transport-driven development mindset, the top-level design of our net uh transport network should be more comprehensive, and our capability to utilize factors should improved.

教师点评：（1）前两句，译员是在阅读 PPT 上的译语，有些令人费解的是，combine 和 explore 被改成了过去时。同前，源语与 PPT 上文字不完全相同，源语中多了一句"准确把握交通运输发展的阶段特征"，该句可处理为 accurately understand the stage-specific features of transportation development。

（2）"甘而不忘苦，安而不忘忧。"的 PPT 译语未能传递出源语信息，与前后句不衔接、不连贯，缺乏交际性，可改为 Having reviewed achievements and experience, we must also look at the challenges。

（3）"交通引导发展理念尚需加强，交通追随发展模式仍占主导"可处理为 We must enhance awareness that transportation leads economic and social progress, but currently transportation follows it.

（4）"综合交通运输体系顶层设计……水平急需提升"可处理为 The top-level design and roadmaps of transportation system must be strengthened. We must enable/empower transportation to play a leading role in guiding land and resources development, industrial distribution, and urban land use。

教师总点评：译员译前准备要更加充分，同传时要以源语听辨为主，加强源语听辨与 PPT 源语视译、译语阅读等任务间的协调性，要加强对译语语言质量的监管，努力减少语法错误，要多运用音韵凸显信息，提升译语可用性，此外，可尝试提升口头表达伶俐性，提高同传加工速度。

剩余源语（源语较长，仅提供部分转写源语和译语供参考）

源语：二是交通运输在区域间、城乡间、运输方式间，新旧业态间，软硬实力间，建、管、养、运间发展还不平衡。三是交通运输在基础设施网络覆盖，运输服务有效供给等方面发展还不够充分，多样化、个性化、高品质的运输服务需求，不能得到有效的满足。四是科技创新、人才带动引领不足，综合交通发展方式相对粗放，运输组织模式单一，交通运输结构不尽合理，物流成本依然偏高。五是交通运输治理体系仍需进一步优化，政府和市场的边界还不够清晰，越位、缺位和错位并存，市场配置资源的决定性作用和更好地发挥政府的作用，都还有较大的空间，等等。

参考译语：Second, between regions, urban and rural areas, transportation modes, new and old business models, soft and hard power, processes of construction, management, maintenance, and operation, transportation development is still unbalanced. Third, infrastructure network coverage and effective supply of transportation services are not yet adequate and the diverse, personalized, and high-quality transportation service needs are yet to be met. Fourth, scientific and technological innovation and human resources have not become the driving force for the sector. The development mode of comprehensive transportation is yet to be intensified, transportation organization model to be diversified, transportation structure to be optimized, and logistics costs to be lowered. Fifth, the governance system still needs further optimization, with government's and market's roles be be defined. The decisive role of market in allocating resources and the better role of the government still have room for improvement.

源语：我们必须坚持目标导向和问题导向的结合，着力推动交通运输发展，由追随发展模式，向交通引领发展模式的转变，由依靠传统要素驱动，向更多地依靠改革创新、开放驱动转变，由各种交通方式并联发展，向融合发展转变，由注重提升供给能力，向注重提升供给质量、效率转变，实现更高质量、更有效率、更加公平、更加安全、更可持续的发展。第二，构建现代交通运输体系面临的形势要求。当今世界正处于大发展、大变革、大调整的时期，中国特色社会主义进入了新时代，中国开启了全面建设社会主义现代化强国的新征程。中国交通运输发展面临的形势、环境和需求都正发生着深刻的变化。

参考译语：We must be both goal-oriented and problem-oriented, and enable transportation to play a leading role in economic and social progress. We should shift from relying on traditional factors to relying more on reform, innovation, and openness. We should transit from the parallel development of various transportation modes to the integrated development. We should shift our focus from improving supply capacity to improving supply quality and efficiency, aiming for higher quality, greater efficiency, fairness, safety, and sustainability. Secondly, we are facing a new context for building a modern transportation system. The world is currently experiencing significant development, transformation and adjustment. China's socialist development with Chinese characteristics has entered a new era, and the country has embarked on a new journey to comprehensively build a modern strong socialist country. China's transportation development is facing a rapidly evolving landscape, environment and demands.

源语：从国际上看，世界经济仍处在后金融危机的调整与构造期，全球产业格局加速重构，全球治理体系深刻变化，新一轮科技革命蓄势待发。特别是近年来，以移动互联网、物联网、人工智能、3D打印、新材料新能源为代表的新一代科技革命和产业革命，正在孕育兴起，将对交通运输传统产业发展和转型升级形成强有力的倒逼机制，同时也带来了新的发展机遇。

参考译语：Internationally, the world economy is still in the post-financial crisis adjustment and reconstruction. The global industrial landscape is undergoing rapid restructuring, and the global governance system is undergoing profound changes. A new round of technological revolution is gathering momentum. In recent years, mobile internet, the Internet of Things, artificial intelligence, 3D printing, new materials and new energy, among other forms of technological and industrial revolutions are emerging. This will push traditional transportation industry to transformation and upgrading. Meanwhile it will also bring new opportunities for transportation development.

源语：从国内看，中国经济已由高速增长阶段转向高质量发展阶段，正处在转变发展方式、优化结构、转变增长动力的攻坚期。进入新时代，中国社会主要矛盾已经转化为人民日益增长的美好生活的需要和不平衡不充分的发展之间的矛盾，这一关系全局的历史性变化，在交通运输领域体现为交通运输供给能力、质量、效率不能满足人民日益增长的美好生活的需要。中国社会主要矛盾的根本性的变化，需要我们着力推动交通运输发展质量变革、效率变革、动力变革，大力推动交通运输高质量发展。

参考译语：Domestically, Chinese economy has transitioned from high-speed growth to high-quality development featuring development mode transformation, structural readjustment and growth driver transformation. In the new era, the main contradiction in Chinese society has shifted from the contradiction between people's growing needs for a better life and the insufficient and imbalanced development. This historic change means for our sector that transportation supply capacity, quality and efficiency fails to meet people's increasing demands for a better life. The fundamental change in the main contradiction of Chinese society pushes us to seek quality, efficiency and new growth drivers in transportation development, and promote high-quality development in the sector.

源语：从行业自身看，目前中国交通运输供给不足的状况已经发生了根本性转变，但人们出行需求已经从有没有转化为好不好。交通运输供给能力和水平与人民群众日益增长的个性化、多样化、品质化、高效率的交通运输需求之间的矛盾日益突出。随着土地利用、资源使用和生态环境的现实条件发生深刻变化，交通运输发展的刚性约束持续增强，传统地依靠大规模要素投入、投资拉动的粗放式发展方式难以为继，交通运输急需要转变发展方式。

参考译语：As for the industry itself, transportation service shortage has been eased and people are expecting convenient and enjoyable mobility.

However transportation supply capacity and quality fall short of meeting people's growing needs for increasingly personalized, diverse, quality, and efficient transportation services. As land use, resource utilization and ecological environment are facing an evolving context, the rigid constraints on transportation development have become increasingly prominent. The development model featuring extensive input of resources and investment is no longer sustainable and there is an urgent need to transform the way transportation is developed.

源语：去年中国共产党第十九次全国代表大会胜利召开，做出了建设交通强国的重大战略部署。建设交通强国，既是全面建设社会主义现代化国家重要组成部分，也是现代经济体系的先行领域和战略支撑。在新的历史起点上，面对新形势和新要求，我们要立足中国国情，坚持以人民为中心，牢固树立创新、协调、绿色、开放、共享的新发展理念，充分借鉴国际经验，遵循交通发展规律，紧扣中国社会主要矛盾的变化，按照高质量发展的要求，以供给侧结构性改革为主线，努力探索新时代中国特色交通运输发展的新路子，全面建成安全、便捷、高效、绿色、经济的现代综合立体交通运输体系，更好地满足人民日益增长的美好生活的需要。

参考译语：Last year the 19th National Congress of the Communist Party of China was held successfully, outlining the strategic blueprint for building China into a strong transportation country. Building a strong transportation nation is not only an important part of comprehensively building a modern socialist country but also a leading sector and strategic support for the modern economic system. At a new historical starting point, facing new contexts and requirements, we should base ourselves on China's national conditions, always put people first, and be committed to innovation, coordination, greenness, openness, and sharing in our development. We should draw on international experience and follow the laws of transportation development. We should also closely follow the changes in the main contradiction of Chinese society, meet the requirements of high-quality development, advance supply-side structural reform so as to explore new paths for the development of China's transportation system with Chinese characteristics in the new era. We aim to comprehensively build a modern, integrated, safe, convenient, efficient, green, and economical transportation system that better meets the growing needs of the people for a better life.